Archaeology of Performance

ARCHAEOLOGY IN SOCIETY SERIES

Series Editors
Ian Hodder, *Stanford University*
Robert Preucel, *University of Pennsylvania*

In the past twenty years, archaeology has expanded beyond a narrow focus on economics and environmental adaptation to address issues of ideology, power, and meaning. These trends, sometimes termed "postprocessual," deal with both the interpretation of the past as hermeneutics and the complex and politically charged interrelationships of past and present. Today, archaeology is responding to, and incorporating aspects of the debates on, identity, meaning, and politics currently being explored in varying fields: social anthropology, sociology, geography, history, linguistics, and psychology. There is a growing realization that ancient studies and material culture can be aligned within the contemporary construction of identities under the rubrics of nationalism, ethnoscapes, and globalization. This international series will help connect the contemporary practice of archaeology with these trends in research and, in the process, demonstrate the relevance of archaeology to related fields and society in general.

Volumes in this series:

Appropriated Pasts: Indigenous Peoples and the Colonial Culture of Archaeology, Ian J. McNiven and Lynette Russell (2005)

Archaeology of Performance: Theaters of Power, Community, and Politics, edited by Takeshi Inomata and Lawrence S. Coben (2006)

Archaeology of Performance

Theaters of Power, Community, and Politics

EDITED BY

Takeshi Inomata and Lawrence S. Coben

ALTAMIRA
PRESS

A Division of
ROWMAN AND LITTLEFIELD PUBLISHERS, INC.
Lanham • New York • Toronto • Oxford

AltaMira Press
A Division of Rowman & Littlefield Publishers, Inc.
A wholly owned subsidiary of The Rowman & Littlefield Publishing Group, Inc.
4501 Forbes Boulevard, Suite 200
Lanham, MD 20706
www.altamirapress.com

P.O. Box 317, Oxford OX2 9RU, UK

British Library Cataloguing in Publication Information Available

Library of Congress Cataloging-in-Publication Data

Archaeology of performance : theaters of power, community, and politics / edited by Takeshi Inomata and Lawrence S. Coben.
p. cm. — (Archaeology in society series)
Includes bibliographical references and index.
ISBN-13: 978-0-7591-0876-9 (cloth : alk. paper)
ISBN-10: 0-7591-0876-5 (cloth : alk. paper)
ISBN-13: 978-0-7591-0877-6 (pbk. : alk. paper)
ISBN-10: 0-7591-0877-3 (pbk. : alk. paper)
1. Social archaeology. 2. Theater and society. 3. Theater—History—To 500. 4. Performing arts—Social aspects. I. Inomata, Takeshi, 1961– II. Coben, Lawrence S. III. Series.

CC72.4.A738 2006
930.1′01—dc22

2005024190

Printed in the United States of America

⊗™ The paper used in this publication meets the minimum requirements of American National Standard for Information Sciences—Permanence of Paper for Printed Library Materials, ANSI/NISO Z39.48-1992.

CONTENTS

ACT III
PUBLIC PERFORMANCE OF POWER AND COMMUNITY

SERIES EDITOR'S FOREWORD

For all the drama and pageantry of Dynastic Egypt, the Classic Maya, and the Inka empire, it is remarkable that archaeology has paid so little attention to the study of performance as a constitutive social practice. The dominant view of performance, spectacle, and ritual is that they are epiphenomenal to fundamental material needs. And yet, it can be argued that performance is characteristic of all known societies and, moreover, that theater and spectacle are the contexts par excellence where power relations are alternatively established, celebrated, mocked, and subverted. Theater and spectacle are commentaries about the contemporary social order and thus metadiscursive acts.

Archaeology of Performance: Theaters of Power, Community, and Politics, edited by Takeshi Inomata and Lawrence S. Coben, is the first attempt to bring together a series of essays on performance in premodern society. The editors define performance along a continuum ranging from individual speech acts to full-blown spectacles and festivals with audiences of thousands. Following Dell Hymes, they favor the view of performance as transcendent of the ordinary course of events, something which is interpretable, reportable, and repeatable within a domain of cultural intelligibility. They make a compelling case that performance in ancient societies can be accessed archaeologically through the study of theatrical space, images, and material objects.

The volume includes a broad selection of case studies addressing public rituals, ceremonies, festivals, and courtly interactions. The case studies include Çatalhöyük (Ian Hodder), Egypt (John Baines), Inka (Lawrence Coben, Jerry Moore), Madagascar (Susan Kus and Victor Raharijaona), Maya (Stephen Houston, Takeshi Inomata), Pueblo Southwest (Daniela

Triadan), and Urartu (Adam Smith). Among the topics they address are the archaeology of experience and the senses, daily life as a form of disciplinary strategy, spectacle as a means to constitute political subjects, audience and nonhuman (supernatural) actors, ritual architecture and social integration, architectural replication and the state, spectacle and monumentality, and public performance and royal discourse. Together, they help chart out new directions for understanding the performative foundations of political power.

Robert W. Preucel
University of Pennsylvania

PROLOGUE

PROLOGUE
BEHIND THE SCENES: PRODUCING THE PERFORMANCE

Lawrence S. Coben and Takeshi Inomata

Writing and editing a volume such as this one is akin to mounting a theatrical production. What the audience eventually reads or witnesses is the result of a long negotiated process, filled with choices and compromises that reflect the power relations among producers/editors, actors/contributors, theater owners/press, critics/reviewers, and of course the marketplace. These interactions continually modify the production's form and often its original artistic visions until opening night/publication.

Our reflection on the interactions among the contributors has only reinforced for us the importance of the production process to the issues with which this volume purports to deal. We need to analyze preparation and rehearsal, including our own, to understand the significance of performance in the establishment and transformation of power relationships and communities. We have thus decided to begin this volume by giving the reader a backstage pass good for entrée into the development of this publication. This behind-the-scenes look also helps highlight the different views of and approaches to performance among the contributors, which might normally be dealt with in the introductory chapter. Because some contributors criticize or refer to our original draft of that section, we have decided not to alter it significantly and to provide an overview of different opinions in this prologue.

This volume grew out of the editors' respective interests in spectacle and performance as integral elements of political processes. Inomata, with Stephen Houston, had recently completed a two-volume study, *Royal Courts of the Ancient Maya* (2001), which had directed his attention to the important role of theatrical performance in courtly settings. After hearing a talk by Inomata at Stanford, Ian Hodder encouraged him to edit a volume on this subject for what evolved into Hodder and Robert Preucel's series at AltaMira Press.

Inomata invited Coben to co-organize a working group at the annual meeting of the Society for American Archaeology (SAA) in 2002 and to coedit the subsequent volume. Coben's research focused on the role of performance in public settings in premodern societies, and more particularly the frequent and varied use of such performance by the Inka as an imperial strategy (see Coben and Stanish 2005; Coben this volume). Coben also studied the theatrical characteristics of ritual and political spaces.

Our goal in organizing the SAA working group, entitled Spectacle, Performance, and Power in Premodern Complex Societies, was to explore the nature and political implications of theatrical performance at public events and their relationship to the exercise of power and the creation of community. We asked participants to examine archaeological evidence of performance in specific cultural and historical contexts with a particular focus on spatial settings and its communicative quality. We selected the working group format because it provides for a session in a closed room with ample opportunity for discussion among the participants. Numerous colleagues criticized this choice as "exclusionary" (or worse), an important reminder of the power relations inherent in and created by the politics of inclusion in and exclusion from a performance's audience.

We "cast" our production with an eye toward outstanding scholarship, geographic and temporal breadth, and theoretical diversity. Most of the volume's contributors, as well as Lynn Meskell and David Romano, accepted this invitation. After the meeting, we invited Baines to contribute a chapter. Our historical contexts ranged from relatively smaller-scale societies with less apparent inequalities (Çatalhöyük, Turkey, and the American Southwest) to the expansive Inka empire.

To ensure a clear focus of the session, prior to the meeting we circulated among the participants a theme paper, which eventually became the introductory chapter of this volume. The differing views of the contributors, nonetheless, grew more evident during the working group, particularly in terms of the definition of spectacle. What the editors had referred to as spectacle may also be called "public performance and public theatrical events." "Public" of course did not assume universal access, but rather the participation of people beyond the circle of daily face-to-face intimate interactions. We sought a focus on these certain qualities and effects of performance that are associated with such public occasions, which may be different from those of quotidian interactions. Hodder, however, described spectacle as just a "showing" and a "looking." For him, this definitional question was related to what he perceived to be certain shortcomings in the theoretical underpinnings of the theme paper. Hodder felt that our approaches assumed that public performance was unique to large-scale societies and that power relations did not operate at the level of intimate, daily practices. Hodder also argued that the theme paper privileged the public and extraordinary spheres over the domestic and ordinary ones, and that insufficient emphasis was placed on the meaning of the performance.

Smith presented a yet different view of spectacle. Following Debord, he suggested that spectacle was a means to constitute political subjects through the formal and codified enactments of relationships. Houston, however, took a position similar to the editors'. He criticized Hodder's definition of spectacle as overly broad and incorporating too many quotidian actions while failing to account for the qualities that differentiate spectacle. The organizers reiterated their original view that performance and power relations took place in diverse forms, ranging from intimate interactions to mass spectacles, and in various kinds of society from small hunter-gatherer groups to vast empires, but that we should have a tighter focus to produce an integrated, meaningful book.

The session made clear that the study of ancient performance is in an early stage of development and that that the production of a coherent book would be an arduous task. In order to clarify our intentions and in an attempt to achieve further coherency, we suggested after the meeting that the contributors focus on "public performance and public theatrical events." Certain contributors perceived our new choice of this term over that of spectacle as a theoretical shift in the volume's focus, which was not our intention. We encouraged these contributors to continue to use the term "spectacle" to the extent they believed appropriate.

With respect to power and community, a greater degree of alignment among the participants led to an engaging debate. Our discussion had raised several important questions in this regard, including why certain societies strongly emphasize public performance by elites and others do not, how large-scale performances relate to small-scale ones, and how some societies incorporate multiple communities through performance. We encouraged the participants to examine the dynamic nature of performance and its role in the creation and negotiation of meaning, identity, and social structures and relations, and noted that stable meanings and static models of performance must be proven rather than assumed.

The diverse views expressed in the working group are preserved in this final volume. Our introductory chapter retains the original form of the session theme paper with minor revisions. Some authors chose to address directly the papers and criticisms of other contributors, while others preferred to allow their approaches to speak for themselves. All papers tackle the theoretical issues of senses, performance, performativity, and spectacle, but discussions on these problems take a prominent place in the chapters presented in Act II (Moore, Hodder, Smith, and Houston). The selections in Act III (Triadan, Inomata, Coben, Baines, and Kus and Raharijaona) focus more tightly on the questions of power and community more or less in the manner originally envisioned by the editors. We declined to present an epilogue or conclusion chapter purporting to unify the diverse views of the contributors.

The production of this book has been and—with the participation of you as readers—continues to be a social drama of archaeological, academic, and performance practice, filled with excitement and uncertainty. You've bought your ticket, so sit back now and enjoy the show. The overture is about to start.

Note

We thank Ian Hodder and Bob Preucel for their strong support of this project. We are particularly grateful to Ian for inviting Inomata to work on this project and for giving us continuous encouragement despite some differences in our respective views. The use of such terms as prologue, overture, act, and scene reflects our view of this project as a social and academic drama, and draws attention to the importance of the organization of a presentation or performance. Yet the requirements of the printed media dictate that scene numbers not strictly follow modern Western theater conventions.

References Cited

Coben, Lawrence S., and Charles Stanish
2005 Archaeological reconnaissance in the Carabaya region, Peru. *In* Advances in the Archaeology of the Titicaca Basin. Charles Stanish, Amanda Cohen, and Mark Aldenderfer, eds. Pp. 243–266. Los Angeles: Cotsen Institute of Archaeology Press.

Inomata, Takeshi, and Stephen D. Houston
2001 Royal Courts of the Ancient Maya. Boulder: Westview.

Act I

CONCEPTS AND APPROACHES

SCENE 1

OVERTURE: AN INVITATION TO THE ARCHAEOLOGICAL THEATER

Takeshi Inomata and Lawrence S. Coben

The traditional focus among archaeologists on the development of administrative and economic systems diverted their attention from the roles of public ceremonies, rituals, and performances, which have often been considered epiphenomenal in terms of political organization. The effects and implications of such gatherings in the past deserve more earnest inquiries. Just think about the importance of dances in Puebloan societies and of carnivals in Brazil. The sense of a community, cultural values, and moral order in those societies can never be adequately understood without the consideration of such theatrical events. Public events and theatrical performance are important for the operation of any society, but we stress that they had critical implications and consequences for the development of centralized polities. Nowhere in the world did the development of a state equipped with impersonal, pragmatic bureaucracy and coercive, disciplinary force happen overnight, leaping directly from a small autonomous village, the integration of which was based primarily on face-to-face contacts among its members. Michel Foucault (1977) suggested that antiquity was a civilization of spectacle whereas modernity is a society of discipline. Although this may be a broad, overarching statement, it is probably true that the development of large, centralized polities would have been impossible in any historical context without frequent public events, in which agents of political power presented themselves in front of a large number of spectators and the participants shared experiences through their bodily copresence.

Richard Schechner (1994:623) has suggested that an actor is a quasi-shaman, a person of power that serves as a conduit for energies liberated by the theatrical event. In many early societies, the roles of religious and political specialists may have overlapped significantly with those of actors in later societies. Even in modern states with highly developed administrative systems, physical enactments of political ideologies and public gatherings continue to play important roles. Many countries, including Britain and Japan, retain monarchs who embody national identities. In the United States, which does not have symbolic figures with deep historical roots, the president, with the help of television and other modern technologies, plays a significant role in public performance by enacting the ideology of the "American way." President Ronald Reagan once observed that he did not know how someone who had not been an actor could be a president.

This volume attempts to bring the question of theatrical performance back to the central stage of archaeological inquiry. We examine the political implications of theatrical performance that took place as spectacles and public events in premodern societies. More specifically, we are interested in performances and events involving multiple individuals or groups, which form a process and arena of political and ideological negotiation, competition, and collaboration. Two issues emerge as critical questions in this study: (1) the moral integration and identities of a community and (2) the creation, maintenance, and subversion of asymmetrical power relations. The examination of these questions requires both a sound theoretical ground and sensitivity to historical particularity.

Conceptual Frameworks

The study of performance has become an important theme in social sciences and humanities, although it is only recently that archaeologists have begun to realize the potential of such an approach. Anthropologists, sociologists, and linguists have become increasingly aware of theatricality in social life, and theater scholars have explored human interactions outside of formal theater buildings. This breakdown of disciplinary boundaries has also created a confusing situation, in which the concepts of performance used by various scholars comprise a wide range of meanings. In an influential paper, Dell Hymes (1975:13) once noted that cultural anthropologists and folklorists tended to confuse matters by lumping what interested them under the term "performance." A similar tendency appears to exist in recent archaeological studies. Restrictive, inflexible definitions of performance, however, are counterproductive. Concepts of performance remain fluid, but the fluidity should not become an excuse for conceptual sloppiness among researchers. What we need is a critical evaluation of our use of the term, concept, and underlying assumptions. As a step toward such critical reflection, here we define our focus for the current study and discuss its relations to various theoretical frameworks.

Performance, Theater, and Theatricality

At one end of the spectrum is the notion of performance as an enactment of what it refers to with an emphasis on what human beings do. This view is represented by the concept of performative utterance in speech act theory, which strongly influenced the analysis of performance by folklorists, anthropological linguists, and culture theorists (see Bauman and Briggs 1990; Parker and Sedgwick 1995). As in the title of a classic book by J. L. Austin (1962), it is about *How to Do Things with Words*. The utterance by a priest in a matrimonial rite, "I hereby pronounce you man and wife," does not simply describe the situation but affects the marriage. Jacques Derrida (1988) and Judith Butler (1990, 1993) have further developed the concept of performativity, emphasizing its aspect of citationality. As she argues that genders are shaped through performative acts, Butler (1993:12–13, 225) characterizes a performative not as a singular act performed through the voluntary will or creativity of an individual, but as a citation of iterable, regulatory norms. Most performatives, such as legal sentences, have a binding power. According to her, as the judge cites the law to authorize and install the situation he or she names, the binding power of a performative derives from the citation of a norm. The regulatory force of a norm is rooted in its own historicity, that is, the repetition and accumulation of processes in which it is cited as a norm (see Joyce 2000; Meskell 1999 for archaeological applications). By emphasizing citationality, Butler focuses on the discursive and explicitly plays down the theatrical aspect of performative acts (Taylor 2003:6), which is a central concern for many performance studies, including this volume.[1]

Also found near this end of the continuum is a broad concept of performance that includes informal daily activities as forms of human interactions and self-presentations. Erving Goffman (1959, 1967) has defined performance as "all the activity of an individual which occurs during a period marked by his continuous presence before a particular set of observers and which has some effect on the observers" (Goffman 1959:22). In this manner, Goffman has explicitly associated social actions in everyday life with theatrical acts, both of which are essentially communicative and expressive acts involving the presence of performers and observers. He has pointed out that a person's identities are flexible and situational in the sense that in everyday life a person presents different identities and images as an actor takes different theatrical roles. Building on the original idea proposed by Gregory Bateson, Goffman (1974) also developed the important concept of "frame," that is, an interpretive framework that is set up by some activities or messages and guides the understanding of other simultaneous or subsequent acts. In a theater, such frames are often marked by the raising and lowering of a curtain, leading the audience to distinguish theatrical acts from others.

Other anthropologists prefer narrower definitions of performance (MacAloon 1984a:6). Hymes (1975:13–19) has argued that performance is not merely behavior but "something creative, realized, achieved, even transcendent of the ordinary course of events," which is interpretable, reportable, and repeatable in a domain of cultural intelligibility. In Hymes's view, what makes performance is qualities that are consciously recognized by performers and observers, whereas Goffman conceptualized performance as something that is not apparent to the actors and that researchers as outsiders find by placing it in their analytical frameworks. Hymes has also noted that performance is cultural behavior for which a person assumes responsibility to an audience. Certain ritual activities can be viewed as performance even when they do not involve the physical presence of an audience, if gods, supernaturals, or performers take the real or symbolic role of an audience (Schechner 1988:30). Thus performance is a mode of communicative behavior (Bauman 1989).

The other end of the spectrum encompasses highly circumscribed and prescribed acts in formalized theaters, in which the performers and audience are consciously concerned with the theatricality of the acts and settings. Richard Schechner (1977:75; 1988:6–16; 1994) has written extensively on the characteristics of theater in comparison with other types of performance, such as rituals, sports, and games. According to him, theater requires the physical presence of an audience who are observers and evaluators, whereas rituals often involve an audience as more active participants who sing, dance, pray, or present offerings. Another defining feature of theater is its focus on symbolic reality, in which the performers represent themselves in roles detached from their lives outside the performance (Beeman 1993:379). As Erika Fischer-Lichte (1992:139–140; 1995) notes, theater has its own semiotic system that utilizes signs made available by a specific culture as its own. Alan Read (1993:10) adds that theater is an expressive practice through the medium of images at the center of which is the human body.[2]

In contrast to the notion of institutionalized theater in modern societies, in which most if not all of the characteristics are prominent, we define theatricality as a more ambiguous, inclusive concept that suggests the degree to which some of these characteristics of theater are present in social action and practice. Hence theatricality is prevalent in human life outside the walls of a theater. A requisite of theatricality is the physical presence of an audience. An audience often has multiple roles of observers, evaluators, and participants, and even a part of the performing group can serve as an audience (Beeman 1993:383–384). Thus one dimension of theatricality concerns the comparative weight of observer and evaluator roles of the audience. This relates closely to another dimension of theatricality, the level of emotional responses, if not entertainment, that performance triggers in the participants and audience. Although theatricality is often associated with the positive elevation of emotions, the spectacle of terror is also possible. Emotional responses of the participants and audience are never homogeneous, and they may at once involve positive and negative feelings, as well as disinterest. Another necessary condition of theatricality is the use of material images in dynamic motion as media of expression and communication. The human body takes a central role in this process. Although such animated objects as puppets, statues, and floats may take important parts, it is ultimately the human body that produces such motions and senses them. Finally, the dimension of symbolic reality is not a categorical marker of theatricality. As Goffman has demonstrated, a certain level of role-playing takes place in day-to-day interactions. In this sense, theatricality refers to the density, rather than the presence or absence, of signs used in a way comparable to formal theater (Pavis 1998:395). Theatricality is a critical concept in examining the communicative potentials of performance, the construction of its meaning, and the emotional impacts on participants. It follows that the political implications of performance, in terms of the reproduction of power relations, the negotiation of ideologies, and the constitution of a community, as discussed below, are closely, but never in a straightforward manner, related to its theatricality.

The focus of our study should build on these diverse theoretical views, tailored specifically for the issues of power and community. In this regard, we believe that Hymes's definition of performance provides a useful conceptual basis. The authors of the volume, with the explicit exception of Hodder, address performance in this sense, including public rituals, ceremonies, festivals, and courtly interactions, which fall between the two extremes of the conceptual continuum. With the foregoing definition of theatricality in mind, we often call these acts theatrical performance. An important goal of the current study is to examine political implications of theatrical performance that are culturally recognized by actors and viewers. Our intention, however, is not to demarcate the categorical boundaries of our inquiry. By using the term "theatrical performance," we suggest a rather arbitrary degree of theatricality. Moreover, we need to recognize that the social significance of any performance we address, from the broadest end of the conceptual spectrum encompassing daily practice or the narrowest end focusing on formal theater, is rooted in both performativity and theatricality.

Spectacles and Public Events

While the foregoing discussion of the conceptual spectrum of performance crosscuts diverse sizes and forms of theatrical events, the scale of interactions, including the number of participants, is also an important dimension of performance that we need to address. In this regard, one end of this continuum represented by the concepts of spectacle and public event figures prominently in our study. For us the primary feature of the spectacle is a gathering centered around theatrical performance of a certain scale in clear spatial and temporal frames, in which participants witness and sense the presence of others and share a certain experience (MacAloon 1984b:243–246).[3] The scale and grandeur of spectacles are not absolute measurements, but depend on the expectations of the participants and the cultural values of the themes presented in these events as shaped in specific social and historical contexts.

Spectacles in this sense comprise many types of rituals, ceremonies, parades, public presentations, festivals, athletic events, and public execution and torture, which overlap significantly with what Don Handelman (1990) calls "public events" (Beeman 1993:380).[4] Because the central figures or protagonists of public events are always highly conscious of the way they present themselves, such occasions inevitably involve certain elements of theatricality. It is our deliberate intention to use the terms "spectacle" and "public event" rather than ritual or ceremony to which anthropologists and archaeologists are more accustomed. In this manner, not only do we consciously apply recent developments in performance theory, theater studies, and dramaturgic analysis to our archaeological cases, but we also examine the common qualities and political implications shared among certain rituals and other types of spectacles (see Moore and Myerhoff 1977).

Again, by primarily addressing spectacles, we do not intend to make a categorical typology. Our point is that the physical forms and settings of a theatrical event are as important as the meaning of performance, as discussed in more detail below. Our focus on large-scale events does not mean that we privilege them over smaller ones in terms of political significance. In this regard, it is suggestive to note certain parallels between the study of spectacle and the more traditional interests of archaeologists in monuments and monumental buildings. The social importance of monumental constructions, as well as that of spectacle, derives partly from their large labor investment (Trigger 1990); the construction of such architecture in itself creates spectacle with planning and managing organizations (Mendelssohn 1974; Baines, this volume, chapter 9). As monuments provide stages for theatrical events, their physical presence creates ordered space that defines social relations of participants (Barrett 1994:57–58; Bradley 1998; Thomas 1999:228–229). Moreover, monuments mediate the construction and negotiation of the meaning associated with landscape and time in a unique manner comparable to spectacle because of its extraordinary nature distinct from buildings tied to daily lives (Bradley 1993).

Communicative and Creative Qualities of Performance

Our goal is not to examine theatrical performance and spectacle as a closed system of their own aesthetics, but as political actions in a broad social context. We need to explore how such acts and events relate to the domains of social relations and the perceptions of society. Important issues include the process of communication through performance and the process in which performance creates identities and social relations.

Communication, Meaning, and Structure

Many early studies of ritual and related subjects dichotomized thought and action and usually assigned the causal primacy to the former (Bell 1997:ix). For example, the study of religion and ritual by Mircea Eliade (1978) proposed that ritual was a secondary reenactment of mythical events and stories told in a preexisting myth. The structuralism of Claude Lévi-Strauss (1969) examined the underlying, abstract structures that were generative of human behavior and organization. Thus the focus in those studies was to read messages and symbols encoded in ritual and to uncover defining structures hidden under observable behavior. Such tendencies are also seen in pioneering work that later led to the development of performance theory. In his "dramatistic" approach to human interactions, Kenneth Burke (1945) focused on the human intent to affect others through symbolic action. His emphasis was on motives that made meaningful symbolic acts. Likewise, Goffman (1959, 1967) addressed the shifting images of an individual managed by him or her, under which the existence of a stable inner core was assumed (MacAloon 1984a:7). Most scholars, however, have acknowledged that the meanings of ritual and other acts are highly complex. Victor Turner (1967:50), in particular, has argued that ritual performance is multivocal, representing different meanings for different people and in different situations. Schechner (1994:621) has also pointed out that the interpretation of performance often falls into the trap of attributing some meaning that belongs to the interpreter's own deeply held prior narratives. Stanley Tambiah (1979:124) and Valerio Valeri (1985:344–345) go further to contend that ritual does not communicate concepts in any direct manner or by conventional means.

Recent studies focus on the way ritual and other types of performance communicate. Valeri (1985:344), for example, has suggested that ritual produces knowledge by producing model experiences because it reproduces dispositions that are at the same time bodily, emotional, and mental. Some scholars turned to semiotics as a theoretical tool, employing Charles Sanders Peirce's concepts of three types of signs: icons that involve formal resemblance, such as some road signs; indices that involve physical or actual connection, such as smoke for fire; and symbols that involve conventional associations, such as most words (Eco 1977; Elam 1980; Fischer-Lichte 1992; Parmentier 1994:129–134, 1997). According to Tambiah (1979:124), ritual produces indexical signs in structured patterns that lead the participants to reproduce concepts in their minds. Roy Rappaport (1999:52–53; see also Robbins 2001) has argued that ritual communicates two types of messages: self-referential messages on the current physical and psychic states of the performer through indices and canonical messages, independent of the performer, about the nature of the world through symbols. Scholars also point out unique potentials of nonverbal communication through bodily performance. Seeing is believing. Images do not deceive while words can be easily manipulated (Rappaport 1999). Thus theatrical performance may sometimes have more persuasive power than verbal communication. Moreover, bodily performance and music may be viewed as a more effective way to communicate with deities, supernaturals, and natural beings that do not talk to humans verbally (Basso 1985).

Practice, Experience, and Creative Processes

The study of performance now emphasizes more strongly its creative quality. Performance not only communicates concepts but creates identities for the participants and constructs the world in which they live. Performance is not only a mode of communication but a mode of social action. We need to focus on the active creation of meaning, identities, cognitive models, and social relations through the experience of doing and seeing (Palmer and Jankowiak 1996). An earlier version of such a view can be found among Cambridge classicists, including Jane Ellen Harrison (1962), who argued that myths, as well as Greek theater and Olympic games, originated in rituals. Also relevant is Victor Turner's (1957, 1972) idea of rituals as social dramas with an emphasis on dynamic processes—rather than static structures—of social relations that unfold in ritual. In this sense, performance not only mirrors social change but also creates change (Schechner 1994:626–632).

Inspirations come from theories of performativity and practice. Some studies of ritual have explicitly applied the Austinian concept of performativity. Tambiah (1979), for example, emphasizes the performative quality of ritual by suggesting that symbolic expressions in ritual simultaneously create the sense of reality and act upon the real world as it is experienced by the participants. In Maurice Bloch's (1974:59–60) view, ritual creates and maintains a certain type of power relations among the participants not by transmitting messages but by catching them in a highly formalized situation that gives no options to challenge authority except by total refusal.

Practice theory proposes that larger structures play out and are reproduced through social practices (Bourdieu 1977). In this theoretical framework, Marshall Sahlins's (1985) analysis of Hawaiian ritual through the death of Captain Cook and Sherry Ortner's (1978, 1989) study of Buddhist ritual among the Sherpas show how ritual practices mediate between enduring structures and the tensions of a particular situation, although they do not emphasize the term performance. Catherine Bell (1992, 1997:72–83, 1998) explicitly employs performance and practice theories and argues that the central quality of ritual is the primacy of the body that, through its movement and senses, not only experiences and receives the values ordering the environment but simultaneously defines and imposes such values. A related issue is the process of preparation and rehearsal. Although anthropologists traditionally focused on performance in ritual or other events, Schechner (1985; 1994:641–643) has shown that rehearsal processes have their own structures and affect relationships among the participants. The cultural importance of carnivals and other festivals, for example, derives not only from the magnificence of the finished products but also from the long process of preparation.

With the emphasis on the experiential aspect of theatrical events, scholars have also directed their attentions to the physical and sensual reality of performing, addressing the concepts of kinesthesia, the sensations experienced by the body in movement, and synesthesia, a stimulus in one sense inducing sensations in other senses (Schechner 1977:99–107; Sullivan 1986:6–8).

The Study of Performance

Early studies of ritual and other performance categories tended to emphasize what specific performance meant. While most types of performance have some conventional meaning shared by multiple individuals, they also are multivocal and ambiguous at deeper levels. An important lesson we learn from recent developments in performance theory as we examine performance in archaeological contexts is to focus more on how theatrical events communicate, how they generate meaning, and how different meanings are negotiated among participants, rather than simply assume the preexistence of fixed meaning.[5] Such examination must include the formal properties of theatrical events. As we prepared this volume, some of our colleagues and reviewers criticized our focus on spectacle. The criticisms of these colleagues, who deemphasize or even ignore such factors as the number of participants and the scale of events, derive from their explicit or unconscious assumption that privileges meaning at the expense of form. We should not connect certain forms of events with specific political effects in a straightforward manner. But it is equally problematic to underestimate the political and social significance of the formal characteristics of theatrical events.

We need to analyze closely the physical acts of performance and its material and social settings. This analysis should consider how such formal processes and characteristics of theatrical events shape, and are shaped by, meaning and emotion. This view also presents important methodological implications for archaeologists. The form, context, and process of theatrical events are accessible through archaeological research. By confronting the social significance of these aspects of performance, we can begin to explore how people create and negotiate meaning through their actions.

Performance, Community, and Politics

The creation and enactment of cultural and moral values through performance take place in a wide range of occasions and contexts. Pierre Bourdieu (1977) and Judith Butler (1990, 1993), in particular, have emphasized the importance of rather unconscious, routine daily practices that shape social relations. Under the influence of these theories, archaeologists have recently directed a significant effort to the study of ordinary, daily lives. While fully embracing the significance of such an approach, we point out that highly conscious acts in extraordinary circumstances, particularly those that contrast with and diverge from daily activities, are equally important in shaping the operation and organization of society. Time and space in traditional societies should not be considered homogeneous, monotonous continua (Bradley 1998:85–100). Spectacles and other public events may provide moments of disjunction from daily routines (Van Gennep 1960; Turner 1972). Practices by sovereigns and courtiers, while often representing the exemplary center of society, also frequently emphasize detachment from the norms of the rest of society. Whereas daily practices reflect—and create—larger structures usually in subtle manners, such extraordinary events and actors ostentatiously dramatize and play out the moral and aesthetic values of a society, and the participants often enact and experience ideologies, cultural ideals, and traditions in uniquely explicit ways (Singer 1959). What we call theatrical performance and spectacles in premodern societies comprise a wide range of activities and occasions, such as polity-wide gatherings with the ruler as the protagonist or sponsor, diplomatic ceremonies involving multiple political units, courtly activities with a relatively small audience, religious rites detached from governmental institutions, festivals at the village level, and pilgrimages that draw numerous participants of diverse political and social affiliations. These events have profound implications for the understanding of any society, particularly in terms of the integration of communities and the establishment and maintenance of asymmetrical power relations, which are intricately intertwined with each other.

Community

Benedict Anderson (1991:6) argues that "all communities larger than primordial villages of face-to-face contact (and perhaps even these) are imagined" in the sense that the members never know most of their fellow members or meet them, yet they bear the image of their communion. No such things as "true" communities exist. The concept of an imagined community implies contradictions and fluidity in identities, expectations, and perceptions of their members. How does a group of people come to bear the image of a community in their mind and to exhibit a certain level of order and coherence in their conduct, while still comprising internal heterogeneity and inconsistency? Anderson (1991:12–19, 37–46) privileges the role of written media both for the rise of modern nationalism and for the preceding religious communities of Christianity, Islam, and Buddhism. In particular, the sacred script of religious communities bound peoples of different languages and customs across time and space. In the premodern world, however, numerous imagined communities developed without the help of writings (see Canuto and Yaeger 2000). Anderson (1991:19–36) adds two more elements that underlie premodern imagined communities: the belief that society was naturally organized around divine centers and monarchs, and the mythical concept that merges the origins of the world and humans. We, however, know that the authenticity of rulership and cosmology cannot be taken for granted. How does the legitimacy of sovereign and myth come to take hold of people's minds?

No organization can exist without associated symbols, which give concrete, sensible forms to community identities (Kertzer 1988:15). In this regard, spectacles ostentatiously dramatize the central value of a community and present it in sensible forms. Milton Singer (1959, 1972) most clearly articulated the role of such events in his concept of cultural performance. According to Singer (1959:xii; 1972), cultural performance is an institution embodying central symbolic aspects of a cultural tradition, such as weddings, temple festivals, dances, and musical concerts, in which the cultural content of a tradition is organized and transmitted through specific cultural media and human carriers. They are reflexive occasions for the participants, for they can stand back and consider their identities, actions, and ideas (Turner 1986b:24). Roberto Da Matta's (1984) study of Brazilian carnival and Handelman's (1990:116–135) analysis of Palio of Siena have shown that, through these unique qualities of spectacles, people and communities reconstitute themselves. Moreover, Paul Connerton (1989:41–71) has argued that what he calls commemorative ceremonies through bodily enactment by participants sustain the social memory of a community.

These arguments of community integration and the perpetuation of its cultural values owe much to the classic study by Emile Durkheim (1965), who proposed that ritual brings together individuals as a collective group and strengthens their bonds to a society through the experience of collective representation and an appeal to communal emotion. Numerous scholars followed and reworked the thesis elaborated by Durkheim. While retaining the essential idea of Durkheim, Max Gluckman (1963:126–131) and Turner (1957, 1972) have emphasized the social tensions expressed through ritual. Turner (1972), with inspiration from Van Gennep (1960), has argued that ritual presents the state of liminality, or antistructure, that detaches people from the normal social order and creates what he calls communitas. Thus ritual is, according to Turner, the process of re-creation of a community rather than the simple perpetuation of its solidarity, involving possibilities for change.

E. E. Evans-Pritchard (1974:207–208), however, criticized Durkheim, arguing that people participating in ritual display a variety of feeling, including indifference, instead of unified collective emotional ethos. What is important, Evans-Pritchard argued, is that the essential acts of ritual be carried out. Tambiah (1979:124) also suggests that ritual does not directly evoke communal emotions; rather, it affords the participants intense experience that reproduces concepts and implicit understanding in their mind. The ambiguity of meaning and the uncertainty of effects are critical aspects of ritual and other public events (Fernandez 1972; Kertzer 1988:57–76; MacAloon 1984a:9). As Bell (1992:221–222) points out, ritual tolerates a degree of internal resistance and indifference among the participants, while requiring their external consent. Ritual becomes effective because it grounds and displays a sense of community without overriding the autonomy of individuals. In this regard, David Kertzer (1988:76) reminds us of the original argument by Durkheim that solidarity is produced by people acting together, not by people thinking together.

The social effects of spectacle derive partly from the physical copresence of participants, whether as performers, audience, or both. Human sociality and identity are rooted in our sensory perceptions of the presence and actions of others. Not only do gatherings facilitate opportunities for exchanging goods, communicating information, and finding mates, but they also create moments of something closest to "true" communities, in which a large number of individuals sense and witness the bodily existence and participation of other members. Performance on such occasions creates objectifications of experience, which makes it accessible to others by transcending the limitations of individual experience (Rogers 1999:5). Public events, thus, do not simply express the solidarity of a group, but they make a community. Communal identities associated with theatrical events are not the expressions of deeply held inner cores of community members but practical accomplishments achieved by means of performance, witnessing, and participation (Rogers 1999:9–10). Preparation and rehearsal leading to the final performance are also important parts of this process. It follows that the authenticity of community traditions and memories is not a timeless entity reenacted in spectacles (Anderson 1991; Hobsbawn and Ranger 1983; Rockfeller 1999:123). Authenticity is something imagined, something created and recreated through the repetition of performance (Bailey 1996:13). This also means that performance has a potential not only of maintaining collective identities but also of transforming them, subverting them, and resisting them.

Although Anderson stresses the importance of written media for the creation of imagined communities, Kertzer (1988) demonstrates that ritual and bodily performance play critical roles even in political organizations of the modern world. Our study is motivated by the assumption that, in premodern societies without writing systems or with a large portion of the population being illiterate, theatrical performance may have had even greater social effects. On a relatively small spatial and demographic scale, we need to examine the centripetal force of spectacle that brings people together beyond the limitations of groups based on daily face-to-face contact. On a larger scale, we should explore the potentials and limitations of theatrical performance in reaching different ethnic groups beyond cultural and linguistic barriers (see Futrell 1997).

Domination and Resistance

The effects of spectacles in creating a community suggest their potential as tools for ideological and political unification and thus for domination. As Adolf Hitler chillingly pointed out, no government can rule by force alone. All forms of power relation necessitate constant affirmation and maintenance through the acts of performance and witnessing (Scott 1990:49). Ideologies that underlie social relations do not appear from thin air, but need to be generated and maintained through practice. While this is true for any society, such processes of the maintenance of power relations are particularly important for the understanding of premodern societies. Many early polities, even ones that may be called states, probably lacked coercive force to control their entire population effectively. In this regard, some early anthropological theories overstated the importance of physical force (see Carneiro 1970). Although warfare and coercive force were critical aspects of virtually all centralized societies, the subordinates in many cases still had an option of fleeing from the spheres of dominant power when subjected to excessive oppression. In addition, military force of states or other centralized political institutions was often directed toward other polities, and a larger concern for central authorities of many early polities was to attract their followers (e.g., Tambiah 1976). Many early states did not have a developed bureaucracy, and the royal court operated as the main apparatus of administration and domination primarily through fluid personal relations (Elias 1983; Inomata and Houston 2001). For such political institutions, one cannot overemphasize the importance of performance in establishing, affirming, manipulating, and maintaining power relations between elites and nonelites, as well as among elites themselves (e.g., Brown and Elliott 1980). According to Foucault (1977:187), in premodern Europe before the technologies of discipline developed, state power was what was seen, what was shown, and what was manifested.

Many studies concerning the relationship between theatrical performance and politics draw to varying degrees on Marxist theory. Elizabeth DeMarrais et al. (1996) have argued that public performance materializes ideologies by giving them concrete forms, thereby facilitating the propagation of dominant ideologies across space and social groups. John Baines and Norman Yoffee (1998:235) have proposed that courtly performance is a part of what they term high culture, that is, the production and consumption of aesthetic items for and by the top elites, through which they appropriate meaning. These views emphasize theatrical performance for and by the dominants as conveyors of their versions of worldviews, history, cultural ideals, value systems, and social order, which serve to define and maintain structured social relations among different classes, genders, and interest groups (see also Demarest 1992). Such messages from the dominant are delivered through the centripetal forces of spectacles, wrapped in the attractions and excitements of theatrical performance. The conspicuous consumption of material goods that often accompanies theatrical performance may also help impress the subjects and force them into the debt of the dominants (Clark and Blake 1994; Hayden and Gargett 1990).

The dominant used theatrical display for their political purposes in many historical contexts. Yet rituals and public events rarely work in completely unambiguous ways. The inherent multivocality of theatrical signs makes the propagation of dominant ideologies difficult, if not impossible. James Scott (1990:77–90) contends that the subordinate rarely subscribes blindly to dominant ideologies. The weak may give the appearance of hegemonic conduct in public, but they often show acts and voices of disobedience behind the scenes. According to Scott (1990:2–19), the "public transcript" enacted on public stages is the presentation of elites as they want themselves to be seen. Both elites and nonelites have their own "hidden transcripts" played out offstage, which diverge from and contradict the public transcript. The gray area between the public and hidden transcripts is a critical arena of political struggles where subordinates express their defiance through disguise and anonymity. The weak may even take advantage of the public transcript that presents elites as their benefactors. The primary purpose of the public transcript, Scott (1990:67–69) argues, is not to gain the agreement of subordinates but rather to awe and intimidate them into a durable and expedient compliance. The dominant is also an audience of the performance of the public transcript, which works as a kind of self-hypnosis within ruling groups to back up their courage, improve their cohesion, and convince themselves anew of their high moral purpose.[6] The rupture of the public transcript may become evident, according to Scott (1990:172–175; see also Bakhtin 1968; Kertzer 1988:144–150), in carnivals and similar public events, in which the populace is released from the normal social order and openly expresses dissent from and resentment toward the dominant. In addition, some theatrical events, particularly when conducted by subjugated or excluded subsections of a society, may generate powerful forms of resistance, as seen in the cases of cargo cult and ghost dance. In short, Scott examines the ambiguity and multiple voices involved in performance, yet he still sees the public transcript essentially as a tool of the elite.

A different approach is seen in the study of divine kingship following the tradition originating from James Fraser (1925). In this view, the ruler, as well as other elites, is also bound by royal ceremonialism and the notion of divine kingship. The primacy of kingship over the king is epitomized in the practice of regicide: the ruler who embodies the well-being of the kingdom must remain strong; thus the ruler must be killed when he or she becomes ill or weak (Feeley-Harnik 1985). Fraser examined the Babylonian rituals of Akitu and Sakaia, in which it is said that the ruler was slapped and humiliated, the roles of slaves and masters switched, and a criminal was put on the throne only to be killed later. Fraser interpreted them as representations of the theme of regicide, in which the king is killed symbolically. Although many scholars questioned the evidential bases of these Babylonian rituals, similar practices can be found ethnographically. Evans-Pritchard (1964:205–206) has noted that in the accession ceremony of the king of the Shilluk in Sudan, the new king conducts a mock battle with the army of the cultural hero, Nykang, in which the king is defeated; thus kingship captures the king. The Shilluk are also said to have practiced regicide. In the royal ceremony of Ncwala of the Swazi kingdom, normal behavior becomes taboo. The main theme of the sacred songs in this ritual is hatred of the king and the rejection of the king by the people

(Kuper 1961:197–225). There has been much debate about the reality of regicide and the interpretation of the Ncwala ceremony (Beidelman 1966; Gluckman 1963:119–225; Lincoln 1987). We just note that these examples show that carnivalesque attitudes can appear even in the public transcript sponsored by the dominant elite. The liminal sphere created through rituals is potentially dangerous for the dominant, as daily social structures may be challenged, threatened, or subverted, at least temporarily. Moreover, the sovereign and other elites may be prisoners of cultural traditions and royal ceremonialism. As much as theatrical pageants are the rights and tools of the ruler and courtiers, they are their duties. In many societies, politically dominant groups do not always cunningly manipulate ideologies through spectacles, but they are bound by their system of cultural and aesthetic values (Bloch 1986:177; Inomata and Houston 2001).

Another important view is the one emphasizing the power and effect of theatrical performance to define the political reality and social relations (Turner 1967). In this approach, theatrical performance is not empty ritual behind which the real mechanism of power works. Performance itself is a critical part of politics (Bell 1992:197–223; Kertzer 1988:77–101). As Mary Douglas (1966:62) has put it, social rituals create a reality which would be nothing without them, for it is impossible to have social relations without symbolic acts. Also relevant is Bourdieu's (1977:95) argument that in daily interactions the concessions of politeness always contain political concessions, and thus such symbolic acts shape political relations. In addition, Bloch (1974:59–60) has suggested that the formalized discourse of ritual, which does not allow deviation, creates and maintains what Max Weber called traditional authority. Clifford Geertz (1980:123–135) goes further to claim that theatrical performance *is* the politics. In the theater state of historical Bali, theatrical performance was the state's primary purpose. In this view, the elaborate and stupendous dramatization of cultural themes through royal ceremonies was not a means to a political end, but the end itself. Thus Geertz has advocated the poetics or aesthetics of power rather than the Weberian notion of the mechanics of power (Smith 2000; Reese-Taylor and Koontz 2001 for archaeological applications).

In the context of emergent centralized polities, the preparation of large-scale spectacles, along with the construction of theatrical space, may also promote the development of hierarchical organization by requiring dramaturgical and logistical organizers (Hill and Clark 2001). In addition, ritual specialists always have potential to become politically powerful figures through their appropriation of the means of symbolic production and objectification.

The opposing themes regarding spectacle and theatrical performance—the appropriation of meaning by dominant groups versus multivocality, the imposition of asymmetrical structures versus the liminal subversion of the daily order, and the theater for the state versus the state for the theater—should not be considered as alternative, mutually incompatible models. Rather, they are the coexisting aspects of every society. The inherent ambiguity in its meaning and effect implies the paradox of theatrical performance that even those designed for the purpose of the dominant simultaneously empower those who are to be subjugated through emotional elevation, the affirmation of their social identities, and the renewed affinities to a community (Fernandez 1972). Theatrical performance does not work for the effect of asymmetrical power relations if it is perceived as not amenable to some degree of individual appropriation (Bell 1992:207, 221–222). Our task is to examine how such multiple dimensions of spectacles and theatrical performance articulate with each other in specific social and historical contexts.

Into the Ancient Theater

The analysis of theatrical performances poses a challenge to archaeologists who cannot directly observe such actions. We, however, should not be pessimistic of the possibilities of our research. In the last few decades such subjects as meaning, ideology, and identity have become central concerns for archaeological studies (Demarest 1992; Hodder 1982; Miller and Tilley 1984; Claessen and Oosten 1996). Our study of theatrical performance places a stronger emphasis on physical acts and the immediacy of material presence, which should be more directly accessible through archaeological research than abstract concepts. Three issues are particularly important for our purpose: theatrical space, images, and objects used in performance. These issues converge at the questions of social contexts and effects.

Performance and Material Culture

As Schechner (1994:618–620) has pointed out, the theater is a cultural place that obtains meanings through performance that takes place there and evokes the memory of past events and thus prior experience, ideological messages, and power relations (Coben 2001). Even the natural landscape can be transformed into a theater by means of the enactment of theatrical themes and the attachment of the lore of performance by ancestors (Schechner 1994:618). The construction of theatrical space, including plazas, certain types of temples, and palaces, is a critical part of preparation for theatrical events. In premodern societies, builders of such architecture were often participants in and audience of spectacles rather than disinterested contract workers. Thus the estimate of labor investment and the cycle of its renovation should not be overlooked in examining the social implications of theatrical events. Moreover, the scale, location, and distribution of such buildings in relation to other structures point to the political importance of theatrical events.

Whether one takes a phenomenological approach or a more "scientific" one, it is essential in the analysis of theatrical space to place the human body as the point of action and sensory perception (Moore 1996:153–167; Pearson and Shanks 2001:134–135; Tilley 1994:16). We need to see such spaces not only from the position of the "God's eyes" (plan views) but also from those of performers and spectators (Bradley 1998:124). Three-dimensional reconstruction of theatrical space with computers is significant in this regard. Proxemics, developed by Edward Hall (1966; Moore 1996:153–164; Pearson and Shanks 2001:127–128), also presents a useful tool. According to Hall, the spatial settings, particularly the distance between the performers and audience, define what kinds of communicative acts—verbal and musical performance, facial expressions, body movements, and so on—were within the capability of human perception. More specific analysis of spatial configurations, including stages, backdrops, lighting, visibility, and acoustics, helps us understand the theatrical effects and actual communicative potential of certain performances (Carlson 1989). The size and configuration of space provide a basis for estimating the number of performers and audience, which is a critical parameter in examining the political implications of theatrical events (Bradley 1998:101–115; Moore 1996:151–153). Moreover, the analysis of visibility between the stage and audience, between performers, and between spectators, provides clues to the nature of performance and to the intended audience (Inomata 2001).

Images of performance preserved as sculptures, figurines, murals, or ceramic paintings provide specific information on certain aspects of theatrical performance, including the identities of performers, the appearance and posture of actors, the spatial settings of performance, and the emic notions of sensory perceptions (e.g., Miller 1986; Houston and Taube 2000). Any representations involve elements of idealized notions of theatrical performance, which may hinder our access to the reality of historical events but may provide clues to cultural notions and ideals in this matter. In addition, graphic representations may be intended as the documentation of specific historical events, serving as the means for reexperiencing theatrical acts or for engraving ephemeral theatrical experiences perpetually in the personal and social memory (Bergman 1999:14). Certain iconographic depictions may have served as guides for future performances. As the analysis of rehearsal is an indispensable part of theater studies, it is equally important to examine processes after theatrical events, that is, how people remembered them and how people maintained or changed their meaning. In this regard, we should note that the production and exhibit of images also constitute performance.

Material objects are often important components of theatrical presentation. Like theatrical spaces and images, such materials may serve as repositories of narrative and practical knowledge associated with theatrical events. These artifacts, however, are rarely left on the localities of performance, which may pose difficulties for archaeological research. The identification and analysis of certain objects used in theatrical events may require the help of iconographic or documentary evidence. Yet performance paraphernalia found in storage, domestic, or mortuary contexts may provide information on performers, sponsors, and their assistants.

Social Contexts and Effects

The inquiry into the political implications and effects of theatrical events needs to be based on a contextualized understanding of the nature and settings of such events. Superficially similar performances with comparable scripts, choreography, and backdrops may deliver significantly different meanings and effects in different social circumstances. Our awareness of and sensitivity to cultural and intersubjective diversity is critical. Instead of assuming the preexistence of fixed meanings, our study should be directed toward the questions of how spectacles provide an arena for the creation of and resistance to dominant discourse, how different groups and individuals use theatrical performance and are bound by its traditions and its performative effects, and in what social contexts such events have social and political effects.

An important question to be considered in the study of social contexts and effects of theatrical events is the relation among participants and the roles they play. In certain theatrical events, the roles of the participants as performers and spectators, and thus the division between them, are relatively well defined. On other occasions, where such roles are not clearly predetermined, a person can potentially assume diverse or multiple roles, or indeed the classification may be without merit. In certain societies participants may not be restricted to humans. Supernaturals, ancestors, animals, architecture, and objects may take central roles as either performers or audience. In many religious ceremonies, deities and the dead often constitute the primary audience, and human spectators become critical participants in the performance. Without the active participation of human viewers, the communication with supernaturals may be unsuccessful. Furthermore, deities and ancestors may assume active roles as performers, often through their material symbols and impersonators, as seen in the processions of mummies in Inka rituals and those of saint statues in Catholic rites.

On a broader framework, we need to examine the relations of theatrical events with their social and natural settings, including their intersections with political institutions, economic activities, and the physical environments. We should not treat performance as a closed system defined by its own aesthetics. This leads to a more dynamic issue of how the nature of theatrical events, their social and political importance, and the relations among the participants changed through time and space in the shifting social and natural environments. This is an area in which archaeology with its long temporal perspective can potentially make a unique contribution. In this manner, we should examine not only what kind of performance specific societies created but also how spectacles and theatrical performance created and transformed society.

Conclusion

Spectacles and other theatrical events are not epiphenomenal for social processes. Nor are they superficial mystifications of the real political machinery that works behind the scenes. Such symbolic events and acts make and transform social relations. They are arenas and processes of collaboration, conflict, and negotiation for the creation, transformation, and subversion of a community and asymmetrical power relations. Although theatrical performance continues to be a critical part of modern politics, its importance in premodern societies cannot be overemphasized. Archaeology should be able to make significant contributions in the study of performance and power through the analysis of theatrical space, iconography, and material objects by placing theatrical events in specific social and historical contexts. We invite the readers to this rich field of inquiry in the archaeological theater.

Notes

We are grateful to Stephen Houston, Michael Smith, and an anonymous reviewer for thoughtful comments on earlier drafts.

1. Butler (1993:2) states that "this [performative] act is not primarily theatrical; indeed, its apparent theatricality is produced to the extent that its historicity remains dissimulated (and, conversely, its theatricality gains a certain inevitability given the impossibility of a full disclosure of its historicity)."
2. Ronald Grimes (1987) also argues the primacy of the human body in rituals.
3. Our definition derives partly from the important work of John MacAloon (1984b), but there are some differences. According to MacAloon, the defining features of spectacle include the primacy of visual sensory, its certain size and grandeur, the institutionalization of distinct roles of actors and audience, its dynamic form, demanding movement and action, and participation by choice as opposed to duty as in the case of ritual. We feel that MacAloon's view is too restrictive, reflecting his focus on the modern spectacle of the Olympic Games, as well as the etymology and common usages of the English word. For a cross-cultural study of premodern societies, we prefer a broader concept of spectacle. In many traditional societies the distinction between duty and choice regarding rituals and other public events was not always clear-cut. In addition, as seen in carnivals and other festivals, a strict division between performers and spectators is not always a defining feature of spectacle. We also place less emphasis on visual sensory as a distinctive feature of spectacles. The primacy of vision is often derivative of the scale of events, in which visual images are generally more effective means of communication to distant audiences than sounds and smells. With the help of modern technologies, such events as rock concerts that maintain the primacy of auditory sense can exhibit qualities comparable to spectacles in premodern societies.

4. Spectacle in our view does not include rituals and games conducted without the physical presence of spectators or the exhibit of static objects without theatrical performance (see Gluckman and Gluckman 1977:227).

5. Robert Wuthnow (1987:332–344) has suggested that what he calls the dramaturgic approach in social sciences with its focus on the observable dimensions of actions, utterance, and interactions in human lives shifts researchers' attentions from the quest of subjective or semantic meaning to a more productive inquiry of the conditions under which symbolic acts are meaningful.

6. Scott (1990:67–69) notes that, during the reign of Louis XIV, for example, a great deal of royal ceremony was no longer performed before the public at all but was presented only to the courtiers and retainers at Versailles.

References cited

Anderson, Benedict
1991 Imagined Communities: Reflections on the Origins and Spread of Nationalism. 2nd edition. London: Verso.

Austin, J. L.
1962 How to Do Things with Words. Oxford: Oxford University Press.

Bailey, F. G.
1996 Cultural Performance, Authenticity, and Second Nature. *In* The Politics of Cultural Performance. David Parkin, Lionel Caplan, and Humphrey Fisher, eds. Pp. 1–17. Providence: Berghahn.

Baines, John, and Norman Yoffee
1998 Order, Legitimacy, and Wealth in Ancient Egypt and Mesopotamia. *In* Archaic States. Gary M. Feinman and Joyce Marcus, eds. Pp. 199–260. Santa Fe: School of American Research Press.

Bakhtin, Mikhail M.
1968[1965] Rabelais and His World. Helene Iswolsky, trans. Cambridge, Mass: MIT Press.

Barrett, John C.
1994 Fragments from Antiquity: An Archaeology of Social Life in Britain, 2900–1200 BC. Oxford: Blackwell.

Basso, Ellen B.
1985 A Musical View of the Universe. Philadelphia: University of Pennsylvania Press.

Bauman, Richard
1989 Performance. *In* International Encyclopedia of Communications, vol. 3. Erik Barnouw, ed. Pp. 262–266. Oxford: Oxford University Press.

Bauman, Richard, and Charles L. Briggs
1990 Poetics and Performance as Critical Perspectives on Language and Social Life. Annual Review of Anthropology 19:59–88.

Beeman, William O.
1993 The Anthropology of Theater and Spectacle. Annual Review of Anthropology 22:369–393.

Beidelman, T. O.
1966 Swazi Royal Ritual. Africa 36:373–405.

Bell, Catherine
1992 Ritual Theory, Ritual Practice. Oxford: Oxford University Press.
1997 Ritual: Perspectives and Dimensions. Oxford: Oxford University Press.
1998 Performance. *In* Critical Terms for Religious Studies. Mark C. Taylor, ed. Pp. 205–224. Chicago: University of Chicago Press.

Bergman, Bettina
1999 Introduction: The Art of Ancient Spectacle. *In* The Art of Ancient Spectacle. Bettina Bergman and Christine Kondoleon, eds. Pp. 9–35. Washington, D.C.: National Gallery of Art, New Haven: Yale University Press.

Bloch, Maurice
1974 Symbols, Song, Dance, and Features of Articulation. Archives européenes de sociologie 15:55–81.
1986 From Blessing to Violence: History and Ideology in the Circumcision Ritual of the Merina of Madagascar. Cambridge: Cambridge University Press.

Bourdieu, Pierre
1977 Outline of a Theory of Practice. Richard Nice, trans. Cambridge: Cambridge University Press.

Bradley, Richard
1993 Altering the Earth: The Origins of Monuments in Britain and Continental Europe. Edinburgh: Society of Antiquaries of Scotland.
1998 The Significance of Monuments: On the Shaping of Human Experience in Neolithic and Bronze Age Europe. London: Routledge.

Brown, Jonathan, and J. H. Elliott
1980 A Palace for a King: The Buen Retiro and the Court of Philip IV. New Haven: Yale University Press.

Burke, Kenneth
1945 Grammar of Motives. New York: Prentice Hall.

Butler, Judith
1990 Gender Trouble: Feminism and the Subversion of Identity. London: Routledge.
1993 Bodies That Matter. London: Routledge.

Canuto, Marcello A., and Jason Yaeger
2000 The Archaeology of Communities: A New World Perspective. London: Routledge.

Carlson, Marvin
1989 Places of Performance: The Semiotics of Theatre Architecture. Ithaca, N.Y.: Cornell University Press.

Carneiro, Robert
1970 A Theory of the Origin of the State. Science 169:733–738.

Claessen, Henri J. M., and Jarich G. Oosten, eds.
1996 Ideology and the Formation of Early States. Leiden: E.J. Brill.

Clark, John E., and Michael Blake
1994 The Power of Prestige: Competitive Generosity and the Emergence of Rank Societies in Lowland Mesoamerica. *In* Factional Competition and Political Development in the New World. Elizabeth M. Brumfiel and J. Fox, eds. Pp. 17–30. Cambridge: Cambridge University Press.

Coben, Lawrence
2001 Signs of the Times: Inca Architecture, Cuzco, and Peircean Replication. Paper given at the annual meeting of the Society for American Archaeology, New Orleans.

Connerton, Paul
1989 How Societies Remember. Cambridge: Cambridge University Press.

Conrad, Geoffrey W., and Arthur A. Demarest
1984 Religion and Empire: The Dynamics of Aztec and Inca Expansionism. Cambridge: Cambridge University Press.

Da Matta, Roberto

1984 Carnival in Multiple Planes. *In* Rite, Drama, Festival, Spectacle: Rehearsals Toward a Theory of Cultural Performance. John J. MacAloon, ed. Pp. 209–240. Philadelphia: Institute for the Study of Human Issues.

Demarest, Arthur A.

1992 Ideology in Ancient Maya Cultural Evolution: The Dynamics of Galactic Polities. *In* Ideology and Pre-Columbian Civilizations. Arthur A. Demarest and Geoffrey W. Conrad, eds. Pp.135–158. Santa Fe: School of American Research Press.

DeMarrais, Elizabeth, Luis Jaime Castillo, and Timothy Earle

1996 Ideology, Materialization, and Power Strategies. Current Anthropology 37:15–31.

Derrida, Jacques

1988 Limited, Inc. Samuel Weber and Jeffrey Mehlman, trans. Evanston, Ill.: Northwestern University Press.

Diamond, Elin

1996 Performance and Cultural Politics. London: Routledge.

Douglas, Mary

1966 Purity and Danger. New York: Praeger.

1973 Natural Symbols: Exploration in Cosmology. New York: Vintage.

Durkheim, Emile

1965[1915] The Elementary Forms of the Religious Life. J. W. Swain, trans. New York: Free Press.

Eco, Umberto

1977 Semiotics of Theatrical Performance. The Drama Review 21:107–117.

Elam, Keir

1980 The Semiotics of Theatre and Drama. London: Methuen.

Eliade, Mircea

1978 The History of Religious Ideas: From the Stone Age to the Eleusinian Mysteries. Willard R. Trask, trans. Chicago: University of Chicago Press.

Elias, Norbert

1983[1969] The court society [Die Höfische Gesellschaf] Edmund Jephcott, trans. New York: Pantheon.

Evans-Pritchard, E. E.
1964 Social Anthropology and Other Essays. New York: Free Press.
1974 Nuer Religion. Oxford: Oxford University Press.

Feeley-Harnik, Gillian
1985 Issues in Divine Kingship. Annual Review of Anthropology 14:273–313.

Fernandez, James
1972 Persuasion and Performances: On the Beast in Every Body . . . And the Metaphors of Everyman. Daedalus 101(1):39–60.

Fischer-Lichte, Erika
1992 The Semiotics of Theater. Abridged translation by Jeremy Gaines and Doris L. Jones. Bloomington: Indiana University Press.
1995 Theatricality: A Key Concept in Theatre and Cultural Studies. Theatre Research International 20:85–89.

Foucault, Michel
1977 Discipline and Punish: The Birth of the Prison. A. Sheridan, trans. New York: Pantheon.

Fraser, James G.
1925 The Golden Bough. Abridged edition. New York: Macmillan.

Futrell, Alison
1997 Blood in the Arena: The Spectacle of Roman Power. Austin: University of Texas Press.

Geertz, Clifford
1980 Negara: The Theatre State in Nineteenth-Century Bali. Princeton: Princeton University Press.

Gluckman, Max
1963 Order and Rebellion in Tribal Africa. New York: Free Press.

Gluckman, Max, and Mary Gluckman
1977 On Drama, Games, and Athletic Contests. *In* Secular Ritual. Sally F. Moore and Barbara G. Myerhoff, eds. Pp. 244–265. Assen, Netherlands: Van Gorcum.

Goffman, Erving
1959 The Presentation of Self in Everyday Life. Garden City, N.J.: Doubleday Anchor.

1967 Interaction Ritual. Garden City, N.J.: Doubleday Anchor.
1974 Frame Analysis. Cambridge: Harvard University Press.

Grimes, Ronald L.
1987 Ritual Studies. *In* Encyclopedia of Religion, vol. 12. Mircea Eliade, ed. Pp. 422–425. New York: Macmillan.

Hall, Edward
1966 The Hidden Dimension. Garden City, N.J.: Doubleday Anchor.

Handelman, Don
1990 Models and Mirrors: Toward an Anthropology of Public Events. Cambridge: Cambridge University Press.

Harrison, Jane Ellen
1962[1912] Themis: A Study of the Social Origins of Greek Religion. 2nd edition. Cleveland: Meridian.

Hayden, Brian D., and R. Gargett
1990 Big Man, Big Heart? A Mesoamerican View of the Emergence of Complex Society. Ancient Mesoamerica 1:3–20.

Hill, Warren D., and John E. Clark
2001 Sports, Gambling, and Government: America's First Social Compact? American Anthropologist 103:331–345.

Hobsbawn, Eric J., and Terrence O. Ranger, eds.
1983 The Invention of Tradition. Cambridge: Cambridge University Press.

Hodder, Ian, ed.
1982 Symbolic and Structural Archaeology. Cambridge: Cambridge University Press.

Houston, Stephen, and Karl Taube
2000 An Archaeology of the Senses: Perception and Cultural Expression in Ancient Mesoamerica. Cambridge Archaeological Journal 10:261–294.

Hymes, Dell H.
1975 Breakthrough into Performance. *In* Folklore: Performance and Communication. Dan Ben-Amos and Kenneth S. Goldstein, eds. Pp. 11–74. The Hague: Mouton.

Inomata, Takeshi
2001 The Classic Maya Royal Palace as a Political Theater. *In* Reconstruyendo la ciudad maya: El urbanismo en la sociedades antigua. Andrés

Ciudad Ruiz, María Josefa Iglesias Ponce de León, and María del Carmen Martínez Martínez, eds. Pp. 341–362. Madrid: Sociedad Española de Estudios Mayas.

Inomata, Takeshi, and Stephen Houston
2001 Opening the Royal Maya Court. *In* Royal Courts of the Ancient Maya, vol. 1: Theory, Comparison, and Synthesis. Takeshi Inomata and Stephen Houston, eds. Pp. 3–23. Boulder: Westview.

Joyce, Rosemary
2000 Gender and Power in Prehispanic Mesoamerica. Austin: University of Texas Press.

Kertzer, David I.
1988 Ritual, Politics, and Power. New Haven: Yale University Press.

Kuper, Hilda
1961 An African Aristocracy: Rank Among the Swazi. Oxford: Oxford University Press.

Lévi-Strauss, Claude
1969 The Elementary Structures of Kinship, James H. Bell, trans. Boston: Beacon.

Lincoln, Bruce
1987 Ritual, Rebellion, Resistance: Once More the Swazi Ncwala. Man 22:132–156.

MacAloon, John J.
1984a Introduction: Cultural Performances, Culture Theory. *In* Rite, Drama, Festival, Spectacle: Rehearsals Toward a Theory of Cultural Performance. John J. MacAloon, ed. Pp. 1–15. Philadelphia: Institute for the Study of Human Issues.
1984b Olympic Games and the Theory of Spectacle in Modern Societies. *In* Rite, Drama, Festival, Spectacle: Rehearsals Toward a Theory of Cultural Performance. John J. MacAloon, ed. Pp. 241–280. Philadelphia: Institute for the Study of Human Issues.

Mendelssohm, Kurt
1974 The Riddle of the Pyramids. New York: Praeger.

Meskell, Lynn
1999 Archaeologies of Social Life: Age, Sex, Class et Cetra in Ancient Egypt. Oxford: Blackwell.

Miller, Daniel, and Christopher Tilley
1984 Ideology, Power, and Prehistory. Cambridge: Cambridge University Press.

Miller, Mary Ellen
1986 The Murals of Bonampak. Princeton: Princeton University Press.

Moore, Jerry D.
1996 Architecture and Power in the Ancient Andes: The Archaeology of Public Buildings. Cambridge: Cambridge University Press.

Moore, Sally F., and Barbara G. Myerhoff
1977 Introduction: Secular Rituals: Forms and Meanings. *In* Secular Ritual. Sally F. Moore and Barbara G. Myerhoff, eds. Pp. 3–24. Assen, Netherlands: Van Gorcum.

Ortner, Sherry B.
1978 Sherpas through Their Ritual. Cambridge: Cambridge University Press.
1989 High Religion: A Cultural and Political History of Sherpa Buddhism. Princeton: Princeton University Press.

Palmer, Gary B., and William R. Jankowiak
1996 Performance and Imagination: Toward an Anthropology of the Spectacular and the Mundane. Cultural Anthropology 11:225–258.

Parker, Andrew, and Eve Kosofsky Sedgwick
1995 Performativity and Performance. New York: Routledge.

Parmentier, Richard
1994 Signs in Society: Studies in Semiotic Anthropology. Bloomington: Indiana University Press.
1997 The Pragmatic Semiotics of Cultures. Special issue of Semiotica 116:1. Berlin: Mouton de Gruyter.

Pavis, Patrice
1998 Dictionary of the Theatre: Terms, Concepts, and Analysis. Christine Shantz, trans. Toronto: University of Toronto Press.

Pearson, Mike, and Michael Shanks
2001 Theater/Archaeology. London: Routledge.

Rappaport, Roy A.
1999 Ritual and Religion in the Making of Humanity. Cambridge: Cambridge University Press.

Read, Alan
1993 Theatre and Everyday Life: An Ethics of Performance. London: Routledge.

Reese-Taylor, Kathryn, and Rex Koontz
2001 The Cultural Poetics of Power and Space in Ancient Mesoamerica. *In* Landscape and Power in Ancient Mesoamerica. Rex Koontz, Kathryn Reese-Taylor, and Annabeth Headrick, eds. Pp. 1–28. Boulder: Westview.

Robbins, Joel
2001 Ritual Communication and Linguistic Ideology. Current Anthropology 42:591–614.

Rockfeller, Stuart Alexander
1999 "There Is a Culture Here": Spectacle and the Inculcation of Folklore in Highland Bolivia. Journal of Latin American Anthropology 3(2):118–149.

Rogers, Mark
1999 Introduction: Performing Andean Identities. Journal of Latin American Anthropology 3(2):2–19.

Sahlins, Marshall D.
1985 Islands of History. Chicago: University of Chicago Press.

Schechner, Richard.
1977 Essays in Performance Theory: 1970–1976. New York: Drama Book Specialists.
1985 Between Theater and Anthropology. Philadelphia: University of Pennsylvania Press.
1988 Performance Theory. Rev. edition. New York: Routledge.
1994 Ritual and Performance. *In* Companion Encyclopedia of Anthropology: Humanity, Culture, and Social Life. Tim Ingold, ed. Pp. 613–647. London: Routledge.

Scott, James C.
1990 Domination and the Arts of Resistance: Hidden Transcript. New Haven: Yale University Press.

Singer, Milton B.
1959 Traditional India: Structure and Change. Philadelphia: American Folklore Society.
1972 When a Great Tradition Modernizes. London: Pall Mall.

Smith, Adam T.
2000 Rendering the Political Aesthetic: Political Legitimacy in Urartian Representations of the Built Environment. Journal of Anthropological Archaeology 19:131–163.

Sullivan, Lawrence E.
1986 Sound and Senses: Toward a Hermeneutics of Performance. History of Religion 26(1):1–33.

Tambiah, Stanley J.
1976 World Conqueror and World Renouncer. Cambridge: Cambridge University Press.
1979 A Performative Approach to Ritual. Proceedings of the British Academy 65:113–169.

Taylor, Diana
2003 The Archive and the Repertoire: Performing Cultural Memory in the Americas. Durham, N.C.: Duke University Press.

Thomas, Julian
1999 Understanding the Neolithic. London: Routledge.

Tilley, Christopher
1994 A Phenomenology of Landscape: Places, Paths, and Monuments. London: Berg.

Trigger, Bruce G.
1990 Monumental Architecture: A Thermodynamic Explanation of Symbolic Behavior. World Archaeology 22:1–32.

Turner, Victor W.
1957 Schism and Continuity in an African Society. Manchester, U.K.: Manchester University Press.
1967 The Forest of Symbols. Ithaca, N.Y.: Cornell University Press.
1972 The Ritual Process. Ithaca, N.Y.: Cornell University Press.
1986a From Ritual to Theatre and Back. New York: Performing Arts Journal Publications.
1986b The Anthropology of Performance. New York: Performing Arts Journal Publications.

Valeri, Valerio
1985 Kingship and Sacrifice: Ritual and Society in Ancient Hawaii. Chicago: University of Chicago Press.

Van Gennep, Arnold
1960 Rites of Passage. Chicago: University of Chicago Press.

Wuthnow, Robert
1987 Meaning and Moral Order: Explorations in Cultural Analysis. Berkeley: University of California Press.

Act II

SENSES, SPECTACLE, AND PERFORMANCE

SCENE 2

"THE INDIANS WERE MUCH GIVEN TO THEIR TAQUIS": DRUMMING AND GENERATIVE CATEGORIES IN ANCIENT ANDEAN FUNERARY PROCESSIONS

Jerry D. Moore

Any attempt to understand prehistoric display and spectacle encounters the problem of reconstructing human sensation. Every analysis of spectacle assumes that it is a dynamic, communicative experience intended to be perceived. This assumption, however, leads the archaeologist to a fundamental problem: Is human sensation universally structured by a shared, evolved, and complex set of neural exchanges (Cosmides and Tooby 1997; Kosslyn 1994; Pinker 1997, 2002), or is sensation a two-stage operation in which sensoral stimuli, processed by generalized mental operations but profoundly structured by learned interpretations of the encountered world, produce irreducibly nonbiological frameworks of culture, language, and learned experience (Sperber and Hirschfield 1999)? This resilient epistemological issue is central for the archaeologist exploring spectacle, performance, or the archaeology of experience (Moore 2005). If the ancient experience was mediated with the same mind and senses that we share, then that experience potentially can be reconstructed. If, on the other hand, the ancient experience occupied completely different "worlds of sense," as Constance Classen (1993) has called them, then the reconstruction of past experience has inevitably and irretrievably eluded us.

This conundrum was discussed recently by Houston and Taube (2000) in their analysis of sensation in the ancient Maya world. "Sight, sound, touch, hearing, and smell are not ordinarily the concern of archaeologists," they observe, "since the senses do not leave vestiges that can readily be accessed" (Houston and Taube 2000:261). Fortunately the ancient Maya encoded their perceptions of the senses in glyphs and, "by means of graphic devices such as speech, scent, and sight scrolls, the Maya and other Mesoamericans communicated the presence, nature, and semantic content of sight, smell, and hearing, to an extent unparalleled in most other parts of the ancient world" (Houston and Taube 2000:261). The authors approach ancient Maya sensation indirectly via the graphic representations of sensations, reading the score, as it were, of music permanently silenced. Having posed the possibility of an archaeological exploration of the senses, Houston and Taube (2000:290) conclude with a wistful coda: "Regrettably, the essay has also set out on a difficult path: an 'archaeology of the senses' can never be possible directly, insofar as it traffics in non-replicable and ephemeral experiences." But is the situation so desperate, especially for archaeologists working on societies without ancient texts or other sensorial scores? Are the doors of perception of prehistoric societies permanently closed?

Faced with such challenges, archaeologists have tended to occupy polarized stances. One position is to ignore issues like the archaeology of sensation and experience and focus on subsistence, settlement, and other "materialist" research domains. The alternative position opts for an idealist and usually relativist position in which archaeological patterns are interpreted in light of other sources of information—texts, artistic depictions, ethnographic and historical accounts—in a cultural historical approach. These distinct positions are reflected in increasingly divergent archaeologies, yet there are solid reasons for synthesis. For example, Bruce Trigger (1998:20) argues,

> Human beings simultaneously inhabit a conceptual environment that exists in their minds and a social and natural environment that exists independently of their wills. A challenge that is faced by archaeologists, other social scientists, and philosophers is to define more precisely the relations between these inner and outer environments.

The challenge, Trigger contends, is to link sensation, cognition, and acquired cultural knowledge:

> Human beings exist by drawing energy from the physical world, and the mind, as a property of the brain, is as material as anything else.

> Archaeologists must study the human mind in terms of both the innate cognitive properties of the brain and the acquired knowledge that allow the organ to interpret sensory observations. The resulting understanding constitutes the conceptualized world to which human beings adapt. Culture in turn must be viewed as a highly flexible mechanism that serves to adapt human beings to the external environment and has enabled them to transform that environment to an ever greater extent. Archaeologists finally must acknowledge the role that the senses play as mediators between the external real world and the inner world of the mind and the ability of sensory observations to alter conceptions relating to the real world. (Trigger 1998:23)

This chapter is an attempt to meet, in a very limited manner, Trigger's challenge by outlining a progressively narrowed argument that begins with an analogy and ultimately arrives at a very specific topic: drumming in pre-Hispanic Andean funeral processions. First, I explore the conflict between universalist and relativist positions on sensation by reference to a well-investigated and illuminating example of this problem: the universality and cultural definition of color sensation and color categories. This leads me to propose an analogous model for other phenomena that vary cross-culturally but nonetheless exhibit less variation than we could imagine. Second, I outline an approach to processions that treats them as a subset of ritual behaviors, focuses on the technology and design logics of processional displays, and finally considers a single aspect of such displays—drumming. I then summarize previous discussions on drumming and its use in defining categories of behavior, specifically in rites of passage. I will then examine the use of drumming in Andean funerary processions and displays expressed in Moche (A.D. 100–750), Chimú (A.D. 900–1470), and Inka (A.D. 1200–1580) societies.

Worlds of Senses or Systems of Sensation? Color Classification and Generative Categories

An established corpus of anthropological literature posits that sensory worlds are culturally relative, linguistically determined, and essentially arbitrary and unfettered by the external world. Franz Boas extended relativism to perception: "The categories of language compel us to see the world arranged in certain definite conceptual groups which, on account of our lack of knowledge of linguistic processes, are taken as objective thoughts" (1920:320). The relativistic approach to sensation is exemplified in Verne Ray's (1952) discussion of color classifications:

> First, the color patterning of man's visual world is not based upon psychological, physiological, or anatomical factors. There is no such thing as a "natural" division of the spectrum. Each culture has taken the spectral continuum and has divided it into units on a quite arbitrary basis. . . . All evolutionary schemes of color vision are shown to be without foundation. (Ray 1952:258–259)

While Ray correctly noted cultural variations in color categories, subsequent research indicates that he overstated the arbitrariness of the schemes. More recently, the thesis of sensoral relativism has been expanded on by Howes (1991a:11), who cites the "evidence of diverse ethnotheories of perception and cognition." Walter Ong's notion of the culturally variable "shifting sensorium" has been very influential:

> Sound and the word itself must thus be considered in terms of the shifting relationships between the senses. These relationships must not be taken merely abstractly but in connection with variations in cultures. In this connection, it is useful to think of cultures in terms of the organization of the sensorium. By the sensorium we mean here the entire sensory apparatus as an operational complex. The differences in cultures which we have just suggested can be thought of as differences in the sensorium, the organization of which is in part determined by culture while at the same time it makes culture. (Ong 1967:6)

Constance Classen (1990, 1993, 1998) extended this relativist position in a set of eloquent essays. Citing historic and ethnographic cases as examples "of the many ways in which culture subverts human biology" (Classen 1993:9), she derives five points from a comparison of sensory orders among the Tzotzil Maya of highland Chiapas, the Ongee of Little Andaman Island, and the Desana of the Colombian Amazon.[1]

First, Classen argues that sensory perceptions are culturally mediated—one culture prioritizing smell, another sight—and the dominance of one sense over the others "can only be understood within the context of a particular culture and not through generalized external sensory paradigms" (Classen 1993:135). Second, a culture prioritizes one sense over the others because of cultural convention, not because of pragmatic advantage or adaptive utility. Third and following directly from this point, Classen argues that there are multiple sensory programs for the same sense, that, for example, "the visualism of the Desana, with its emphasis on integrating and animating colour energies, is surely very different from the visualism of the West, with its emphasis on detached observation and surface appearance" (Classen 1993:135). And if Western visualism leads us to think falsely that the eye is the dominant sense, understanding non-Western "worlds of sense" requires us to consider "the multi-sensory dimensions of other cultures" (Classen 1993:136):

> Finally, sensory models are conceptual models, and sensory values are cultural values. The way a society senses is the way it understands. . . . It is not simply that a society's mode of thinking and acting is ordered by the cultural consequences of the sensory properties it emphasizes, however. Sensory values not only frame a culture's experiences, they express its ideals, its hopes and its fears. (Classen 1993:136)

I contend that Classen has confused sensory classifications with sensation. It is well established—nearly an anthropological commonplace—that different cultures employ distinct cultural frameworks to describe and classify sensation, but this does not mean that different societies have infinitely distinct sensory perceptions. The study of color classifications provides an example of how humans can apprehend similar phenomena employing an identical mental apparatus yet devise varied—but not *infinitely* varied—classification schemes.

A recent estimate suggests that the human eye can distinguish 2.3 million colors (Pointer and Attridge 1998), but we classify colors into a relatively narrow range of categories. Berlin and Kay (1969), in their well-known study, *Basic Color Terms: Their Universality and Evolution*, established that while different cultures distinguished colors in varying schemes, the variation was neither arbitrary nor infinite (Hardin and Maffi 1997). Berlin and Kay found that basic color terms reflect categories with a central or focal color. The boundaries between colors are less well defined than their central focal tendencies, but color categories, though culturally different, are not infinitely varied. The color categories marked by distinctive color terms are equivalent to the English terms black, white, red, yellow, green, blue, brown, purple, orange, and gray. Societies that employ fewer color categories assemble them in a regular way. If a society employs a two-category scheme, the colors are always black and white or more correctly "dark" and "warm." If a third color is employed, it is always red. A four-color scheme may add yellow, blue, or green to the black/white/red triad, but orange, purple, pink, or gray will never be the fourth color.

Color categories are neither arbitrary cultural schemes nor direct reflections of objective reality. Color, Zeki notes (1999:83), "is a construction of the brain. There are no colours in the outside world." Issac Newton recognized this in the seventeenth century, as he apologized for the fictions of common speech:

> And if at any time I speak of light and rays as coloured or embued with Colours, I would be understood to speak not philosophically and properly, but grossly, and according to such conceptions as vulgar People in seeing all these Experiments would be apt to frame. For the Rays to speak properly are not coloured. In them there is nothing else than a certain power and disposition to stir up a sensation of this or that Colour. (Quoted in Wade 1998:116)

Normal human color vision depends on three types of cones in the retina that respond to different but overlapping light wavelengths: S cones tend to respond to high-frequency light, L cones to low-frequency light, and M cones to light at intermediate frequencies. Humans share this trichromatic color vision with Old World apes and monkeys, but not with New World monkeys or other primates (Jacobs 1996). Optical cones differ in light receptivity because of pigment molecules that maximally absorb light of different wavelengths. For humans with normal color vision, the average peak value for S cones is 410–430 nanometers (nm), while peak values for M cones are 530 *or* 535 nm and peak values for L cones are 556 *or* 562 nm; the alternative peak values for M and L cones are the product of genetic polymporphisms discussed below. The shift from dichromatic vision (S and L cones) to trichromatic vision (S, M, and L cones) is thought to result from selective pressures associated with fruit selection in a forested environment: trichromatic vision allows for readily seeing yellow and orange fruits hidden in a green forest (Jacobs 1996:580). It is estimated that the evolution of trichromatic primate vision occurred approximately 30 million years ago (Jacobs 1996).

The spectral maxima of different retinal cones are determined by a pigment molecule. The pigment molecule contains two parts: a large protein molecule, opsin, and a form of vitamin A, retinal. Analyses of the opsin molecule have identified their genetic sequences (Nathans et al. 1986), and if specific genes are missing or defective, color blindness occurs. One of the most common forms of color blindness—the inability to distinguish red and green—is caused by the abnormal sequence in the opsin molecule in which the gene for L pigment is absent. The gene for the L pigment lies on the X chromosome, which also determines the sex of the individual; since males are XY and females are XX, there is a lower chance for females to suffer from red-green color blindness. Further, even among males who have the gene for L pigment, there are alternate forms of the genetic sequence. One form has the amino acid alanine at position 180 in the opsin sequence; the alternative has serine at that same position. Alanine has peak response to light at 552.4 nanometers; serine's peak response is at 556.7 nanometers. Of males with "normal" color vision, some 62 percent have the serine allele, while 38 percent have the alanine allele, and the two groups differ slightly in the ways they perceive the red wavelength and green wavelength color to "see" yellow (Hoffman 1998:132–133).

> The significance of these discoveries for psychologists cannot be exaggerated. Here is a case where a difference of a single nucleotide places people in distinct phenomenal worlds and where we know almost all the steps in the causal chain from gene to molecule to neural signals; only the final steps from cortical activity to sensation elude us. It is the first such case in psychology. It cannot be the last. (Mollon 1990:378)

It is extremely unlikely that the twenty-two different combinations of basic color categories discovered by Berlin and Kay (1969)—out of a maximum possible 2,048—are the results of variations in the amino acid sequences in rods. Alternatively, if color categories were simply the culturally determined and arbitrary divisions of a continuous light spectrum, then we would expect more than twenty-two different combinations.

So how then can we conceptualize the link between sensation and classification, neural excitation and cultural categories? Again, color research suggests an answer. Kay and McDaniel (1978) developed a model linking color classifications to the response of color-sensitive cells in the retina, cones, that responded to different wavelength modes within the visual spectrum. While the specific association between percept and neural response may be more complex than Kay and McDaniel anticipated, the basic thesis is supported: color combinations reflect varying responses of S, M, and L cones to light of different wavelengths. However, the correlations between wavelength and color are not "categorical" but based on approximations to a norm. Rather than forming a standard set, of which an element either is or is not a member, Kay and McDaniel argued, color categories approximate "fuzzy sets" whose elements approximate a central value. This model best describes the central tendencies, the focal shades of color categories; it does not describe well the boundaries between color categories. There are, however, maximal limits to which every person with normal vision agrees (yellow is not blue).

Kay and McDaniel's "fuzzy set theory" has implications for the classification of other domains of human experience. The cognitive scientist George Lakoff writes:

> The Kay-McDaniel theory has important consequences for human categorization in general. It claims that colors are not objectively "out there in the world" independent of any beings. Color concepts are embodied in that focal colors are partly determined by human biology. Color categorization makes use of human biology, but color categories are more than merely a consequence of the nature of the world plus human biology.
>
> *Color categories, thus, are generative categories*. . . . They have generators plus something else. The generators are the neurophysiologically determined distribution functions, which have peaks where the primary colors are pure: black, white, red, yellow, blue and green. These generators are universal; they are part of human neurophysiology. The "something else" needed to generate a system of basic color categories consists of a complex cognitive mechanism incorporating some of the characteristics of fuzzy set theory union and intersection. This cognitive mechanism has a small number of parameters that may take on different values in different cultures.
>
> It is important to bear in mind that it is not just the names for colors that vary. The color names do not just attach to the neurophysiologically determined distribution functions directly. Cognitive mechanisms . . . must be postulated in addition. There are general characteristics of the cognitive mechanisms, for example, the use of something like fuzzy set theory union and intersection. *But . . . color cognition is by no means all the same*

> *across cultures. Nor is it by any means arbitrarily different across cultures. The possible color ranges depend upon limited parameters within the cognitive mechanism.* (Lakoff 1987:29–30; emphasis added)

As empirical support for this position, Robert MacLaury's monumental (1997) *Color and Cognition in Mesoamerica* analyzes color categories employed by speakers of indigenous Mesoamerican languages, and confirms and deepens Lakoff's proposition. "Color categorization is both perceptual and cognitive," MacLaury (1997:86) concludes. The perception of color is grounded in universal human perception and cognition, and elemental color combinations are varied but limited (Kay 1999).

I have discussed the problem of color categorization in such detail because it may be analogous to how humans process other specific classes of information. This research suggests that humans may employ a series of fuzzy sets rooted in neurobiology, shaped by cultural practice, codified in language, and exhibiting variation but less than imaginable. Some of these domains may include conceptions of time (Boroditsky 2001), modes of expressing spatial relationships (Haviland 1996; Levinson 1998; Lewis 1976; Reiger 1996; Talmy 1983), and the symbolic associations of olfaction (Gell 1977; Howes 1991b). I suggest that the complex, multileveled, and connective research on color perception and classification may serve as a model for other realms of ancient experience. Those realms are not reducible to universal human neurobiology, but neither are they endlessly varied nor hermetically sealed by individual experience. Rather, there is a complex connective web between physical sensation, cultural categories, and experience. It may be possible, I contend, for the archaeologist to explore some of the connections, to partially penetrate specific domains of ancient experience—realizing that any insights we arrive at will be incomplete. In the balance of this chapter, I discuss the ritual characteristics of processions, emphasizing their performative aspects and technologies of display, then turn to a specific comparative case of the role of drumming in pre-Hispanic Andean funeral processions.

Rituals, Processions, Design Logics, and Technologies of Display

Processions, Richard Schechner reminds us, are a form of theatrical production, a kind of "natural" theater. "In a procession—which is a kind of pilgrimage—the event moves along a prescribed path, spectators gather along the route, and at appointed places the procession halts and performances are played" (Schechner 1988:159–160).

> Usually a procession moves towards a goal: the funeral to the grave, the political march to the speakers' stand, the circus parade to the big top, the pilgrimage to the shrine. The event performed at the goal of the procession . . . is well planned for, rehearsed, ritualized. (Schechner 1988:160)

Processions share the characteristics of ritual. A thorough theoretical review of ritual is beyond the scope of this chapter, but Bell (1997:23–59) notes six general characteristics of "ritual-like activities" that are relevant to Andean processions: formality, traditionalism, disciplined invariance, rule governance, sacral symbolism, and performance (Bell 1997:138–169).

Rituals are characterized by *formality*, and they typically employ more restricted and defined codes of verbal and nonverbal communications than "ordinary" behavior: for example, stylized speech, verbal tones, gesture, etiquette, and attire. Also, rituals often, but not always, call on past practice to make present acts consistent with cultural precedence, a characteristic Bell (1997:145) refers to as *traditionalism.* Such efforts may range from carefully following historically prescribed routes, the incorporation of ancient regalia in modern settings, the use of archaic language, or specific appeals to past practice (actual or invented) invoking the authority of an earlier age to explain ritual coherence and continuity. *Invariance* is another characteristic of ritual (Bell 1997:150–153). Ritual practice often must include disciplined repetition and control if it is to be efficacious—ensuring desired outcomes, isolating the contemplative from distractions, or forging shared experience. Similarly, ritual is often marked by *rule governance.* The rules of ritual are generally perceived "as formulated norms imposed on the chaos of human action and interaction" (Bell 1997:155). The most essential aspect of ritual is also its most complex: *sacral symbolism,* the connection between ritual and the sacred (Bell 1997:155–159). Rituals connect participants to larger cultural themes generally considered to be outside or greater than the individual's corporeal or commonplace existence.

Finally, rituals are often *performative* (Bell 1997:159–164; Tambiah 1985). Ritual performance is identified by several elements. It often employs public, self-aware, and deliberate acting out of symbolic behaviors in overlapping fields of multisensory experience. For example, Victor Turner (1985:295) wrote of

> that great multifaceted system of preindustrial ritual which embraces ideas and images of cosmos and chaos, interdigitates clowns and their foolery with gods and their solemnity, and uses all the sensory codes to produce symphonies in more than music: the intertwining of dance, body languages of many kinds, song, chant, architectural forms (temples, amphitheaters), incense, burnt offerings, ritualized feastings and drinking, painting, body painting, body marking of many kinds, including circumcision and scarification, the application of lotions and the drinking of potions, the enacting of plots drawn from oral traditions.

To reiterate, rituals tend to be characterized by formality, an appeal to tradition, attempted and often realized invariance of performance, rule governance, sacral symbolism, and their performative aspects.

From a dramaturgical perspective, Kirshenblatt-Gimblett and McNamara (1985:2–5) have outlined some characteristics of processions. Simply defined as "a performance in motion through space," the movement becomes an essential aspect of the display's "ceremonial and symbolic importance." As with rituals, the performance is framed "to distinguish it from everyday movement through space," employing costumes, props, scenography, music, and choreography. Processional performance must compete with the surrounding distractions of life. The symbolic contents of the procession

> are generally presented in ways that are comprehensible to spectators. Usually they are familiar, simply stated and easily visible in an environment that was not designed as a "theatre" for processional performance and which may contain other activities that could draw focus away from the performance. The procession, however, is designed to compete with the existing environment around it, becoming for a time the dominant element. (Kirshenblatt-Gimblett and McNamara 1985:2)

Perhaps because of this need to compete with and dominate its surroundings, processions employ a variable, but limited repertoire of performance strategies: movement as transition, ascents and descents marking changes in statuses, the use of large emblems (e.g., banners, pennants, flags) as group "badges," costumes marking roles and memberships, and elevated displays and tableaux. In his excellent *Models and Mirror: Towards an Anthropology of Public Events*, Handelman (1990) has argued that the form of public displays—as distinct from their meanings or significance—are linked to the social orders of the societies which create them. His useful model warrants extensive quotation:

> There may be generalizable features that underlie, and that may help to constitute public events—but . . . these can be demonstrated only comparatively. Moreover, these features or forms are neither the significance nor the meaning of public events. Instead, form contributes to the formation of public events, setting broad parameters of likelihood—the likelihoods of certain operations being accomplished through certain forms of public events. *Thus, my position is closer to a technology of events, of the identification of the logics of their design, themselves embedded in cultural matrices that imbue these designs with significance and that put them to work in cultural ways.* Therefore, these designs are never static, nor complete in themselves. They are configurations of potential dynamism that both exercise and limit possibilities of empowerment within social orders. Their status as grounded phenomena, their fullness and their substance, always are constituted and empowered culturally and historically. Put differently, what I am after are logics of meta-design that potentially enable social orders to act upon or to relate to themselves in radically different ways through the substantive media of public events. . . . I am not arguing that some social orders have ways of relating to themselves that others lack, but that *different logics of design in the constitution of public events index social orders that themselves are organized in radically different ways.* (Handelman 1990:7; emphasis added)

To this point, I have argued the following. Like other rituals, processions are characterized by formality, traditionalism, disciplined invariance, rule governance, sacral symbolism, and performance. Processions and other public performances employ specific technologies of display and design logics, and these vary among societies. However, while there is variation in the design logics of processions, there is actually less variation than one could potentially imagine. This is so, I suggest, for reasons analogous to those discussed by Lakoff for color categories and other generative categories: there are neurobiological bases for the perception and sensation of specific elements of processions, and while design logics are not reducible to neuronal activity, neither are they infinitely varied, "arbitrary" cultural conventions.

Rather, specific design logics are employed in processions because they are generators that operate within variable but limited parameters. One design logic that creates a generative category is drumming.

Drumming and Rites of Transition

The relationship between drumming and rites of transition is a commonplace of New Age websites, but it also has a long-posed issue in anthropological literature.[2] In addition to its frequent discussion in ethnographies, the relationship between percussion and transition was first articulated by Rodney Needham (1967:606), who asked, "Why is noise that is produced by striking or shaking so widely used in order to communicate with the other world?" This question, Needham states (1967:606), was triggered by

> the common report, encountered again and again in the ethnographical literature, that a shaman beats a drum in order to establish contact with the spirits. It is so well described, and has been so thoroughly recognized as a characteristic form of a shaman's activities, that the question seems not to have been asked (so far, at least, as I can discover) just why he beats a drum, and why this banging noise is essential if he is to communicate with spiritual powers.

Needham's original question underwent several modifications: he broadened the category from "drum" to a broad set of "percussive noise-makers": drums, gongs, bells, cymbals, rattles, rasps, anklets and bracelets, hand clapping, and so on (Needham 1967:607). The other side of his question, "communicate with spiritual powers," was extended to include an array of rites of passage, including "healing, prophylaxis, hunting, warfare, and funerals" (1967:611). Needham observed that

> one has only to review ethnographical literature to appreciate that percussion is typical of a remarkably wide range of other situations such as birth, initiation, marriage, accession to office, sacrifice, lunar rites, calendrical feasts, declaration of war, the return of head-hunters, the reception of strangers, the inauguration of a house or a communal building, market days, sowing, harvest, fishing expeditions, epidemics, eclipses, and so on. Often the instruments are identified with the events, and are themselves

> the material symbols of them; their players may not be just normal participants but indispensable officiants at the rites and ceremonies which are distinguished by the sounds. (1967:611)

The widely distributed relationship between percussion and rites of transition led Needham to suggest a psychological explanation, arguing that

> the more nearly a cultural phenomenon approaches the universal the more necessary it becomes to seek the grounds of it in the general psychic characters of mankind. In the present case, the remarkably wide distribution of percussive noise-makers, employed in communication with the other world, indicates that an historical or sociological interpretation would be quite inappropriate. (Needham 1967:609)

Needham concluded his article without answering his question, taking refuge in the notion that social anthropology is better at posing questions than answering them (1967:613), but his ideas stimulated a variety of responses. Sturtevant (1968:133) criticized Needham for the imprecision of the terms "percussion" and "transition," terms so broad that any "correlation is an artefact of the typologies." Arguing for greater precision, Sturtevant cited experimental data (Neher 1962), which Sturtevant (1968:133–134) claimed suggested (1) that the percussion involved was specifically drumming on a steep-sided drum that would produce low frequencies that would stimulate the basilar membrane of the ear and be transmitted to a wide area of the brain and (2) required drumming at a rhythm of seven to nine cycles per second, "near the basic alpha brain wave frequency" and thus creating an "abnormal" psychological state. "Seven to nine cycles per second," Sturtevant (1968:134) acknowledges in a fine bit of understatement, "is distinctly rapid drumming."[3]

More recently Sullivan (1988:790) chided Needham for disregarding "the seriousness of answers provided by cultural traditions" as reflecting "the unexamined presumption that answers of firm value are forthcoming only from 'science,'" a provocative point that sidesteps any exploration of universality. A potentially more useful argument is advanced in a short note by Knauft (1979:189), who suggests that percussion operates as a nonverbal metaphor that "not only reports category change but motivates it in a deeply experiential manner." Knauft's subtle argument deserves extensive quotation:

> *The use of percussion to generate and energize movement between social categories, as it does in rites of passage, is an obvious analog to the use of metaphor in bridging the gaps between conceptual/semantic categories.*
>
> Percussion works as a metaphor not only because it links social categories via strong sensory experience, but also because its synthesis of sonic burst and repetition, of force and form, recapitulates the structure of the metaphor itself. This is especially evident in rhythmic percussion, such as drumming, where analogic/sensory experience is intrinsically linked to an ordered digital pattern of sound. (Knauft 1979:189; emphasis added)

Unlike verbal metaphor, the sonic metaphor of drumming suppresses semantic logic, keeping categories distinct but simultaneously blurring rigid boundaries.

> Percussion thus seems to be part of "the relatively undifferentiated prelinguistic pool of motor and emotive experience on which semantic codes are later built." The control of percussive rhythm is one of the few ways in which clear markers and boundaries can be unambiguously established in perceptual/sensory experience . . . and percussion as a context marker in ritual helps in a non-semantic manner to juxtapose and superimpose ritual phases. Thus, *percussion is a kind of primordial metaphor*, immensely expressive and instrumental, whose internal structure can be easily linked with that of larger social and semantic categories. In a Durkheimian perspective, percussion as a metaphor makes an important contribution to ritual "effervescence." Moreover, because of its unique capacity to entrain collective activity (e.g., marching, clapping and dancing), percussion can easily be used for functional ends—to manage social transitions and foster collective solidarity. (Knauft 1979:190; emphasis added)

To summarize the argument to this point, processions share a number of characteristics with ritual, including performance. Processional performances tend to employ a varied but not infinite set of design logics and technologies of display, including drumming. Drumming has been associated with a large variety of rites of transition, in part because it can be used to aurally define a social time and space. It can coordinate and entrain collective action, and volume, tempo, timbre, and silence can be used to mark the boundaries of social categories (Benzon 2001; McNeill 1995). In this, drumming may serve as a generative category, to recall Lakoff's earlier discussion, and this seems to be the case in funerary processions in three pre-Hispanic Andean societies—Moche, Chimú, and Inka.

Drumming in Andean Funerary Processions

A rich array of ethnohistoric sources documents the importance of Andean public performances, variously and somewhat indiscriminately referred to as processions, penitences, fastings, fiestas, and *taquis*, the last a communal musical celebration. Such public ceremonies were targets of postconquest extirpations of idolatry, and so it is remarkable how resilient Andean knowledge of processions remained. In what must be only the fragment of a taxonomy, the seventeenth-century mestizo chronicler Felipe Guaman Poma de Ayala described some of the marvelous "processions of the Inkas":

> Procession to drive out diseases and pestilence, they throw fire from slings, as if they were fighting in battle, and thus they drive diseases and pestilence out of the cities and towns and pueblos of this reign at the Inka's command.
>
> Procession of tempests, they march with pennants on their weapons and chonta lances, wailing until the hills and peaks echo.
>
> Procession of hail and ice and lightening, that they drive away with arms and drums and flutes and trumpets and bells, shouting, astaya zuua runa uacchachac cunyaqui cuchuscayque amaricuscayquichu. (Guaman Poma 1993: 1:213; translation mine)

In addition to upright flutes, pan pipes, conch shell trumpets, bells, and rattles, drums were an essential instrument in Andean ceremonies (Fig. 2.1). The colonial chronicler Bernabe Cobo writes:

> The Indians were much given to their taquis, which is what they call their songs and dances.... For these celebrations they had many musical instruments which were played only at their dances and drinking bouts. The sound of all their instruments was rather harsh and not very artistic. In just one lesson, anyone will learn to play their instruments like an expert. Their most widely used instrument is the drum, which they call *huancar*. They made their drums both large and small, of a hollow log covered on both ends with llama hide like thin, dry parchment. The largest ones are like our war drums, but longer and not as well made, the smallest ones are like a very small box of preserves, and the medium-sized ones

Figure 2.1. Inca Processions (Guaman Poma de Ayala 1993 [1615])

were like our timbrels. The drum is played with a single drumstick . . . The drum is played by both men and women, and there are dances done to the rhythm of a single drum and other dances in which they each carry their own little drum, dancing and playing at the same time. (1990:243–244)

The seventeenth-century priest Arriaga wrote that there were three main ceremonies (actually there were many more):

On all these occasions there are fastings and confessions; when these are over, they drink and dance and sing. The women play little drums,

> which they all have, and some sing and others respond, and the men play instruments called succhas, made from deers' heads, which they call guaucu [i.e., the camelid, guanuco], and of these instruments and horns they have a great supply . . .
>
> While they are singing these songs, they tell foolish things about their ancestors, they invoke the huaca by name, raising their voices and reciting a single verse, or they raise their hands or turn around, according to the custom of the region. (Arriaga 1968:49–50)

The religious importance of these songs and dances was belatedly recognized a century after the Spanish conquest by Catholic priests intent on the extirpation of idolatry. "No one who saw them performing these celebrations thought there was any malice in it" Arriaga (1968:70) complained, "but considered them pastimes, traditional dances, and so forth."

> Nor had it been observed that they owned various instruments used to summon the people for the festivals and celebrations of the huacas, such as the many ancient trumpets of copper or silver, of different shape and appearance from ours, the great coiled horns which they play, called *antari* and *pututu*, and other instruments called *pincollos*, which are bone or cane flutes. . . . Nor was any attention paid to the quantity of small drums used to accompany their drunkenness. (Arriaga 1968:69)

Drums were used in a variety of *taquis:* harvest ceremonies, war dances, the *guacon* danced only by "men who wear masks and go jumping around while carrying in their hand the skin or dried-out body of a wild animal" (Cobo 1990:244), a *pas de trois* danced by the Inka and two noblewomen, a circle dance joined by men and women dancing hand in hand, and the Inkas' own *taqui,* danced by members of noble lineages who moved to the beat of a single large drum in a dance that was "solemn and dignified without any hopping or jumping" (Cobo 1990:245).

Drums were also used in specific phases of Inka funerary spectacle (Fig. 2.2). Depictions of actual interments do not include drums, while subsequent festivals honoring and including the dead explicitly included drumming. What we know of Inka funerary corteges seems to be characterized by weeping and sacrificial offerings but not drumming. Guaman Poma (1993:216; translation mine) wrote that upon the death of the Inka, "all in the kingdom made great cries *[lloros]* and lamentations *[llantos]* with song and music, dancing and waltzing *[bailando y danzando]* as they wept,

Figure 2.2. Inca Funeral Processions (Guaman Poma de Ayala 1993 [1615])

and after a month had passed they would bury him and carry him to the crypt that they called pucullo, with great and solemn processions." In contrast, when the mummies of the Inka and other ancestors were brought out to participate in other ceremonies, drumming was used to honor the dead. The mummies would be brought out into the plaza, given offerings of llamas, *chicha,* cloth, feather work, precious metals, and other items (Arriaga 1968:19; Molina 1964:44–45), and then the *taquis* would begin with songs and drumming.

Although the evidence is less rich than for the Inka case, there are interesting similarities to earlier funerary practice for the Chimú and Moche of the north coast of Peru. Sixteenth-century chronicler Pedro Cieza de Leon (1989:39) recounts that the lord of each valley along the north coast "had within his house a large plaza where they made their dances and songs," but he does not mention the musical instruments. A more detailed view of Chimú practice is provided by a set of remarkable artifacts from an intrusive Chimú burial at the site of Huaca de la Luna in Moche, excavated under the direction of Santiago Uceda (1999). The artifacts consist of five sets of carved miniature figures depicting a ceremony in a plaza, two funeral corteges, and two sacrificial processions—one of llamas, the other of a human. Not only are these objects elaborately carved and inlaid with shell, but they were stitched with thread onto their bases; in other words, the relative position of the objects has been preserved as intended.

The plaza ceremony occurs within an architectural model depicting a patio inside a Chimú royal compound (Fig. 2.3). The objects of the ceremony are a male and two female mummies, who are offered *chicha* and music in a final fiesta. Uceda (1999) has interpreted this ceremony as similar to the Inka celebrations honoring mummies discussed above. I differ with this interpretation; I believe the patio ceremony occurred relatively soon after the individuals' deaths and before their interment—not years or decades later—since the Chimú buried their dead in tombs that were permanently sealed from which mummies could not be retrieved (Moore 2004).

Of the twenty-six figures in the plaza ceremony, seven play musical instruments (Fig. 2.4). Three large side drums are played by males wielding large drumsticks. Two of the drummers are flanked by musicians playing side horns, a relatively large tube held horizontally and blown from the middle. Given the size of the drum and the length of the drumstick, a

Figure 2.3. Chimú Architectural Model Showing Funerary Ritual (Uceda 1999). Courtesy of Santiago Uceda

relatively slow bass rhythm is suggested; this would also seem to be true of the side horns. Uceda (1999) suggests that one of the figures depicts a conductor, and it is reasonable to infer that the music was coordinated. Given the placement of the musicians in the three corners of the patio, the drumbeats would have created overlapping fields of sound. In sum, the plaza ceremony created a space immersed in low-pitched, rhythmic, slow, and reverberating sound. This is not true of other phases in the ceremony (Fig. 2.5). The sacrificial processions were led by a single musician playing a *quena,* the high-pitched, multinote, Andean upright flute. In contrast, the actual funeral cortege advances without drums, side horns, or *quenas,* the mummy bundle strapped to a pole carried on the shoulders of two pall-bearers (Fig. 2.6). As in the Inka case, different soundscapes are associated with different phases of the Chimú funeral ceremony—drumming with

Figure 2.4. Chimú Wooden Figurines of Drummers and Trumpeters (Uceda 1999). Courtesy of Santiago Uceda

offerings of *chicha* in a fiesta for the dead, but silence in the actual burial procession.

An analogous audial distinction is suggested by Moche fine-line drawings. Mold-made ceramics depict Moche drumming with remarkable naturalism, and fine-line drawings show musical processions and dances (Donnan and McClelland 1999:101, 120, 164–165, 236). Some vessels portray processions in which musicians play medium-size side drums, upright *quenas* with six finger holes, coiled trumpets, and large panpipes; warriors and other figures dance in a long line hand in hand. When these scenes portray a Moche ruler, he is clearly alive: eyes opened, arms in midair gesture or joined in the dance (Fig. 2.7). In stark contrast, in another recognizable theme, the burial ceremony (Fig. 2.8) portrays the interment of a noble but in these ceremonies, musical instruments are never played, although conch

Figure 2.5. Chimú Figurines Showing Procession of Llama Sacrifice. Courtesy of Santiago Uceda

Figure 2.6. Chimú Figurines Showing Funerary Procession. Courtesy of Santiago Uceda

Figure 2.7. Moche Fine-line Drawing Showing Noble, Warriors, and Musicians in Dance (Donnan and McCleland 1999)

Figure 2.8. Moche Fine-line Drawing Showing Burial Ceremony (Donnan and McCleland 1999)

shells—which could be transformed into trumpets—are always exchanged (Donnan 2002). It seems that as with the Inka and Chimú cases, Moche burials were silent, but fiestas were noisy, syncopated, communal affairs.

Several points regarding this comparison require clarification. First, a variety of archaeological evidence, including architectural spaces, osteological remains, and artifactual assemblages, strongly support the idea that the artistic representations of funerary processions were not merely figurative conventions but reflections of actual practice. Second, although the Inka, Chimú, and Moche were all Andean societies, there is no reason to think that the common use of drumming in funeral processions was the product of historical connections or trait diffusion, that, for example, the Inka had "borrowed" their practice from earlier traditions. Inka, Chimú, and Moche funeral practices differ in fundamental ways in funerary architecture and conceptions of the relationships between dead and living (Moore 2004), and also in the design logics of other processional performances (Moore 2005). But to reiterate, neither is the use of drumming in Andean funerary processions completely dissimilar. Drums mark specific phases in the ritual displays, but are silenced in the procession to the grave.

Conclusion

I have attempted to make a series of points connecting a specific aspect of Andean performance—drumming in funerary ceremonies—to a larger set of issues concerning the archaeological exploration of sensation and experience. Drawing on the ideas and investigations of anthropologists, cognitive scientists, and neurophysiologists, I have suggested that "drumming" shares some of the "fuzzy set" properties of color categories: it is based on sensation and it varies cross-culturally, but the range of the variation has limited parameters. Drumming, as a prelinguistic and primordial metaphor (Knauft 1979:190), is incorporated into Andean processions as a means of generating categories—in this case, categories of mortuary spectacle. That drumming is employed in these and other cross-cultural settings must, at a basal level, reflect the evolved neurophysiology of the human brain, although we cannot claim that those relationships are well understood. However, that does not suggest that "drumming" as defining a category is a straight reflection of neuronal activity or even a simple audial stimulation of the neurons. Rather, there is a limited range of possibilities linking drumming and rites of transition that underlies the original observation made by Needham and others since.

Undoubtedly, I have overlooked numerous issues; other issues I have seen but cannot address. Drumming was only one element of these Andean funerary ceremonies; other dimensions such as human sacrifice, alcohol consumption, and weeping were also important. Further, I cannot precisely state what drumming meant in Moche, Chimú, and Inka funerary processions. Did drumming drive away evil spirits, encourage the soul on its flight, summon the spirits, create social solidarity? Did drumming occur in other, nonfunerary contexts and symbolically resonate with other meanings? I lack answers to those important questions.

Thus the above is a first approximation of an approach to the archaeology of ancient experience, including that of spectacle and performance (Moore 2005). Such an approach is a response to Trigger's (1998:9) charge that archaeologists should recognize that "idealist, positivist, and realist epistemologies are not alternative explanations, but account for various aspects of human behavior in ways that complement one another." This synthetic approach is not motivated by a desire to avoid theoretical conflicts, but because it accords with what we know about human existence and by a conviction that it will lead to new insights about ancient societies.

Notes

Earlier versions of this chapter were written while I was a scholar (2001–2002) at the Getty Research Institute, Los Angeles, whose support I gratefully acknowledge. I also thank Dr. Lawrence Krueger (UCLA), Dr. Dennis Sepper (University of Dallas), and Dr. Andrew Parker (Oxford University) for their insights. I also thank Dr. Janine Gasco (CSUDH) for commenting on earlier drafts of this chapter. All errors and oversights are, of course, my own.

1. The ethnographic cases are based on studies by G. Gossen, *Chamulas in the World of the Sun: Time and Space in a Maya Oral Tradition*; E. Vogt, *Tortillas for the Gods: A Symbolic Analysis of Zinacanteco Rituals*; V. Pandya, *Above the Forest: A Study of Andamanese Ethnoamenology, Cosmology, and the Power of Ritual*; and various works by Gerardo Reichel-Dolmatoff, including *Amazonian Cosmos: The Sexual and Religious Symbolism of the Tukano Indians,* and "Brain and Mind in Desana Shamanism" in *Journal of Latin American Lore.*

2. I was introduced to this literature while reading *Planet Drum: A Celebration of Percussion and Rhythm* by Mickey Hart, longtime drummer with the Grateful Dead.

3. A tempo probably impossible to achieve with hand drumming.

References Cited

Arriaga, Jose de
1968 The Extirpation of Idolatry in Peru. L. Clark Keating, trans. Lexington: University of Kentucky Press.

Barkow, Jerome, Lida Cosmides, and John Toobey, eds.
1992 The Adapted Mind: Evolutionary Psychology and the Generation of Consciousness. New York: Oxford University Press.

Beck, Brenda
1978 The Metaphor as Mediator between Semantic and Analogic Modes of Thought. Current Anthropology 19:83–97.

Bell, Catherine
1997 Ritual: Perspectives and Dimensions. Oxford: Oxford University Press.

Benzon, William
2001 Beethoven's Anvil: Music in Mind and Culture. New York: Basic.

Berlin, Brent, and Paul Kay
1969 Basic Color Terms: Their Universality and Evolution. Berkeley: University of California Press.

Boas, Franz
1920 The Methods of Ethnology. American Anthropologist 22:311–321.

Boroditsky, Lera
2001 Does Language Shape Thought? Mandarin and English Speakers' Conceptions of Time. Cognitive Psychology 43:1–22.

Cieza de Leon, Pedro
1989[1553] La Cronica del Peru. *In* Cronistas del Perú Antiguo. Francisco Carillo, ed. Lima: Editorial Horizonte.

Classen, Constance
1990 Sweet Colors, Fragrant Songs: Sensory Models of the Andes and the Amazon. American Ethnologist 17(4):722–735.

1993 Worlds of Sense: Exploring the Senses in History and across Cultures. London: Routledge.
1998 The Color of Angels: Cosmology, Gender, and the Aesthetic Imagination. London: Routledge.

Cobo, Bernabe
1990[1653] Inca Religion and Customs. Austin: University of Texas Press.

Cosmides, Leda, and John Toobey
1997 Evolutionary Psychology: A Primer. Electronic document, www.psych.ucsb.edu/research/cep/primer.html. Accessed August 28, 2005.

Donnan, Christopher
2002 Personal communication, January.

Donnan, Christopher, and Donna McClelland
1999 Moche Fineline Painting: Its Evolution and Its Artists. Los Angeles: Fowler Museum of Cultural History, University of California.

Gell, Arthur
1977 Magic, Perfume, Dream. *In* Symbols and Sentiments: Cross-cultural Studies in Symbolism. I. M. Lewis, ed. Pp. 25–38. London: Academic.

Gossen, Gary
1974 Chamulas in the World of the Sun: Time and Space in a Maya Oral Tradition. Cambridge: Harvard University Press.

Guaman Poma de Ayala, Felipe
1993[1615] Nueva Crónica y Buen Gobierno. Mexico City: Fondo de Cultura Económica.

Handelman, Don
1990 Models and Mirrors: Towards an Anthropology of Public Events. Cambridge: Cambridge University Press.

Hardin, C. L., and Luisa Maffi, eds.
1997 Color Categories in Thought and Action. Cambridge: Cambridge University Press.

Hart, Mickey, and Frederic Lieberman
1991 Planet Drum: A Celebration of Percussion and Rhythm. New York: HarperSanFrancisco.

Haviland, John
1996 Guugu Yimnithirr Cardinal Directions. Ethos 26(1):25–47.

Hoffman, Donald
1998 Visual Intelligence: How We Create What We See. New York: Norton.

Houston, Stephen, and Karl Taube
2000 An Archaeology of the Senses: Perception and Cultural Expression in Ancient Mesoamerica. Cambridge Archaeological Journal 10(2):261–294.

Howes, David
1991a Introduction: To Summon All the Senses. *In* The Varieties of Sensory Experience: A Sourcebook in the Anthropology of the Senses. Pp. 1–21. Toronto: University of Toronto Press.
1991b Olfaction and Transition: An Essay on the Ritual Uses of Smell. *In* The Varieties of Sensory Experience: A Sourcebook in the Anthropology of the Senses. Pp. 128–147. Toronto: University of Toronto Press.

Jacobs, Gerald
1996 Primate Photopigments and Primate Color Vision. Proceedings of the National Academy of Sciences 93:577–581.

Kay, Paul
1999 Color Categorization. *In* MIT Encyclopedia of the Cognitive Sciences. Robert Wilson and Frank Keil, eds. Pp. 143–145. Cambridge, Mass.: MIT Press.

Kay, Paul, and Chad McDaniel
1978 The Linguistic Significance of the Meanings of Basic Color Terms. Language 54:610–646.

Kirshenblatt-Gimblett, Barbara, and Brooks McNamara
1985 Processional Performance: An Introduction. The Drama Review 29(3): 2–5.

Knauft, Bruce
1979 On Percussion and Metaphor. Current Anthropology 20(1):189–191.

Kossyln, Stephen
1994 Image and the Brain: The Resolution of the Imagery Debate. Cambridge, Mass.: MIT Press.

Lakoff, George
1987 Women, Fire, and Dangerous Things: What Categories Reveal about the Mind. Chicago: University of Chicago Press.

Levinson, Steven
1998 Studying Spatial Conceptualizations across Cultures: Anthropology and Cognitive Science. Ethos 26(1):7–24.

Lewis, David
1976 Observations on Route Finding and Spatial Orientation among the Aboriginal Peoples of the Western Desert Region of Central Australia. Oceania 46:249–282.

MacLaury, Robert
1997 Color and Cognition in Mesoamerica. Austin: University of Texas Press.

McNeill, William H.
1995 Keeping Together in Time: Dance and Drill in Human History. Cambridge, Mass.: Harvard University Press.

Mithen, Steve
1998 The Prehistory of the Mind. New York: Oxford University Press.

Molina, Christobal
1964[1873] An Account of the Fables and Rites of the Yncas. *In* Narratives of the Rites and Laws of the Yncas. Clement Markham, trans. and ed. Pp. 3–64. New York: Burt Franklin.

Mollon, John
1990 Worlds of Difference. Nature 356:378.

Moore, Jerry
2004 The Social Basis of Sacred Spaces in the Prehispanic Andes: Ritual Landscapes of the Dead in Chimú and Inka Societies. Journal of Archaeological Method and Theory 11(1):83–124.
2005 Cultural Landscapes in the Ancient Andes: Archaeologies of Place. Gainesville: University of Florida.

Nathans, Jeremy, D. Thomas, and D. Hogness
1986 Molecular Genetics of Human Color Vision: The Genes Encoding Blue, Green, and Red Pigments. Science 232:193–202.

Needham, Rodney
1967 Percussion and Transition. Man (new series) 2:606–614.

Neher, Andrew
1962 A Physiological Explanation of Unusual Behavior in Ceremonies Involving Drumming. Human Biology 34:151–160.

Ong, Walter
1967 The Presence of the Word: Some Prolegomena for Cultural and Religious History. New Haven: Yale University Press.

Pandya, Vishvajit
1987 Above the Forest: A Study of Andamanese Ethnophenomenology, Cosmology, and the Power of Ritual. Ph.D. dissertation, Department of Anthropology, University of Chicago.
1990 Movement and Space: Andamanese Cartography. American Ethnologist 17(4):775–797.

Pinker, Steve
1997 How the Mind Works. New York: Norton.

Pointer, M. R., and G. G. Attridge
1998 The Number of Discernible Colors. Color Research and Applications 23:2–54.

Pollan, John
1999 Color Vision: Opsins and Options. Proceedings of the National Academy of Sciences 96:4743–4745.

Ray, Verne
1952 Techniques and Problems in the Study of Human Color Perception. Southwestern Journal of Anthropology 8:251–259.

Reichel-Dolmatoff, Gerardo
1971 Amazonian Cosmos: The Sexual and Religious Symbolism of the Tukano Indians. Chicago: University of Chicago Press.
1978 Desana Animal Categories: Food Restrictions and the Concept of Color Energies. Journal of Latin American Lore 4(2):243–291.
1979 Desana Shamans' Rock Crystals and the Hexagonal Universe. Journal of Latin American Lore 5:117–128.
1989 Brain and Mind in Desana Shamanism. Journal of Latin American Lore 7(1):73–98.

Reiger, Terry
1996 The Human Semantic Potential: Spatial Language and Constrained Connectionism. Cambridge Mass.: MIT Press.

Schechner, Richard
1988 Performance Theory. New York: Routledge.

Sperber, Dan, and Lawrence Hirschfield
1999 Culture, Cognition, and Evolution. In MIT Encyclopedia of the

Cognitive Sciences. Robert Wilson and Frank Keil, eds. Pp. 111–132. Cambridge, Mass.: MIT Press.

Sturtevant, William
1968 Categories, Percussion, and Physiology. Man (new series) 3:133–134.

Sullivan, Lawrence
1988 Icanchu's Drum: An Orientation to Meaning in South American Religions. New York: Macmillan.

Talmy, Leonard
1983 How Language Structures Space. *In* Spatial Orientation: Theory, Research, and Application. Herbert Pick and Linda Acredolo, eds. Pp. 225–283. New York: Plenum.

Tambiah, Stanley
1985 Culture, Thought and Social Action: An Anthropological Perspective. Cambridge: Harvard University Press.

Trigger, Bruce
1998 Archaeology and Epistemology: Dialoguing across the Darwinian Chasm. American Journal of Archaeology 103:1–34.

Turner, Victor
1985 The Anthropology of Performance. *In* On the Edge of the Bush. Edith Turner, ed. Pp. 177–204. Tucson: University of Arizona Press.

Uceda, Santiago
1999 Esculturas en miniatura y una maquesta en madera: El culto a los muertos y a los ancestros en la época Chimú. Beiträge zur allegemeinen und vergleichenden Archäologie 19:259–311.

Vogt, Evon
1976 Tortillas for the Gods: A Symbolic Analysis of Zinacanteco Rituals. Cambridge: Harvard University Press.
1977 On the Symbolic Meaning of Percussion in Zinacanteco Ritual. Journal of Anthropological Research 33:231–244.

Wade, Nicholas
1998 A Natural History of Vision. Cambridge, Mass.: MIT Press.

Zeki, Semir
1997 Inner Vision: An Exploration of Art and the Brain. Oxford: Oxford University Press.

SCENE 3

THE SPECTACLE OF DAILY PERFORMANCE AT ÇATALHÖYÜK

Ian Hodder

Çatalhöyük (Mellaart 1967) presents a number of challenges to archaeological theorizing about spectacle. The Neolithic east mound, dated from 7400 to 6000 B.C., contained densely packed houses and a population of around 5,000 people at the height of occupation. There are about eighteen layers of occupation. Between groups of houses in any one layer there are midden areas that were primarily used for discard—there is little of the trampling that would suggest public gatherings. Movement seems to have been on roofs, and there is no evidence as yet of centralized public architecture, specialized ceremonial or ritual spaces or buildings, and elite residences. So far, there is no evidence of any space within the settlement at which large gatherings could occur, and no evidence of the type of centralized elite authority that might have organized public spectacles and theater.

It is possible that public architecture and elite residences remain to be found. On other and earlier village sites in Anatolia, such buildings have been found at Çayönü, Göbekli Tepe, Nevali Çori, Asıklı Höyük, and so on (Özdoğan and Özdoğan 1998). But in all such cases, the ritual buildings are small scale and are not associated with a large theatrical setting. The surface layer of the eighteen-layer mound at Çatalhöyük has been subject to intense geophysical survey, surface pickup, and surface scraping (Hodder 1996), and there has been testing of some anomalies found. All this work has simply reinforced the picture of a dense packing of houses and midden areas. Even if specialized ritual buildings are in future found at Çatalhöyük, it remains the case that the organization of production and ritual is highly decentralized. Evidence from the excavation of individual houses shows that storage occurs at the domestic scale, as does much tool production, brick construction, and food consumption. Burial and probably painting and sculpture are carried out in each house. Even when some specialization of production can be identified, as in some forms of obsidian manufacture, it is low level and house centered.

Are we to say, then, that spectacle and theater do not occur at Çatalhöyük? I think not. Rather, Çatalhöyük forces a consideration of some of the assumptions that underlie theorizing about this domain. First, our definitions of spectacle often seem based on the much critiqued separation of public from private or domestic. Inomata and Coben (this volume) emphasize the agents of political power presenting themselves in front of large numbers of people at public events. While accepting that small numbers of people may be involved, and that the role of performer and audience may often be blurred, they still place the emphasis on gatherings of a "certain scale." They make the distinction between ordinary, daily lives and exceptional actions in extraordinary circumstances. I will argue that at Çatalhöyük this distinction is difficult to make. Rather, I would prefer to see spectacle as just a showing and a looking. The processes that lie behind such showing and looking, such as staging, performance, theatricality, and so on, occur however large the audience and however public or private that audience might be. So spectacle as such is not confined to the public realm, even if the mechanisms involved will change depending on the size of the audience and the scale over which performances are to be seen and heard.

Second, spectacle is often linked to power and to different forms of power. For example, some understanding of spectacle seems to assume that societies of spectacle can be separated from disciplinary societies. Many have accepted the view of Michel Foucault that antiquity was a civilization of spectacle, in contrast to modern societies which are run through by a dispersed discipline. For example, Thomas (2001:764) discusses Foucault's notion of biopower, through which multiple state mechanisms administer the lives of human subjects. He argues that "this swarming of modern society by the mechanisms of 'governmentality' is very different from the kinds of power relations that have been proposed for the Neolithic" (Thomas 2001:764). For the Neolithic in Britain, he and others such as

Barrett (1994) and Edmonds (1999) have reconstructed a society in which public rituals in monuments produced forms of authority that were contingent or temporary. "Far from imposing a continuous discipline on docile bodies, Neolithic monuments were experienced discontinuously, in performances which saturated the senses in ways that were otherwise unfamiliar" (Thomas 2001:764). I want to argue instead that premodern societies, at least at Çatalhöyük, contained both spectacle and discipline as necessarily integrated. I do not think that "in premodern Europe before the technologies of discipline developed, state power was what was seen, what was shown, and what was manifested" (Inomata and Coben, this volume, p. 26). On the contrary, power was often hidden, bodily, practical, and disciplinary in premodern societies, at least at Çatalhöyük. Of course, the institutions and governmentality that "swarmed" through society in the Neolithic were very different from today. But it is not clear to me why family, clan, and lineage cannot be seen as mechanisms every bit as disciplining and pervasive as the structures of the modern state. Docile bodies were produced by the mechanisms of power working within the daily practices of social life.

Another indication that discussion of spectacle is still infused with remnants of evolutionary thinking about forms of power is that spectacle is linked to complex societies. In fact, noncomplex societies hold public events. This is clear from the archaeological evidence in Europe, where Neolithic societies constructed major arenas such as causewayed enclosures (Barrett 1994). Despite recognizing the view of Bakhtin that spectacles can be carnivalesque and disruptive of power, Inomata and Coben tend to return to the notion that spectacle is linked to community unification and domination. Certainly in small-scale societies spectacle is linked to power and domination too. But I also think we need to consider whether theater and spectacle may be components of all societies, and we should consider Geertz's point that spectacle may not exist solely in the service of power. Rather, it may be better seen as a dimension of human experience.

Third, it seems that much discussion of spectacle assumes that we can separate the meaning of spectacle from its politics and bodily practice. It is assumed that we can separate the study of meaning, ideology, and identity from the physical acts of performance and the immediacy of material presence. In many places, Inomata and Coben separate spectacle as a closed aesthetic system from spectacle as political action. They want to look at the way performance communicates rather than the meaning of specific symbols.

They say that we should shift the focus of research from the content or message of theatrical events to their forms and context, which are more accessible through archaeological research. They suggest we should concentrate on the conditions under which symbolic acts are meaningful. This is very much the claim made by Barrett (1994), which has been subjected to criticism by Thomas (2000), and I wish to reinforce those criticisms here.

Inomata and Coben (this volume) and Barrett claim that instead of asking what specific performance means, we should study the conditions which lead to acts being meaningful. But how can one study the politics and practice and form of performance without knowing what the performance means? Surely each side of this duality implies the other. Take, for example, a play in a theater. The content of the play may be supportive of existing structures of power. But a very similar play in the same theater may, by perhaps the slightest inflection of meaning, be ironic or wholly critical of those power structures. Now, of course, we must examine the conditions which allow a play to be pro- or antigovernment. But such an examination depends on knowing what the message of the play is. The meanings and politics of performance are inextricably intertwined. We cannot study one without the other. Another example can be taken from an archaeological case such as Stonehenge. There has been much discussion recently of the "theater" of Stonehenge. But the layout of Stonehenge in relation to the summer solstice is an integral part of that theater. The acts that took place there are given a higher authority by the link to the rising sun in midsummer. Thus the politics and mechanics of the theater of Stonehenge are inextricably linked to its meaning in relation to the solstice.

I have presented a similar critique of the attempt to separate bodily practice from meaning in much phenomenological writing in archaeology. The notion that we can describe bodily movements somehow divorced from meaning (whether discursive or nondiscursive) simply reasserts the mind/body dichotomy from which such accounts strive to escape. The result is accounts of bodily movements and ritual practices and performances that present universalized bodies with universalized responses (Hodder 1999; Meskell 1996). An adequate account of bodily practice needs to situate bodies as biological/cultural within specific historical and cultural contexts. A similar critique of phenomenological approaches has been made by Brück (2001a, b). She notes that certain postprocessual archaeologists have argued for a move away from approaches in which attribution of symbolic meaning is a fundamental part:

> An understanding of what architecture *does* rather than what it *means* has been a significant element within this school of thought. . . . Within this conceptual framework, only the impact of the immediate physical context in which people find themselves can be taken into consideration; the interpretations, values and concerns which people bring with them from other areas of practice are *de facto* excluded. (Brück 2001b:766)

Although she notes that other postprocessual archaeologists working on Neolithic monuments are concerned with meaning (e.g., Thomas and Tilley 1993; Edmonds 1999; Richards 1993), the difficulty with attempts to bypass meaning is clear. The same materialities of monuments can produce very different ways of being (Brück 2001a). The world and the body through which it is experienced have social and cultural as well as physical dimensions.

In my view, our definition of performance needs to accept its dual nature as both meaningful and practical, bodily and political. I would define performance as a dimension of action that bridges to meaning and communication. Performance is an interpretation acted out for someone (including oneself). It is always, consciously or not, staged, and it is thus always theatrical.

The Staging of Performance at Çatalhöyük

At Çatalhöyük there is indication of large-scale participation in public events. There are depictions in the wall paintings of gatherings of considerable numbers of individuals. In some cases, all the individuals are bearded and very few can be clearly identified as women. The individuals are often aligned in rows, moving or dancing, sometimes with dogs and often with objects that could include clubs or bows or musical instruments. Many of the actors in these scenes are wearing garments around their waists that are spotted and have been interpreted as leopard skins because of the prevalence of leopards in the mural relief sculpture. The rows of people break up around various wild male animals. People are shown pulling the tongues and tails, and scratching the backs of bulls, stags, wild boars, and bears. Several animals have erect penises and some have their hackles raised. The people seem to be making the animals angry, teasing them, or baiting them.

We cannot be sure that such scenes depicted a contemporary reality. There is undoubtedly a mythical element to the art of Çatalhöyük. This can be seen most clearly in the images of vultures picking the flesh from headless corpses. Most of the bodies found beneath the floors in the houses were buried fully fleshed (Andrews, Molleson, and Boz 2005). There is no evidence of marks on the bones that might come from vultures or carnivores. On the other hand, we have found some headless burials beneath the Çatalhöyük floors. So the art presents a partial representation of the reality of burial at the site. It is possible that the public gatherings seen in the art may have a similar, partial relationship to events that occurred during the occupation of the site. There are also some indications onsite of larger-scale events, such as feasting. Russell and Martin (2005) have suggested that the faunal data at the site indicate a range of meat consumption practices varying from frequent small-scale consumption to less-frequent large-scale feasting.

Any large-scale gathering of parts of the community at Çatalhöyük must have taken place off-site. There is no evidence of open and trampled areas onsite, and the roofs were divided into small activity areas. Large groups of people baiting wild animals must have happened off-site. But there are mnemonics of it on the site. The depictions of baiting wild animals in the mural art at Çatalhöyük emphasize animals that are less frequent on-site. For example, by far the dominant meat source at the site, throughout its occupation, is the domesticated sheep and goat (Russell and Martin 2005). There are few sheep and goats shown in the mural paintings, and perhaps none that are domesticated. On the other hand, the main animals shown in the art are often rare onsite. No leopards have been found, and few bears. Deer are common in the art but they are mainly found onsite in the form of antlers. The cattle at Çatalhöyük seem to be morphologically wild. It is the heads of the animals that are shown in the baiting scenes that are given prominence in the relief sculpture at the site. The heads or horns, antlers, or teeth are brought into the house. The skulls of bulls and rams are plastered and set on pillars and on the walls. The horns are set in benches. Bears' skins and claws are brought in, and the tusks of wild boars are set in walls. The traces of public outside events such as ritual baiting and feasting are placed inside the house. Indeed, it could be said that they are used to create a focus of attention (Renfrew 1985) around which a theater could be created inside the house. Bulls' heads are plastered and set on pillars and in central places on walls and upright posts. Focus is created around items that memorialize past events in the public realm.

We shall see below that there is much evidence that a wide range of daily and/or ritual activities took place inside the houses. These activities are staged by the arrangement of the inner space. In general terms this is done with light, sound, platform height, whiteness, painting and relief sculpture, framing, and so on. All these theatrical techniques are being used to orchestrate daily/ritual activities. Of the 160 or so buildings that have been excavated at Çatalhöyük, the vast majority have a floor plan in which the main hearth or oven and the entrance are in the south of the main room. There is usually little painting or sculpture in this southern area. The people entering and the smoke from the fire used the same hole in the roof, and the ladder entry went through the rising smoke. Once inside, the main room was divided into platforms or segments by raised floors and lips between areas (Figs. 3.1, 3.2). The inner platforms tend to have burials beneath them and the main concentrations of painting and sculpture are in the inner northern areas. The different platforms are distinguished by their height, by being bounded by ridges or columns and pillars, by bucrania, and by color and covering. Different platforms in the main room use plaster with

Figure 3.1. Reconstruction of Building at Çatalhöyük by John Swogger

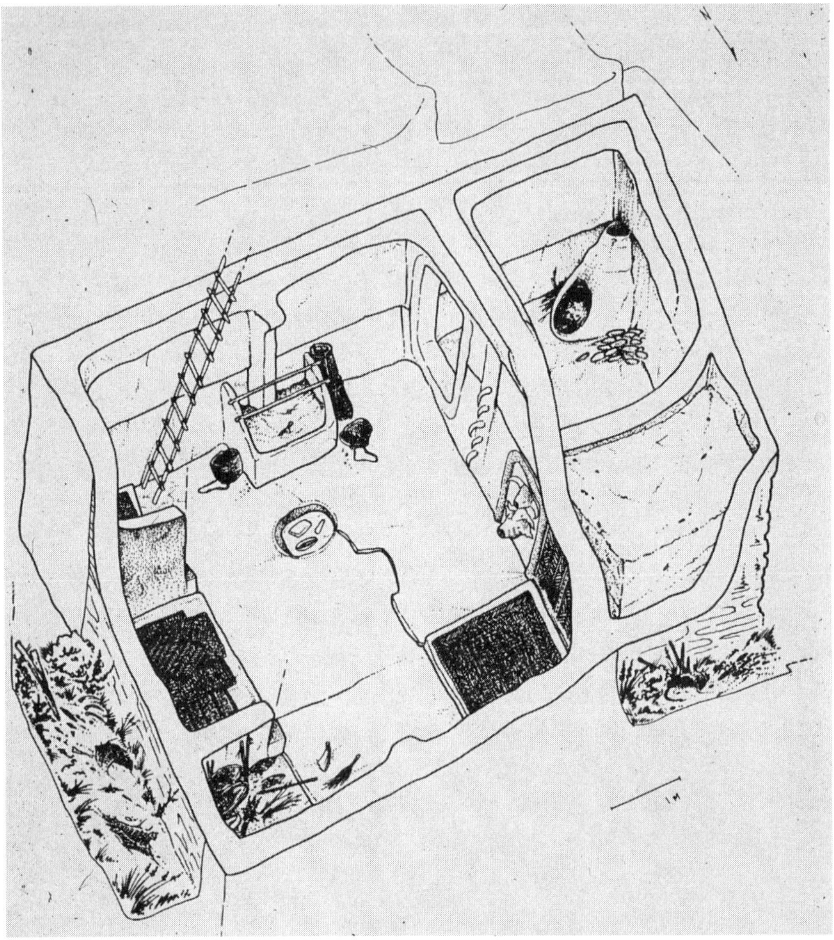

Figure 3.2. Building 1 at Çatalhöyük as Drawn by John Swogger

different makeup and with different color. The higher and more elaborate platforms are often whiter, but they are sometimes surrounded in red ochre. The different platforms also have evidence of different types and degrees of covering, usually well-woven reed mats.

The walls too partake in this staging of the inner space. The walls are divided by upright posts. There is little evidence that these upright timbers had much structural function. They do not seem essential to the construction of the house. What they do very effectively is provide a frame to the divisions in the house. They always occur at the boundaries between platforms, and they often are used to affix bucrania. They are always hidden behind multiple layers of plaster. The same emphasis on framing is found in the plastering of the walls themselves. In Building 1 and in Mellaart's Building 10 (Level VI) the main bucrania are set within a plaster frame. This is formed by vertical ridges on either side of the relief sculpture; the ridges separate or frame off the sculpture from the rest of the wall.

All this careful staging occurs in a small space. The main room is normally only 3.5 meters by 3.5 meters in size. The staging also uses light. We believe that the main source of light was single: during the day from the entrance hole, and at night from the oven. As one moved into the main room, the space would have been lit from these single sources, but as soon as one moved into the small side rooms, light and sound traveled less well. These dark, cut-off side rooms were used for food and tool preparation, storage, and a range of other activities. The arrangement of space within the main room was often repetitive; similar focal points are found in similar places in different houses. For example, major relief sculpture (of bucrania or supposed goddess figures) often occurs on the west wall, and benches of bucrania on the east wall. In both Buildings 1 and 3, the northwest platform was the main burial platform and was surrounded by geometric painting on the lower part of the walls. All this suggests a careful and repeated knowledge about how space and bodily movement within that space was to be staged (Last 1998).

We have seen then that movement and action inside the buildings at Çatalhöyük always had a quality of performance in that they could only take place in a setting constructed around focal points: large mnemonics from external events. The bucrania, relief sculpture, and art were part of an elaborate staging. Every act was willy-nilly interpreted in relation to the stage setting. What are the meanings of this microtheater? There are two central themes I would emphasize, although in fact a complex set of meanings can be discussed. The first concerns the presencing of ancestors. There are different numbers of burials beneath the floors of the buildings, as we will see below. Many have an average of four to eight burials, but some houses have up to sixty-two burials. The platforms with burials beneath them are continually replastered as new burials are added, and there is a clear ability to remember who is buried beneath each platform throughout the life of the house, which may be up to 150 years. This is seen in the fact that different types of people are buried beneath different platforms. Thus in Building 1, younger people are buried beneath the northwestern platform and older people beneath the eastern platform. There is some evidence (see below) that in Building 1 the geometric art around the northwestern platform is related to the occurrence of burials there. But the ancestors are also presenced directly by the removal and circulation of skulls. In two cases in the recent excavations, burials were found of bodies lacking skulls and with evidence of cut marks on the upper vertebrae for the removal of the skulls. We have also found individual skulls in abandonment and foundation deposits in houses. To some degree these skulls must have been circulated and reused.

This emphasis on using skulls as markers of links to ancestors is part of a wider practice of head removal and circulation that is seen also in figurines. Some of them have removable and replaceable heads. The bucrania in the houses were often treated in similar ways—removed and replaced. In a number of cases excavated by Mellaart in the 1960s, the major sculptures on the west wall had been removed as part of the abandonment process. In the recent excavations of Building 1 (Cessford 2005a), there was clear evidence that after the house was abandoned and cleaned out, it was filled in with clean clays and silts. Some decades later, a pit was dug down through this fill to remove a relief sculpture, probably a bucranium, from the western wall. It is possible that animal skulls too were used as mnemonics of past events or individuals. Such links to the past suggest an emphasis on continuity of the social group, probably based around kin and ancestry.

So one theme in the art is ancestry, and this is of course a wider trend in the Neolithic of the Near East and Europe. The plastering and circulation of skulls is a wider practice in the PPNB, and again a concern with ancestry seems the best interpretation. A second theme in the meaning of the art at Çatalhöyük concerns an emphasis on certain parts of animals and birds. It is not just that wild animals are brought in from the outside. Only parts of certain animals are brought in or given emphasis in the relief sculpture. We have seen the bull bucrania, the antlers, the tusks of wild boars, and the claws of bears. Mellaart noted that behind protuberances on the walls were vulture beaks and the teeth of foxes and weasels. Prominence is not given in the art to sheep, goat, and cattle postcranial parts or to equids (which were also hunted regularly). There is evidence that weasel droppings were collected and placed in human burials. It is not easy to explain this particular set of preoccupations. There is an image from the site of a naked woman sitting on felines, probably leopards, her hands on their heads. This association could be read as the woman as powerful, controlling the leopards, but also associated with them. More generally, we could argue that of the canines and carnivores, the horns and teeth were brought into the house and were controlled within the repeated practices and structures of daily life in the house. The beaks and teeth within the walls were repeatedly plastered over, and the leopards on the walls were repeatedly painted. But the objects from the outside also gave a power and force to those repeated practices. In other words, they created action as performance by referring to a set of meanings related to powerful images and memories of, for example, outside rituals.

An important part of any play is timing. This is partly controlled by the rise and fall of the curtain, and by the changes of stage setting. The temporality of activities in space at Çatalhöyük is very important. There is continual erasure and restaging. The plasters on the walls and the floors often show numerous replasterings, in some cases up to 150 major replasterings (Matthews 2005). Because of a general correspondence between the number of replasterings of walls in houses and the dendrochronological estimates of length of use of houses (Kuniholm and Newton 1996), it is assumed that the main replasterings occurred annually. However, there is also evidence of seasonal or even monthly replastering (Matthews 2005). In all cases only some of these replastered walls were painted. In other words, most paintings were short term and soon covered up, although in some cases (e.g., the repaintings of leopards) paintings were repeated several times. The relief sculptures existed throughout the life of a building and they seem to have been connected more closely to the construction of continuity and ancestry. The paintings, on the other hand, were more often short term and may have been involved in staging particular events. For example, as already noted, in Building 1 there is some microstratigraphic evidence that the geometric paintings occurred when young people were buried beneath the northwestern platform. The paintings may have been apotropaic or may have allowed communication with the dead in some way. Thus, the paintings and the replasterings created a sense of rhythm to the practices in the house. They changed the setting in which performances of certain types could occur. But it should also be noted that there is more evidence of replastering in certain rooms and platforms. The side rooms usually have fewer layers of plaster. In the main rooms, it is the higher, whiter platforms, those that often contain burials, that are more frequently replastered. It is not easy to argue that these areas were more carefully maintained. Rather, their special nature was created by continual renewal. These areas were set up as special through the manipulation of timing.

The Staging of Discipline at Çatalhöyük

So far I have described the ways in which actions inside houses were given a quality of performance by being staged within a carefully constructed architecture, and by being constituted as meaningful within a particular set of themes. Few people would have seen these performances. They were primarily designed for family groups that we estimate as five to ten people, although slightly larger numbers could have been crammed in on special occasions. The spectacle was small scale, but what it lacked in scale was made up for in terms of intensity, detail, and meaning. I will return later to the question of actor and audience, but for the moment I want to focus on how the spectacle created disciplined bodies.

The Cambridge–Stanford team working at Çatalhöyük has come to excavate buildings in phases with little or no use of baulks and running sections. This is because of the enormous complexity of the archaeology and stratigraphy in these spaces. There is multiple flooring, reflooring and replastering, scouring, rebuilding, cleaning out, abandoning, and filling in. The best way to understand a phase is to excavate it by digging in plan and in phase. When excavating, we try and clean off onto sets of contemporary floors and platforms. As we work within such a phase of floors in a building, we find that our bodies become attuned to the complexities of the space. We become accustomed to the changes in platform height, the ridges and lips. The body moves around carefully so as not to tread on and destroy fragile plaster features and platform edges.

We cannot assume that bodies in the past were similarly constrained by these spaces. But there is evidence that they were. There are marked differences between the surfaces of the different platforms and floors in any one building. Near the ovens the floors are rich in charcoal and a wide range of residues from obsidian knapping debris to animal bone scatter to potsherds and charred wood and basketry. But there are also other types of floor, including the white plastered platforms. There are also nonwhite clean plasters and unplastered floors.

On the whole these different types of floors are associated with different densities of material (Cessford 2005b). This is shown in Table 3.1,

Table 3.1. The Densities of Heavy Residue Material in Floors of Different Types in the North Area at Çatalhöyük.

	White Clay Floors (48 Samples)		*Non-White Laid Floors (20 Samples)*		*Occupation Floors (42 Samples)*		*All Floors (176 Samples)*	
Bone 4mm	0.210667	0.73	0.241111	0.84	0.653909	2.28	0.287152	1.00
Chipped Stone 4mm	0.001176	0.24	0.006667	1.38	0.004915	1.02	0.004833	1.00
Bone 2mm	0.026136	0.65	0.059952	1.50	0.053000	1.32	0.040000	1.00
Chipped Stone 2mm	0.002083	0.65	0.008333	2.60	0.005227	1.63	0.003200	1.00
Bone 1mm	0.016771	1.00	0.013810	0.82	0.020275	1.20	0.016852	1.00
Chipped Stone 1mm	0.000000	N/A	0.000833	N/A	0.001278	N/A	0.000000	N/A

Note: After Cessford 2005a. All densities are expressed in grams per litre. For ease of comparison the overall median density value for all units can be expressed as a nominal value of 1.00 and the median values for specific types of units can be expressed as a second figure.

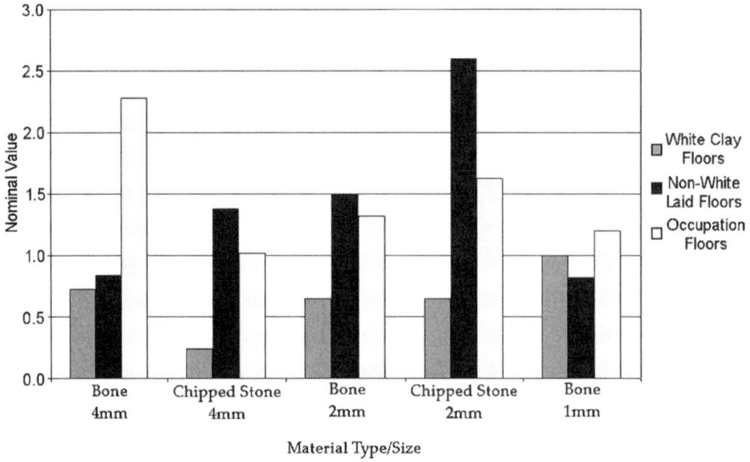

Figure 3.3. Median Densities of Bone and Chipped Stone in Different Types of Floor in the North Area at Çatalhöyük

Figures 3.3 and 3.4; an example of a plot of artifacts is shown in Figure 3.5. These artifact plots are based mainly on microresidues—densities of material that have been collected in 4-millimeter, 2-millimeter, and 1-millimeter sieves. Macroartifacts are rarely found on floors at Çatalhöyük, which are swept scrupulously clean on abandonment in most cases. Because each floor replastering is so thin, it is difficult to know whether the microartifacts in

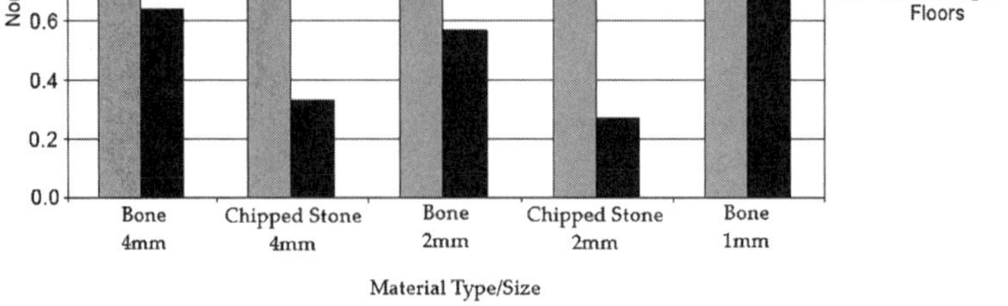

Figure 3.4. Densities of Bone and Chipped Stone in General and Raised-Height Floors in the North Area at Çatalhöyük

Figure 3.5. Example of Heavy Residue Plots for Microartifacts in and on Floors in Building 1 at Çatalhöyük

floor contexts derive from the use of floors or from their construction. We have examined this question by comparing floor plasters with wall plasters and by a wide range of studies of artifact size, fragmentation, and abrasion. Our overall conclusion is that at least a part of the variation in densities seen in Figures 3.3 and 3.4 may be the result of variations in use. But it is more clearly the case that the differences result from the fact that each platform was made of rather different clays from different sources and with different amounts of residual material in them. The chemical differences between platforms are also marked (Middleton et al. 2005), and again the explanation is a mixture of use and makeup variation.

Given the extreme differences between the charcoal-rich floors near ovens and the clean white platforms, it is remarkable that there is not more spreading or scuffing of charcoal and microartifacts from one area of the house to another. Any messiness might be masked by the use of floor coverings; there is phytolith evidence that the floors were covered with mats for at least part of the time (Rosen 2005). But micromorphological study of the surfaces of the platforms shows that microartifacts and residues were getting through these mats onto and into the soft plaster floors (Matthews 2005). The materials on and in the floors thus give some indication of the amount of spreading and scuffing that took place.

On the whole, the division between floor areas is marked. We talk colloquially onsite of "clean" and "dirty" floors, an inaccurate shorthand but indicative of the ease of identification of the differences. If movement around the spaces in the rooms was frequent and unstructured, we would expect to find more spreading and scuffing. The careful attention to detailed differences between platforms and spaces in terms of both construction and use suggests that as bodies moved around these spaces they moved carefully and in a controlled manner. In addition, the different platforms were used for the burial of different social groups. Such differences likely had some reflection in life, regarding who could sit, sleep, eat, and so on in the different spaces. It seems likely that one learned social rules through the way in which the body was trained to move through these small spaces.

This evidence of a disciplining or socializing of the body in the house might be said to contrast with an outer world in which such restrictions did not occur. For example, perhaps there was free movement on the house roofs. In Building 3 a collapsed roof has been found (Tringham and Stevanovic, personal commmunication) that had multiple floorings and showed differences between clean and dirty areas. The structuring of the body inside the house may have been repeated outside, at least in some contexts.

If there is not a high degree of centralization of power at Çatalhöyük, it may be that social rules were constructed not through the imposition of central authority but through the dispersed construction of docile bodies within small social units. This disciplining was sanctioned and given force by being staged within a small-scale but powerful everyday spectacle. Action became performance by being given meaning and being interpreted within a complex set of myths about ancestors and outside rituals concerning wild animals.

The Powers of the Daily Spectacle

The daily spectacle at Çatalhöyük socializes and disciplines, insofar as it also regulates how the body moves and learns to move. It derives its power from historical associations and meanings, but it cannot be reduced to power. It derives its power also from effective performance. The spectacle and the performance are dimensions of social life. They serve the interests of power but cannot be reduced to it. In whose interests are these bodies staged and disciplined? Who is the theater director and who the audience?

Even if we cannot identify central buildings and ceremonial centers at Çatalhöyük, it must be presumed that groups or alliances, say of elders, held some sway or authority in joint decision making at the site. Presumably it was in their interests to promote myths and performances associated with disciplinary practices. Many of the motifs used in the art are common to the site as a whole, and there may have been some regulation of practices within buildings.

Slightly more visible to us are groups of buildings that seem to function in some way as a unit. These groups of three to six contiguous houses can be identified in a number of ways (Farid 2005). First, there are openings or entrances that sometimes link adjacent houses, allowing access without going onto the roof. Second, there are major differences between the numbers of people buried in adjacent houses. In a number of cases, a central house with thirty to sixty burials is surrounded by houses with few or no burials. In the case of the sixty-two burials in Building 1, it is clear that this number of burials could not have been produced from the inhabitants of the house, which in this case only lasted for about forty years. Apparently people were buried in central houses from other houses. Third, these central houses often are more elaborate in terms of numbers of platforms, painting, sculpture, benches, pillars, and so on. Fourth, the central houses show more continuity than surrounding houses. While surrounding houses may go in and out of use, the central houses tend to endure and be stable over centuries. In fact, Mellaart's Building 10 ended up being considerably lower than surrounding houses; one would have had to step down onto the roof of this central building.

There is some slight evidence that the central houses had preferential access to the production of certain types of obsidian blade (Conolly 1996), and there may be concentrations of figurines. But these buildings are mainly differentiated by their greater elaboration. That is, they focus especially on the staging and performance of daily activities and those associated with ancestors. It is in these more elaborate buildings that we find headless burials. Any concentration of power in these central buildings seems to be based primarily on power/knowledge—the manipulation of meanings that surround performances in the daily practices of social life.

Another aspect of the power of microspectacle at Çatalhöyük that might be considered is gender. There is a strong male theme in much of the art, especially that associated with large-scale outside group events. As already noted, all of the people in some of the ritual baiting scenes have beards and several of the animals have erect penises. At an earlier site to the east at Göbekli, all the animals in the art seem to be male, many with erect penises (Schmidt 2001). At Çatalhöyük the image of the female is more common in individualized contexts (as figurines), often sitting. The contrast between the active dancing men in the baiting scenes and the folded arms and legs of the static female figurines could be said to imply a difference in disciplinary strategy. Perhaps it was a male interest to discipline female bodies. But the evidence does not support such an interpretation. The traces of repetitive action and posture on the skeletons from Çatalhöyük suggest, if anything, greater varieties of posture for women than for men (Andrews, Molleson, and Boz 2005). There is no evidence that males and females controlled different areas of the house and no real evidence that one gender controlled the house. The area around the oven is used for food preparation and obsidian knapping, and there is no evidence for a gendered use of space or for men and women being buried in different ways in different parts of the house. All the evidence for diet from tooth wear to isotopes indicates a similar diet for men and women (Pearson and Richards 2005). Both male and female skulls were removed from bodies and were used in the founding and abandoning of houses. This suggests that lineal ties through both men and women were seen as important. There is no evidence that gender relations were involved in the disciplinary strategies embedded within the staging and performance of daily/ritual practices at Çatalhöyük.

Conclusion

At Çatalhöyük it is difficult to separate public from private domains, and we can argue for spectacle within the domestic context. But this spectacle is intimately linked to a disciplinary power that is all pervasive and is structured to produce a particular form of docile body. We have also seen that spectacle and discipline are used to create a concentration of power in certain houses, but there is no evidence to suggest that we can reduce spectacle to power. Rather, spectacle is involved in an elaborate set of meanings that extend out into a social and mythical world. It is this rich world of meanings that makes Çatalhöyük what it is.

Note

Providing citations for this chapter was difficult, as many of the ideas and data derive from discussions among members of the Çatalhöyük team. Publications of team members will appear in the volumes produced by the project over the next few years. I have indicated specific sources in these volumes, but team influence is pervasive. However, many would take a different line from that taken here and I do not mean to imply that those referred to would agree with my views as presented here. I am deeply in debt to the team as a whole for its openness of discussion and its sharing of data.

References Cited

Andrews, P., T. Molleson, and B. Boz
2005 The Human Burials at Çatalhöyük. *In* Inhabiting Çatalhöyük: Reports from the 1995–1999 Seasons. I Hodder, ed. Pp. 261–278. Monograph of the McDonald Institute of Archaeology and the British Institute of Archaeology at Ankara.

Barrett, John C.
1994 Fragments from Antiquity. Oxford: Blackwell.

Brück, Joanna
2001a Monuments, Power, and Personhood in the British Neolithic. Journal of the Royal Anthropological Institute 7:649–667.
2001b Comment: Monuments, Power, and Personhood in the British Neolithic. Journal of the Royal Anthropological Institute 7:766–767.

Cessford, C.
2005a Excavations in the North Area. *In* Excavations at Çatalhöyük: The 1995–1999 Seasons. Ian Hodder, ed. Monograph of the McDonald Institute and the British Institute of Archaeology at Ankara.

2005b Heavy Residue Analysis. *In* Changing Materialities at Çatalhöyük: Reports from the 1995–1999 Seasons. Ian Hodder, ed. Monograph of the McDonald Institute and the British Institute of Archaeology at Ankara.

Conolly, J.
1996 The Knapped Stone. *In* On the Surface: Çatalhöyük, 1993–1995. Ian Hodder, ed. Pp. 173–198. Monograph 22, McDonald Institute for Archaeological Research and the British Institute of Archaeology at Ankara.

Edmonds, M. R.
1999 Ancestral Geographies of the Neolithic. London: Routledge.

Farid, S.
2005 Excavations in the South Area. *In* Excavations at Çatalhöyük: The 1995–1999 Seasons. Monograph of the McDonald Institute and the British Institute of Archaeology at Ankara.

Hodder, Ian
1999 The Archaeological Process. Oxford: Blackwell.

Hodder, Ian, ed.
1996 On the Surface. Monograph 22, McDonald Institute and the British Institute of Archaeology at Ankara.

Kuniholm, P., and M. Newton
1996 Interim Dendrochronological Progress Report 1995/1996. *In* On the Surface: Çatalhöyük 1993–1995. Ian Hodder, ed. Pp. 345–348. Monograph 22, McDonald Institute for Archaeological Research and the British Institute of Archaeology at Ankara.

Last, Jonathan
1998 A Design for Life: Interpreting the Art of Çatalhöyük. Journal of Material Culture 3:355–378.

Matthews, W.
2005 Micromorphological and Microstratigraphic Traces of Uses and Concepts of Space. *In* Inhabiting Çatalhöyük: Reports from the 1995–1999 Seasons. Ian Hodder, ed. Monograph of the McDonald Institute and the British Institute of Archaeology at Ankara.

Mellaart, James
1967 Çatal Hüyük: A Neolithic Town in Anatolia. New York: McGraw-Hill.

Meskell, Lynn
1996 The Somatisation of Archaeology: Institutions, Discourses, Corporeality. Norwegian Archaeological Review 29:1–16.

Middleton, William, D., T. Douglas Price, and David C. Meiggs
2005 Chemical Analysis of Floor Sediments for the Identification of Anthropogenic Activity Residues. *In* Changing Materialities at Çatalhöyük: Reports from the 1995–1999 Seasons. Ian Hodder, ed. Monograph of the McDonald Institute and the British Institute of Archaeology at Ankara.

Özdoğan, M., and A. Özdoğan
1998 Buildings of Cult and the Cult of Buildings. *In* Light on Top of the Black Hill: Studies Presented to Halet Cambel. G. Arsebuk, M. Mellink, and W. Schirmer, eds. Pp. 581–601. Istanbul: Ege Yayinlari.

Pearson, J., and M. Richards
2005 Stable Isotope Evidence of Diet at Çatalhöyük. *In* Inhabiting Çatalhöyük: Reports from the 1995–1999 Seasons. Ian Hodder, ed. Monograph of the McDonald Institute and the British Institute of Archaeology at Ankara.

Renfrew, Colin
1985 The Archaeology of Cult. London: Thames & Hudson.

Richards, Colin
1993 Monumental Choreography: Architecture and Spatial Representation in Late Neolithic Orkney. *In* Interpretative Archaeology. Christopher Tilley, ed. Pp. 143–178. Oxford: Berg.

Rosen, Arlene
2005 Phytolith Indicators of Plant and Land Use at Çatalhöyük. *In* Inhabiting Çatalhöyük: Reports from the 1995–1999 Seasons. Ian Hodder, ed. Monograph of the McDonald Institute and the British Institute of Archaeology at Ankara.

Russell, N., and L. Martin
2005 The Çatalhöyük Mammal Remains. *In* Inhabiting Çatalhöyük: Reports from the 1995–1999 Seasons. Ian Hodder, ed. Monograph of the McDonald Institute and the British Institute of Archaeology at Ankara.

Schmidt, K.
2001 Göbekli Tepe, Southeastern Turkey: A Preliminary Report on the 1995–1999 Excavations. Paléorient 26(1):45–54.

Thomas, Julian
2000 Introduction: The Polarities of Post-Processual Archaeology. Interpretive Archaeology: A Reader. Julian Thomas, ed. Pp. 1–18. London: Leicester University Press.
2001 Comment: Monuments, Power, and Personhood in the British Neolithic. Journal of the Royal Anthropological Institute 7:763–766.

Thomas, Julian, and Christopher Tilley
1993 The Axe and the Torso: Symbolic Structures in the Neolithic of Brittany. *In* Interpretative Archaeology. Christopher Tilley, ed. Pp. 225–324. Oxford: Berg.

SCENE 4

REPRESENTATIONAL AESTHETICS AND POLITICAL SUBJECTIVITY: THE SPECTACULAR IN URARTIAN IMAGES OF PERFORMANCE

Adam T. Smith

Carved into an exposed piece of windswept bedrock, approximately 7 kilometers northeast of the modern city of Van and the ancient Urartian capital of Tushpa, is an open-air monument known as Meher Kapısı (Fig. 4.1). Although much of what might have been the architectural features of the site are today eroded away, the central feature of the complex—a rectangular niche, or false door, 4 meters high and 2.6 meters wide—remains intact along with the extensive inscription of the Urartian kings Ishpuini and Menua (who ruled as father–son coregents). The inscription begins:

> To Haldi, the Lord, Ishpuini, son of Sarduri, and Minua, son of Ishpuini, erected this door. They established the following order (ardiše): in the month of the sun god must take place a ceremony (?) (aşuse) in favour of Haldi, the Weather God, the Sun God, and the assembly of the Gods. (Salvini 1994:205–206)

The text then continues with a detailed list of sacrifices required for each of the members of the Urartian pantheon:

> Six kids were slaughtered for the God Haldi, 17 bulls (and) 34 sheep for the God Haldi (as) sacrifices; for God Teisheba—6 bulls (and) 12 sheep, for God Shivini—4 bulls (and) 8 sheep, for God Khutuini—2 bulls (and) 4 sheep, for God Turani—a bull (and) 2 sheep, for God Ua—2 bulls (and) 4 sheep, for God Nalaini—2 bulls (and) 4 sheep, for God Shebitu. (After Melikishvili 1960: no. 27)

Figure 4.1. Meher Kapısı Monument (Photo: Adam T. Smith)

The list continues in this manner, listing the sacrifices owed to eighty-one distinct deities, aspects of deities, or groups of deities. This evocative text has been discussed as a key to the hierarchy of the Urartian pantheon (Belli 1999; Riemschneider 1963) and as a syncretic cartography of an expanding empire's appropriation of local divinities (Salvini 1994). The text is more superficially, yet perhaps no less significantly, an account of a dramatic political spectacle held on the rock terrace below. By the end of this procession of sacrifice, 99 bulls, 277 sheep, 6 kids, and 6 cows had been killed, uniting the kings of the realm and the rulers of the cosmos in a massive festival of death and consumption.

Aside from providing the vocabulary necessary to produce an impressionistic sense of the scale of the performance that culminated in pools of animal blood seeping into the weathered rock, contemporary approaches to political spectacle in early complex societies lend us little help in broaching a more profound discussion of the Meher Kapısı monument. What were the central political perspectives at play in the Meher Kapısı spectacles? What made them compelling? How do they relate to the constitution of authority more generally? As Inomata and Coben point out in their introduction to this volume, part of the problem lies in the lack of attention that archaeologists have paid to spectacles in the ancient world. However, the reluctance of archaeologists to take on public performances in antiquity is symptomatic of a larger uncertainty within the social sciences as to how we should grapple with aesthetic dimensions of political life—with the practices and processes of authorization and subjectification that draw upon a sensibility beyond the empirical, on frisson rather than functional rationality.

In another context I discussed the built environments that served as backdrops to scenes of conquest and devotion conveyed in both texts and images generated by Urartian political authorities (Smith 2000). In this chapter I want to attend more closely to the relations between figures and actions that provide the central representational foci for Urartian pictorial images of spectacle. The goal of this discussion is to provide not only some insight into the relation between the aesthetics of spectacle and the reproduction of Urartian political authority, but also a more general theoretical orientation to the political aesthetic. Can such representations provide us with not just a sense of the instrumentality of ways of seeing, but also a point of entry for a discussion of the sublime in subjectification and thus a sense of the polity beyond interest and strategy?

A Brief Account of Urartu

The kingdom of Urartu (Fig. 4.2) apparently emerged during the early first millennium B.C. from a collection of local polities in the highlands of eastern Anatolia centered in cyclopean stone masonry fortresses perched atop steep rock outcrops. Formal similarities in settlement patterns, built

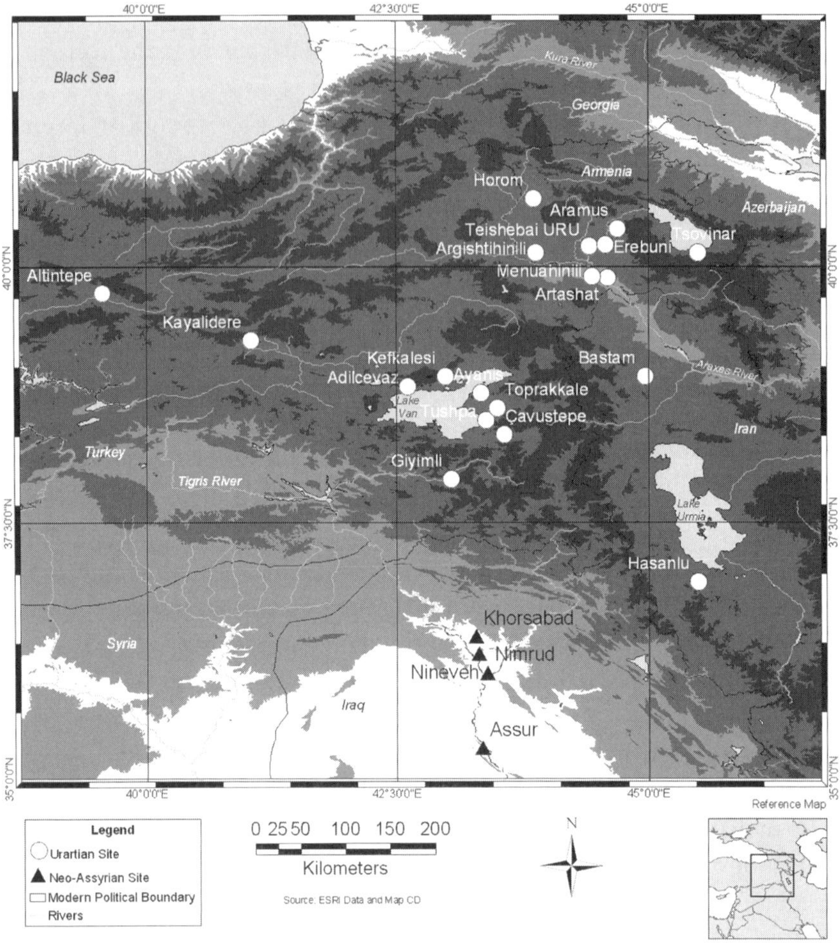

Figure 4.2. Southern Caucasia and Eastern Anatolia with the Locations of Major Urartian Sites of the Ninth to Seventh Centuries B.C.

environments, and institutional complexes strongly suggest that Urartu developed out of a southern Caucasian political tradition that began to flourish during the second half of the second millennium B.C. (Badalyan et al. 2003; Smith et al. 2004; Smith and Thompson 2004; cf. Çilingiroğlu 1991; Kushnareva 1997; Martirosian 1964; Pogrebova 1977).

By the mid-ninth century B.C., the Urartian kingdom controlled an as yet uncertainly defined territory in the highlands around the eastern shore of Lake Van from their capital at Tushpa (Van), just west of the modern city of Van. During the imperial period (between the mid-ninth and late eighth centuries B.C.), the Urartian kings embarked on a program of imperial expansion, conquering rivals from the headwaters of the Euphrates to the south shore of Lake Urmia. As they expanded, the Urartian kings inscribed declarations of their presence on stone outcrops and stele and built large stone masonry fortresses across the occupied territories (Barnett 1982; Piotrovskii 1959; Salvini 1995; and Wartke 1993).

The archaeological record for the period that followed Rusa I's defeat indicates a reconsolidation of much of Urartu's territory, a resurgence of Urartian resolve to challenge Assyrian pretensions in the highlands, and a reinvigoration of the power of Urartian authorities. The reign of Rusa II during the mid-seventh century B.C. was the apogee of this period of reconstruction. Thanks to foundation inscriptions, five major fortresses, accomplished on a grand scale, are directly attributable to him (Zimansky 1995:94), including Ayanis (Çilingiroğlu and Salvini 1995, 2001), Bastam (Kleiss 1979, 1988), and Karmir-Blur (Oganesian 1955; Piotrovskii 1955).

Dynastic succession following Rusa II is unclear, leaving some confusion over the last rulers of the empire and the dating of collapse. The fate of Urartu during the late seventh century B.C. is not well understood, but an inscription of the Assyrian King Ashurbanipal, dated to 643 B.C., records the submission of the king of Urartu (Thompson and Mallowan 1933:95). Although not an adequate date for collapse, Urartu was never again a significant force in the geopolitics of southwest Asia (Salvini 1995:109ff).

A number of surviving sources from the Urartian era bear directly on the problems of politics and performance at issue in the present discussion. In addition to the door of Haldi at Meher Kapısı, investigations at several sites have uncovered places of spectacle and performance. Excavations at the seventh-century B.C. fortress of Ayanis, a construction of Rusa II on the eastern shore of Lake Van, have uncovered a remarkable temple complex (Çilingiroğlu 2001:37–48) that was built around an exterior pillared courtyard and an internal *cella*. The complex as a whole was constructed as a 30-meter by 30-meter square at the topographically highest point of the citadel. A series of rectangular buttressed pillars outlined a portico around the edges of the courtyard. The roughly square *cella* is 4.58 meters by 4.62 meters. An extraordinarily long cuneiform inscription on the stones that surround the doorway dedicates the temple to Haldi and describes, in terms highly reminiscent of the Meher Kapısı monument, the ceremonies that must attend each stage in the process of temple construction:

> When one performs (= the ceremony?), one young kid must be slaughtered for Haldi, (and) an ox has to be sacrificed to Haldi, and a cow to (the Goddess) 'Arubaini. When they build *pahazuli* one young kid has to be slaughtered to Haldi, one ox must be slaughtered to Haldi, and a cow to (the Goddess) 'Arubaini. (Salvini 2001:259)

The interior walls of the *cella* were decorated with extraordinary stone inlays in the shape of winged deities, geometric shapes, and winged animals. Thrusting forward from the center of the *cella*'s rear wall was an alabaster podium incised with motifs depicting mythical winged animals (Çilingiroğlu 2001).

A more explicitly political place of spectacle was documented at the ninth-century site of Erebuni (Fig. 4.3), political capital of the Urartian occupation in the Ararat plain. Adjacent to the main entrance to the fortress, the excavators uncovered a large columned hall which has been repeatedly described as an audience chamber for the king or resident governor.[1] Aside from the large circular column bases that litter the floor, the most

Figure 4.3. The Columned Hall at Erebuni (Photo: Adam T. Smith)

remarkable feature of the room must have been the brilliantly colored mural thought to have covered the wall behind the throne (Oganesian 1961, 1973). Remains of painted plaster were carefully recovered by the excavators and elaborated into a large mural that employed geometric designs, chased floral motifs, and simplified fortress elements (Smith 2000:144) interspersed with repeated renderings of human figures bearing (sacred?) trees and attending to livestock (sacrifices?). Among these motifs the excavators also recovered plaster remains bearing images of winged animals with human torsos, wheeled vehicles, wild animals, and horses. Like the temple complex at Ayanis, the columned hall at Erebuni provides us with a sense of the aesthetics of Urartian spectacle as they orbit around central figural relationships among deities, humans, and the natural world both beyond immediate human control (the wild) and, more profoundly, as it arises within pastoral production.

As already noted in the introduction, Urartian inscriptions are rich sources of information on the role of performance in constituting Urartian authority. Aside from the evocative descriptions of devotional spectacles such as those held below the Meher Kapısı monument, many texts render the martial heroics of the king in terms that were simultaneously highly restricted in form and yet evocative enough to verge on *ekphrasis*. Urartian display inscriptions generally have a very limited narrative range, focusing most resolutely on warfare and construction (Arutyunian 2001; Diakonoff 1963; Melikishvili 1960, 1971). The most extensive display inscriptions are the annals of kings Argishti I and Sarduri II, which provide summaries of major military and architectural accomplishments (e.g., Melikishvili 1960: no. 127, 155). The majority of stone inscriptions are short military declarations, usually erected in outlying districts after a campaign, that record specific lands and cities defeated and tribute taken in rather standardized terms.[2] By describing royal activities with a very limited vocabulary and highly structured narrative form, these inscriptions arguably transformed the unscripted activities of war into ritualized spectacles. That is, the contingent actions of an immediate historical moment were filtered through the tropic conventions of textual expression such that the event became spectacular in retrospect, as a now materialized official memory, and provided a referent for future spectacles as reperformance. The relation between event and spectacle is thus both past and future looking, simultaneously retrospective and prognostic.

While both the archaeological and epigraphic records warrant closer scrutiny for the perspectives they can provide on performance, in this discussion I want to focus specifically on Urartian images of spectacle as carried in pictorial media. Urartian pictorial media provide a perspective on political spectacles that opens up ways of seeing the aesthetics of subjectification and authorization, allowing us to think about both the instrumentality of images and the formulation of the aesthetic. To do so, however, requires that we come to terms more explicitly with the overlapping places in the theorization of three critical concepts—spectacle, image, and aesthetics—as they are deployed within a general account of the political.

The Spectacle, Aesthetics, and Political Authority

Enlightenment aesthetic theory—particularly the Kantian concern to formalize a philosophical understanding of beauty, taste, sublimity, and pleasure—arose from a broad certainty that even the most ineluctable elements of human passion could be made intelligible.[3] In contrast, high modernist aesthetic theory was born in large measure out of a sense of political despair. In the early decades of the twentieth century, forms of representation retained a sense of emancipatory possibility, both within Marxist avant-gardism (e.g., debates in Adorno et al. 1977; Horkheimer and Adorno 1993) and liberal cultural progressivism (e.g., Santayana 1896; Dewey 1934). Art, and more specifically a highly politicized art, offered a "promised happiness of adventure" (Adorno 1997:1), or at least possibilities for the radicalization of consciousness. However, a note of disquiet regarding the potential confluence of aesthetics and politics was sounded by Benjamin, who presciently anticipated a reactionary appropriation of the image into spectacle when he pointed out that "traditional" life had proven remarkably compliant in its transformation from genuine experience into commodified tourist show. Political events within this industrialized traditional had been aestheticized, recast into festivals that affirmed rather than critiqued the contemporary order (Benjamin 1987:4:312; Buck-Morss 1989:27).

In the wake of the aestheticization of totalitarian violence under both fascist and Stalinist regimes, Benjamin's caution transformed itself in the work of Adorno into a deep cynicism regarding the ties between politics and representation. In Adorno's *Aesthetic Theory*, a dark portrait of the loss of the avant-garde, art can no longer aspire to radicalism and certainly cannot hope to alleviate suffering. The best it can do is express an element of the "correct consciousness" of the historical moment (Adorno 1997:191). Although Adorno provides us with a foundation for understanding the autonomy of the aesthetic (though not the image) from politics, his account of representation is ultimately a trap in that it provides a sense of the appropriation of art but no account of the relationship between image and political practices. That is, Adorno links art straight to political authority without an account of the image in practice. But where Adorno leaves representation in a highly attenuated political position, Guy Debord, French painter and situationist, focused resolutely on the politics of images by confronting the aesthetics of performance.

In *Society of the Spectacle*, Debord argued that the spectacle is "an instrument of unification" (Debord 1994: no. 3), but not in the Durkheimian sense of social solidarity that has so profoundly shaped anthropological accounts of political ritual. For Debord the essence of spectacle was not its affirmation of the social but rather its negation of the self beyond its status as political subject:

> The agent of the spectacle placed on stage as a star is the opposite of the individual, the enemy of the individual in himself as well as in others. Passing into the spectacle as a model for identification. The agent renounces all autonomous qualities in order to identify himself with the general law of obedience to the course of things. (Debord 1994: no. 61)

The political spectacle for Debord is not intelligible as a collection of images, either in the sense of modernist montage or even theatrical scene, but rather describes a "social relation among people, mediated by images" (Debord 1994:4). These images serve, in more contemporary terms, to narrow broad horizons of vision into ways of seeing fundamental to the operation of authority.

To the extent that Debord's account of spectacle has made an impression on contemporary theorizations of politics and aesthetics, he has generally been faulted for his tendency to totalize culture, to obscure the mechanics of power, and to misread the historical role of rationality in Western politics (Crary 1984; Clark 1985; Houston this volume). These are by and large entirely fair criticisms despite attempts by Greil Marcus (1989) to rehabilitate Debord through the legacy of punk. However, Debord does provide a set of useful theoretical links between the political aesthetic described by Adorno and the representation of public performances in media through the mediating aesthetics of spectacle. These links are particularly crucial for archaeological studies of the ancient world, where spectacle has long resided at the center of our imagination of the political. From Gibbon's accounts of sacrificial Christians to Ridley Scott's recent staging of Roman politics as read through the gladiatorial contest, the spectacle as aestheticized politics looms large in the popular understanding of ancient governance. Furthermore, there is a close link between the theatrical moment of spectacle and images of the spectacular, as both are highly self-conscious representations removed some distance from their referent and filtered through a politicized set of orienting tropes.

If, as Debord argued, spectacle is a means to constitute political subjects through formal and codified enactments of relationships—performances of position—then the aesthetics of spectacle provide a point of entry to where the work of subjectivization really gets done. Through the transformation of mechanical reiteration into profound liturgy, the aesthetics of spectacle allow theatrical roles to be recast as positions in the social world and cosmic order. Yet such a description, as Debord well knew, entails a redescription of spectacle in relation to representation. In one of the few attempts to probe the relationships between spectacles and their representation, Bettina Bergman (1999) has argued that images of spectacle in the classical world should be understood as techniques of memory that both served a historical purpose as record and a political purpose as a technique of reproducing and sustaining the awe generated within the event itself. That is, such renderings are both retrospective, as a medium of memory, and prognostic, as a medium of political desire and regulation. Pictorial images of spectacle thus provide us with ways of seeing that are, in effect, images of images, distillations of political practices focused not simply upon an instrumental authorization, but more profoundly on the aesthetics of subjectivity, on what we might call the pleasure of polity.

Urartian Images of Spectacle

Figural images are known from across a variety of media in Urartian art, including stone reliefs, stone and metal sculpture, and wall paintings. However, the most extensive corpus of what we might term "images of spectacle" are known from bronze belts and bronze plaques. There are three primary elements that I have utilized to define the group of images of spectacle.

1. Figures are drawn as instantiating unique social positions.
2. Figures are engaged in some form of action that establishes each in a specific practical relationship.
3. This action occurs in place. That is, the images provide a setting for action.

Few of these images have secure proveniences as most have come to us from the relentless depredations caused by the antiquities market.

As discussed above, the first problem in approaching spectacle through the medium of art lies in establishing the social context of artistic production. Despite the considerable limitations that arise from problems of context, we can, as I have argued elsewhere, describe the large majority of Urartian art recovered to date as "state art" (Piotrovskii 1967:15; Van Loon 1966:166). While too little is known about the relations between political authorities and the artisans who accomplished artistic production in Urartu, the limited contexts in which representations have been recovered suggest that we are on relatively safe ground in treating the extant corpus of Urartian images of spectacle as works of the political apparatus (Smith 2000:143).

The most straightforward Urartian images of spectacle center on a direct encounter between supplicant and deity. These images set two figures in profile against the backdrop of a fortress. The deity is recognizable by the wings attached to the figure's back and by its penchant to receive the approaching figure while standing atop a lion or other animal. The second figure, which I have taken to calling the supplicant because it is their entreaties which provide the narrative force for the scene, typically approaches the deity with offering in hand, usually in the form of a sacrificial animal. The fortress is rendered in varying levels of detail ranging from highly elaborated architectural elements to the use of stylized features, most notably stepped crenellations atop the battlements, zigzag friezes on the cornice, and high, narrow towers projecting from recessed curtine walls. Kleiss (1982:54) has suggested that these three architectural elements comprise the core repertoire of symbolic elements in Urartian fortress representations.[4] The core elements are complemented by a more variable set of details, such as rectangular windows in the curtine wall and tower base and arched, double-winged gateways (often with one side open).

Images of spectacles assembled on these figurative lines appear in a series of bronze plaques, such as two currently in the collections of the Louvre (Figs. 4.4, 4.5). The spatial convention used in the scenes places a stepped crenellation along the top border of the plaque, thus tying the scene to the built environment of the fortress. The architectural elements

Figure 4.4. An Urartian Bronze Plaque (Photo: Réunion des Musées Nationaux/Art Resource, N.Y.)

Figure 4.5. An Urartian Bronze Plaque (Photo: Réunion des Musées Nationaux/Art Resource, N.Y.)

rendered in plaques are highly stylized but recognizable as part of Kleiss's core elements of fortress representation. The crenellations are always two-tiered and are typically either inscribed or cut out of the top of the plaque. A cornice is a more variable feature that is often left out of the composition. Cornices are embossed or incised. Despite their generally stylized form, both the crenellation and the cornice (when included) are still recognizable as elements of the core repertoire of fortress features that were mustered individually as fortress elements or as details of fortress images.

The figures which comprise the narrative content of the scene occupy the remaining lower space of the composition. The scenes presented in the plaques show deities and supplicants engaged in devotional ritual. While all of the scenes in these plaques carry a nominal sense of action—a devotional ritual—what appears to be of greatest significance was simply the portrayal of the deity in front of fortress walls. Indeed, in many examples, the supplicant, whose entreaties would presumably comprise the narrative focus, is left out of the composition.

A more developed version of this form of representation is presented by a third bronze plaque from the collections of the Louvre (Fig. 4.6). In front of the walls of a fortress rendered in great detail, two figures approach a figure enthroned in front of a tower temple. Circular tack holes remain on each side of the plaque to indicate how they were affixed to a wall surface. A much more elaborately rendered fortress provides the image's sense of place. In addition to the cut-out crenellated battlements along the top edge of the work, three towers were incised into the plaque, one at each edge of the composition and one in the center. The towers were tied to each other by cornices, one decorated in the standard zigzag style, the

Figure 4.6. An Urartian Bronze Plaque (Photo: Réunion Des Musées Nationaux/Art Resource, N.Y.)

other marked only by a line of embossed rings topped by evenly spaced crenellated battlements. Identical embossed rings define the groundline of the scene and stretch between the surmounting crenellated battlements at the top of each tower.

The figures in the scene occupy the rectangular space of the lower curtine walls. To the left, two figures rendered in profile face right. The leftmost figure, dressed in a long skirt with an angular cuff decorated with embossed rings, carries pails in both hands, standard items in the repertoire of Urartian ritual paraphernalia strongly reminiscent of those used in Assyrian fructification scenes. The second figure in the left panel also wears a long skirt decorated with embossed rings, but this garment lacks the angular cuff, descending the body in a much looser line. Unlike the taller figure to the left, which is rendered with close-cropped hair, the right-hand figure appears to have long hair flowing down what we might fairly gender as her back. This apparently female figure carries in her left hand a raised rectangle on a staff which has been interpreted to be a standard. In her right hand she carries what appears to be a string of beads.

The figures in the left-hand panel are gazing and perhaps moving forward toward the right panel, where a deity sits on a throne with lion paw feet (Merhav 1991:249). The deity sits in a strangely flexed position with its knees against its chest; its hair is rendered in a manner that either gives the figure a fiery aura or simply appears unkempt. Its arms are rendered out of proportion to the rest of the body, and in the left and right hand it holds a flail and a cup, respectively. The cup is raised as if in anticipation of the offerings borne by the approaching figures while the flail is lowered. Behind the deity is inscribed the front profile of a tower temple *cella* with an arched doorway and elevated crenellated battlements that link the building into the larger built environment of the fortress. Taken together, what we see here is a devotional spectacle centered on the care and feeding of the gods that most likely took place in the courtyard immediately outside of a temple's *cella*—such as the large courtyard excavated at Ayanis. The composition centers on relations between three primary elements: the deity and its temple at right, the supplications of subjects at left, and the overarching authority of the Urartian political apparatus represented in the embracing sense of place provided by the fortress. As I have argued elsewhere (Smith 2000), the fortress in these images stands in for the political apparatus of the Urartian state.

In order that the relationships depicted in this rendering of Urartian devotional spectacle not appear too idiosyncratic, we can locate a similar set of relationships in a different medium assembled on slightly different compositional lines. Although similarly unprovenienced, a bronze belt in the collections of the Lands of the Bible Archaeology Foundation in Jerusalem provides a similar vision of Urartian spectacle (Fig. 4.7; Kellner 1991a: no. 279). The belt, 78 centimeters long and 6.5 centimeters wide, is divided into a series of seven scene panels separated by six panels of prancing herd animals (goat, sheep, and ram). The center panel of the composition depicts a scene very much like that in the plaque above. On the left, a deity sits on a throne with lion paw feet. The deity sits in a flexed position with its legs against its chest. In both hands it holds small cups. Behind the throne, a male attendant in a decorated long skirt with an angular cuff holds a pail in his left hand and a fan in his right. The center of the panel is taken up by a large table on which sits a collection of offerings in bowls. Two supplicants approach the table from the right and appear to bear cups to the offering table. Thus in the center panel we find a similar devotional scene as to that in the foreground of the plaque described above.

The center panel is flanked on both sides by panels of prancing sheep. If we continue to move outward from the center, the panels beyond these sheep contain mirror image renderings of Urartian fortresses depicted using the canonical architectural elements: high towers capped by crenellated battlements, zigzag decorated cornices, and an arched, double-winged doorway. A sense of place is thus again interjected into the scene that centers on the position of the Urartian political apparatus within devotional spectacle. Flanking the two fortress panels are identical panels of prancing goats followed by panels of supplicants shown in profile with their gazes focused inward toward the devotional scene at the center of the composition. The figures appear to be males, with cropped hair and cuffed long skirts. They carry with them bowls, pails, and goblets as offerings for the deity's table.

Moving outward toward the panels at either end of the belt, we encounter identical final animal scenes of three prancing rams. At each end of the belt is a final pair of supplicants. With their gaze and movement fixed on the center scene, these figures extend the central relationships of the spectacle out to the edges of the belt. These figures also appear to be males and carry the same instruments of offering—cups, pails, and goblets—seen in the adjacent panels. As a rendering of devotional spectacle,

Figure 4.7. An Urartian Bronze Belt (Kellner 1991a: no. 279). Permission to Reprint Courtesy of Franz Steiner Verlag, Stuttgart

we see similar figurative elements at work on this belt as on the previous plaque. The key relationships are those established in the center panel between a deity and supplicants who provide offerings. This relationship is drawn across the composition as a whole through the parade of paired supplicants who approach the center from both directions. But mediating these relationships is a third figure, that of the fortress. The renderings of fortresses not only provide a sense of place for the action but inject a third figure—the state—into the scene that must be triangulated into the action. A number of other representations of spectacle can be provided that were assembled on very similar aesthetic lines in diverse media, including a bronze helmet (Calmeyer 1991), bronze pectorals (Van den Berghe 1982: no. 89, 59), and a bronze medallion (Van den Berghe 1982: no. 90), in addition to other belts (Kellner 1991a: no. 256; 262, 263, 269) and plaques (Kellner 1991b).

The most remarkable image of spectacle from the extant corpus of Urartian art comes from a bronze belt (6.8–7.0 cm by 79.2 cm) recorded in the photo collections of the Prähistorische Staatssammlung in Munich (Fig. 4.8; Kellner 1991a: no. 282). Divided vertically into two registers, this composition is both detailed and complex. The composition portrays a long parade of figures that link together an array of scenes of devotion and production. The parade generally proceeds away from fortresses located at the upper left and lower right of the composition, toward images of an enthroned deity at the center of the belt. Beginning at the top left, we see a large and detailed fortress with five foreground towers, zigzag cornices, curtine walls surmounted by crenellated battlements, and double-winged doorways (one arched, one rectilinear). Proceeding away from this fortress, rendered in profile, are thirteen figures depicted in the now familiar position with one leg forward to suggest movement and both forearms raised—one slightly above the other. Each figure carries an item of ritual paraphernalia: bowls of goods, pails, jugs. The short hair and angular cuff of the skirts suggest all of these figures are male, though there are slight variations in the decorations of the garments. After this processional of thirteen figures, we see the profiles of two figures in front of a slanted apparatus. The long hair of the figure in the foreground suggests that she is female. She holds in her left hand a tool of some kind linked to the apparatus by a thin line that suggests a thread. If so, it seems quite plausible to suggest that the

Figure 4.8. An Urartian Bronze Belt (Kellner 1991a: no. 282). Permission to Reprint Courtesy of Franz Steiner Verlag, Stuttgart

apparatus is a loom on which the two figures are weaving. Below the loom is a basket that would hold the thread.

Moving away from the scene of weaving, ten male figures process to the right. Like the previous parading figures, these are rendered in profile bearing the same array of materials in their hands. This parade culminates at the center of the belt, where a seated deity facing a table of offerings is fanned by an attendant standing behind. To the right of the table we see a supplicant, now rendered facing to the left to denote the shift in the center of gravity of the composition. Beyond this figure, two supplicants face each other from either side of a massive decorated cauldron. Continuing to the right, another pair of figures face each other, one holding what looks to be a panel, or perhaps what in other contexts we have described as a standard, while the other figure applies a substance, perhaps paint, to it. Four processional figures are then interposed between these figures and a second pair of pairs engaged in similar activities—decorating a panel and attending a large cauldron. Moving past three processional figures facing left toward the seated deity, we come to another weaving scene focused on a figure with a loom. The remainder of this upper register is composed of ten processional figures interrupted by a third scene of a pair of figures decorating a rectangular panel.

The lower register of the belt is organized around a similar set of parading figures and interposed scenes. The composition seems to carry over from the upper right to lower left, where we see two figures facing each other across a peculiar apparatus. It is unclear exactly what this apparatus is—and hence what sort of activity is represented—but one possibility might be offered. If we think that the theme of cloth production might be carried over, then perhaps this image represents the cleaning of the wool. Moving to the right of these figures, we find a parade of nine figures facing to the right toward the center of the composition. Following them, two figures face each other over a different apparatus that seems to reintroduce the loom again, although this time rendered from behind rather than from the side. Here, two figures gather the cloth from the loom. To their right, two processional figures lead into a scene of two seated, female figures on either side of a decorated rectangular panel. They appear to be working on the panel, and thus we can perhaps understand them as embroidering a piece of cloth. Two additional processional figures are to the right of this scene, and then we find a series of three figures bearing aloft what by now we might fairly understand as the embroidered cloth that has been the center of the productive scenes thus far. Two male figures hold the cloth above their head while an intervening female figure walks beside them. The parade continues from left to right as three figures lead us to an upturned figure or acrobat, an element that reminds us of the carnivalesque nature of spectacle. The acrobat seems to be paired with a figure, perhaps a musician. To their right, three more parading figures lead us to the center of the lower register where we again find an enthroned deity, fanned from behind by an attendant, facing an offering table. To the right, we see the repetition of the paired figures around a large cauldron visible in the same position in the upper register.

Similarly, the subsequent pair mirrors that above as one holds a rectangle and the other a small cup. This repetition from the upper register ends with the next pair of figures who together appear to be holding a decorated rectangular item, perhaps a bolt of cloth to follow the dominant theme. The parade moves toward its end as the figures again face to the left, toward the central scene of the deity. In the final set of images, we see the repetition of the figures gathering cloth off the loom and the figures working with the same unknown apparatus that opened our discussion of this register. Between them, parading figures bear the familiar array of goods and items. The register ends at the lower right with a second fortress image, this one slightly less elongated with only four foregrounded towers, but with three doorways—one in each of the curtine walls.

The preceding detailed descriptions of select Urartian images of spectacle provide us with a sense of the compositional elements and core features at play in a highly political corpus of representations. How can we move from these images to an account of Urartian political aesthetics?

The Urartian Political Aesthetic

If our interest lies in recreating Urartian spectacles, the existing corpus of images does provide some resources for positing certain lines of mimesis that we might bring to the archaeological record. For example, the plaque incised with a deity enthroned outside of the temple *cella* might well recall the space of courtyards such as that found at Ayanis. However, the interest of this chapter lies in bringing forward the dominant aesthetics of Urartian spectacle and thus providing a view onto the web of social relationships and the images that mediated them. Thus the work of interpretation lies in setting forth the rubrics for building an account of the various perspectival horizons at play in Urartian spectacle and how the media wove these together to provide a way of seeing.

But whose way of seeing was at issue in Urartian images of spectacle? The problem of audience is one of the most difficult issues that face analyses of ancient media (cf. Michalowski 1990, 1994; Postgate et al. 1995). I have suggested elsewhere (Smith 2000) that a large share of Urartian royal media was directed to fellow elites. Pictorial representations are primarily known from within Urartian fortresses and thus would have been viewed only by those allowed within its walls, an undoubtedly restricted corps of imperial officials, foreign emissaries, local governors, and courtiers. And literacy in Urartu was likely restricted to an elite scribal class, severely limiting the number of people who could directly read the words of the king. However, a large proportion of the media carrying images of spectacle are highly portable belts and plaques, suggesting that such images were not cloistered within the privileged spaces of palace or temple. And the open public space of the Meher Kapısı monument suggests the possibility that public readings might have accompanied large public events, thus further diminishing the conceptual distance between spectacle as theatrical performance and spectacle as media representation.

It is a relatively straightforward problem to come to terms with the style of Urartian images of spectacle, by which I mean the formal lines of composition that were carried over from media to media and from work to work. Description of the style of these images would center on the regular depiction of figures in profile set in linear parades or in symmetrical face-to-face encounters. These positional relationships among the figures are given a concrete sense of place through the use of fortress images and architectural elements that clearly draw the apparatus of Urartian governance into the action along with the deity and the supplicant.

The aesthetics of the images—the socially situated understanding of affect that they promote—is less immediate though no less straightforward to theorize, thanks to the remarkable turn in the study of ancient art led by Irene Winter and fellow specialists in neo-Assyrian art (Marcus 1987, 1995; Russell 1991; Winter 1983, 1987, 1995, 1997). Here our analysis would center on the utilization of images to inscribe and distill memory, reinforcing a particular way of seeing that positions the observer within a specific set of social relationships (Bergman and Kondoleon 1999). It is in this sense that we can interpret Urartian images of spectacle as instrumental to programs and strategies of governance in that they frame the authorization of the royal regime and subjectivization of the populace in relation to the order of the intervening cosmos. If there is one "message" communicated by images of spectacle (and there are undoubtedly many more than one), it is that the demands of the regime and the acquiescence to these demands by subjects are not direct but rather mediated by deities. As a result, demand and acquiescence are more than simply dialectical stratagems of power; they are right, good, beautiful, desirable, and sublime in their accordance of the particular individual with the course of the universe. They are, in a word, aesthetic, in the sense that they appeal to value over fact, imagination over experience, sentiment and sensibility over sense.

And here we come to the heart of the problem that Urartian images of spectacle pose for theories of ancient politics. By establishing the instrumentality of images of spectacle in ancient political life, we must presume that their efficacy, or at least legibility, derives from a historically located shared understanding of the aesthetic in Adorno's terms rather than Debord's—what Jameson (1981) referred to as "the political unconscious," the beautiful as lived order. The strategic instrumentality of program, message, and style can clearly be tied to the Urartian regime (as both privileged cultural producer and hence primary target of resistance). But the *aesthetics* of the images demands a trans-sociological moment; producer and viewer, regime and subject, are dissolved into a totality wherein affect subsumes the logic of fragmented sociopolitical positions. That is, a theory of the aesthetic presumes an enduring shared sense of beauty and the sublime beyond the immediacies of power and strategy. What we are inquiring into, then, are the sensibilities at work in images of spectacle on which Urartian statecraft was predicated; how were they allowed to be instrumentally deployed? In other words, what were the emotional foundations for politics under the Urartian regime? Like Adorno, I do not presume this aesthetic to be either historically stable nor categorically a priori. Nor do I suggest that calculation and fact are not working in parallel with the aesthetic. But to attempt to understand political spectacle without an understanding of the visions that not only strike the eye but stir the imagination, would seem to miss something fundamental about the phenomenon.

I do not propose to provide a full account of the Urartian political aesthetic here, but rather would like to examine one possible route into an admittedly dense terrain. The epigraphic record, particularly the text from Meher Kapısı, centers on animal sacrifice and consumption. This vision of spectacle is again emphasized in the images that portray supplicants leading animals up to the deity. But I think we would be incautious if we jumped precipitously to read consumption as a form of the sublime (even though it might resonate with the contemporary world). The long procession on the belt pictured in Figure 4.8, if we have described it correctly, places the deity's consumption within the context of scenes of production. At all points in the composition, the face-to-face figures engaged in production are surrounded by parades of supplicants carrying goods to the table of the god. It would seem that what we have here is an ideology of the aesthetic, in Eagleton's (1990) term, that presumes an emotional response to the instantiation of political subjectivity within an embracing order of production and consumption.

What sentiment of the beautiful did these images appeal to in their viewers? What is at work, I suggest, is a pleasure of position, a sublime rooted in a sense of practical place, where daily productive activities (particularly those closely associated with pastoralism, but that is another discussion) are positioned in relation both to polity and to cosmos. This is less an aesthetic of negation than one of incorporation and hence has a dimension that runs beyond the instrumental. This is not by any means to argue that the frisson of Urartian images of spectacle was experienced by all. Indeed, as a number of chapters in this volume point out, following Bloch (1987) and Bell (1992), among other anthropologists, the appearance of consent implied by bodily enactment may well mask emotions of resentment and repression rather than pleasure. However, an account of moments of resistance does not substitute for a theory of politics. The inevitable diversity of emotional responses need not frustrate an account of the aesthetic as value deployed in representation just as the diversity of modern American responses to a presidential State of the Union address need not preclude an understanding of the sublime in American political oratory.

Conclusion

What I have suggested in this chapter is that considerations of the instrumentality of images in the ancient world allow us to confront the configuration of the underlying aesthetic. In the case of Urartian images of spectacle, we can theorize their instrumental efficacy quite directly since they focus with profound immediacy on redescribing political relationships as mediated by the divine. That said, a new and difficult question arises as to the sense of the sublime that these images targeted in viewers, such that they might be intelligible beyond now established tropes of media manipulation. I have suggested that the political aesthetic in these works was a pleasure of position, a sense of emotional commitment to the polity that involved not the sublimation of the individual to the mass but rather an effective locating of quotidian practices of subjectivity within a cosmic order. The pleasure of Urartian images of spectacle lay not in a dissolution of the self for the polity, but in a chorographic positioning of the self in the polity. Such a conclusion of course begs a host of attendant historical and sociological questions that call for an account of the formation of political aesthetics within public culture. Such an exploration would undoubtedly explore the mutual coconstitution of intertwined sites of cultural production and consumption (cf. Baines and Yoffee 1998 on "high culture"). However, such a vital enterprise lies just beyond the scope of this chapter and must await a different forum.

Notes

1. There is some uncertainty over the configuration of the columned hall at Erebuni during the Urartian period due to later reuse of the site during the Achaemenid era. However, the fragments of painted plaster from the wall mural are more securely assignable to the Urartian occupation based on art historical parallels.

2. For examples of Urartian military declarations, see Benedict (1965:7, 39), Hmayakyan et al. (1996:142), or Salvini (1982:98).

3. Throughout this chapter, I use the term "aesthetics" to refer to a general theory of affect that has been explored most profoundly in relation to the arts and media but today ranges broadly as an investigation of representation.

4. Kleiss (1982:54) points out that the zigzag friezes depicted on the cornices are a distinctly Urartian artistic element, unknown elsewhere in contemporary southwest Asia.

References Cited

Adorno, Theodor W.
1997 Theory and History of Literature, vol. 88: Aesthetic Theory. Minneapolis: University of Minnesota Press.

Adorno, Theodor, Walter Benjamin, Ernst Bloch, Bertolt Brecht, and György Lukács
1977 Aesthetics and Politics. London: Verso.

Arutyunian, N. V.
2001 Korpus Urartskikh Klinoobraznykh Nadpisej. Izdatel'stvo "Gitutyun" Yerevan: NAN RA.

Badalyan, Ruben S., Adam T. Smith, and Pavel S. Avetisyan
2003 The Emergence of Socio-Political Complexity in Southern Caucasia. *In* Archaeology in the Borderlands: Investigations in Caucasia and Beyond. Adam T. Smith and Karen Rubinson, eds. Pp. 144–166. Cotsen Institute of Archaeology, UCLA.

Baines, John, and Norman Yoffee
1998 Order, Legitimacy, and Wealth in Ancient Egypt and Mesopotamia. *In* Archaic States. Gary Feinman and Joyce Marcus, eds. Pp. 199–260. Santa Fe, N.M.: School of American Research Press.

Barnett, Richard D.
1982 Cambridge Ancient History, vol. 3: *Urartu.* J. Boardman, I. E. S. Edwards, N. G. L. Hammond, and E. Sollberger, eds. Pp. 314–371. Cambridge: Cambridge University Press.

Bell, Catherine
1992 Ritual Theory, Ritual Practice. Oxford: Oxford University Press.

Belli, Oktay
1999 The Anzaf Fortress and the Gods of Urartu. Istanbul: Arkeoloji ve Sanat Yayinlari.

Benedict, Warren C.
1965 Two Urartian Inscriptions from Azerbaijan. Journal of Cuneiform Studies 19:35–40.

Benjamin, Walter
1987 Gesammelte Schriften. Frankfurt am Main: Suhrkamp.

Bergmann, Bettina
1999 Introduction: The Art of Ancient Spectacle. *In* The Art of Ancient Spectacle. Bettina Bergmann and Christine Kondoleon, eds. Pp. 9–35. Washington, D.C.: National Gallery of Art.

Bergmann, B., and C. Kondoleon, eds.
1999 The Art of Ancient Spectacle. Washington, D.C.: National Gallery of Art.

Bloch, Maurice
1987 The Ritual of the Royal Bath in Madagascar: The Dissolution of Death, Birth, and Fertility into Authority. *In* Rituals of Royalty: Power and Ceremonial in Traditional Societies. David Cannadine and S. Price, eds. Pp. 271–297. Cambridge: Cambridge University Press.

Buck-Morss, Susan
1989 The Dialectics of Seeing: Walter Benjamin and the Arcades Project. Studies in Contemporary German Social Thought. Cambridge, Mass.: MIT Press.

Calmeyer, Peter
1991 Helmets and Quivers. *In* Urartu: A Metalworking Center in the First Millennium B.C.E. Rivka Merhav, ed. Pp. 123–133. Jerusalem: Israel Museum.

Çilingiroğlu, Altan
1991 The Early Iron Age at Dilkaya. *In* Anatolian Iron Ages: The Proceedings of the Second Anatolian Iron Ages Colloquium Held at Izmir, 4–8 May 1987. Altan Çilingiroğlu and D. H. French, eds. Pp. 29–38. British Institute of Archaeology at Ankara, Monograph no. 13. Oxford: Oxbow.
2001 Temple Area. *In* Ayanis I: Ten Years of Excavations at Rusahinili Eiduru-Kai, 1989–1998. Altan Çilingiroglu and Mirjo Salvini, eds. Pp. 37–65. Rome: Istituto per gli studi micenei ed egeo-anatolici CNR.

Çilingiroğlu, Altan, and Mirjo Salvini
1995 "Rusahinili in Front of Mount Eridu": The Urartian Fortress of Ayanis (7th Century B.C.). Studi Micenei ed Egeo-Anatolici 35:111–124.
2001 Ayanis I : Ten Years of Excavations at Rusahinili Eiduru-Kai, 1989–1998. Documenta Asiana 6. Rome: Istituto per gli studi micenei ed egeo-anatolici CNR.

Clark, T. J.
1985 The Painting of Modern Life: Paris in the Art of Manet and His Followers. New York: Knopf.

Crary, Jonathan
1984 Eclipse of the Spectacle. *In* Art after Modernism: Rethinking Representation. Brian Wallis, ed. Pp. 282–294. New York: New Museum of Contemporary Art.

Debord, Guy
1994 The Society of the Spectacle. New York: Zone.

Dewey, John
1934 Art as Experience. New York: Minton Balch.

Diakonoff, Igor M.
1963 Urartskie Pis'ma i Dokumenty. Moscow: Izdatel'stvo Akademii Nauk.

Eagleton, Terry
1990 The Ideology of the Aesthetic. Oxford: Blackwell.

Hmayakyan, Simon G., Valerij A. Igumnov, and Hovhannes H. Karagyozyan
1996 An Urartian Cuneiform Inscription from Ojasar-Ilandagh, Nakhichevan. Studi Micenei ed Egeo-Anatolici 37:139–151.

Horkheimer, Max, and Theodor W. Adorno
1993 Dialectic of Enlightenment. New York: Continuum.

Jameson, Fredric
1981 The Political Unconscious: Narrative as a Socially Symbolic Act. Ithaca, N.Y.: Cornell University Press.

Kellner, Hans-Jörg
1991a Gürtelbleche aus Urartu. Prähistoriche Bronzefunde XII(3). Stuttgart: Franz Steiner Verlag.
1991b Votive Plaques. *In* Urartu: A Metalworking Center in the First Millennium B.C.E. Rivka Merhav, ed. Pp. 285–299. Jerusalem: Israel Museum.

Kleiss, Wolfram
1979 Bastam I. Berlin: Gebr. Mann Verlag.
1982 Darstellungen Urartäischer Architektur. Archaeologische Mitteilungen aus Iran 15:53–77.
1988 Bastam II. Berlin: Gebr. Mann Verlag.

Kushnareva, Karine K.
1997 The Southern Caucasus in Prehistory. Philadelphia: University of Pennsylvania.

Marcus, Greil
1989 Lipstick Traces: A Secret History of the Twentieth Century. Cambridge: Harvard University Press.

Marcus, Michelle I.
1987 Geography as an Organizing Principle in the Imperial Art of Shalmaneser III. Iraq 49:77–90.
1995 Geography as Visual Ideology: Landscape, Knowledge, and Power in Neo-Assyrian Art. *In* Neo-Assyrian Geography. Mario Liverani, ed. Pp. 193–202. Rome: University of Rome.

Martirosian, A. A.
1964 Armenia v Epokhu Bronzi i Rannego Zheleza. Yerevan: Akademiya Nauk Armyanskoi SSR.

Melikishvili, G. A.
1960 Urartskie Klinoobraznye Nadpisi. Moscow: Izdatel'stvo Akademii Nauk SSSR.
1971 Urartskie Klinoobraznye Nadpisi, II. Vestnik Drevnej Istorii 4:267–294.

Merhav, Rivka
1991 Secular and Cultic Furniture. *In* Urartu: A Metalworking Center in the First Millennium B.C.E. Rivka Merhav, ed. Pp. 246–271. Jerusalem: Israel Museum.

Michalowski, Piotr
1990 Early Mesopotamian Communicative Systems: Art, Literature, and Writing. *In* Investigating Artistic Environments in the Ancient Near East. Ann C. Gunter, ed. Pp. 53–69. Washington, D.C.: Sackler Gallery Smithsonian Institution.
1994 Writing and Literacy in Early States: A Mesopotamianist Perspective. *In* Literacy: Interdisciplinary Conversations. Deborah Keller-Cohen, ed. Pp. 49–70. Cresskill, N.J.: Hampton.

Oganesian, K. L.
1955 Karmir-Blur IV: Arkitektura Teishabaini. Yerevan: Akademii Nauk Armianskoe SSR.

1961 Arin-Berd I: Architektura Erebuni. Yerevan: Akademii Nauk Armianskoe SSR.
1973 Rospisi Erebuni. Yerevan: Akademii Nauk Armianskoe SSR.

Piotrovskii, B. B.
1955 Karmir-Blur III: Resultat Reskopok 1951–1953. Yerevan: Akademiya Nauk Armianskoe SSR.
1959 Vanskoe Tsartsvo (Urartu). Moscow: Vostochnoe Literaturi.
1967 Urartu: The Kingdom of Van and Its Art. P. S. Gelling, trans. New York: Praeger.

Pogrebova, M. N.
1977 Iran i Zakavkaze v Rannem Zheleznom Veka. Moscow: Nauka.

Postgate, Nicholas, Tao Wang, and Toby Wilkinson
1995 The Evidence for Early Writing: Utilitarian or Ceremonial? Antiquity 69(264):459–480.

Riemshneider, Margarete.
1963 Die Urartaischen Gottheiten. Orientalia 32:148–169.

Russell, John M.
1991 Sennacherib's Palace without Rival at Nineveh. Chicago: University of Chicago Press.

Salvini, Mirjo
1982 Die Felsinschrift Sarduris II in Seqendel (Libliuni). Archaeologische Mitteilungen aus Iran 15:97–100.
1994 The Historical Background of the Urartian Monument Meher Kapisis. *In* Anatolian Iron Ages 3. Altan Çilingiroğlu and David H. French, eds. Pp. 211–220. Ankara: British Institute of Archaeology at Ankara.
1995 Geschichte und Kultur der Urartäer. Darmstadt: Wissenschaftliche Buchgesellschaft.
2001 The Inscriptions of Ayanis. Cuneiform and Hieroglyphic. *In* Ayanis I: Ten Years of Excavations at Rusahinili Eiduru-Kai, 1989–1998. Altan Çilingiroğlu and Mirjo Salvini, eds. Pp. 251–319. Rome: Istituto per gli studi micenei ed egeo-anatolici CNR.

Santayana, George
1896 The Sense of Beauty: Being the Outlines of Aesthetic Theory. New York: Scribner's.

Smith, Adam T.
2000 Rendering the Political Aesthetic: Ideology and Legitimacy in Urartian Representations of the Built Environment. Journal of Anthropological Archaeology 19:131–163.

Smith, Adam T., Ruben S. Badalyan, Pavel Avetisyan, and Mkrtich Zardaryan
2004 Early Complex Societies in Southern Caucasia: A Preliminary Report on the 2002 Investigations by Project ArAGATS on the Tsakahovit Plain, Republic of Armenia. American Journal of Archaeology 108:1–41.

Smith, Adam T., and Tiffany T. Thompson
2004 Urartu and the Southern Caucasian Political Tradition. *In* A View from the Highlands. Antonio Sagona, ed. Pp. 557–580. Herent: Peeters.

Thompson, R. Campbell, and Maxwell E. L. Mallowan
1933 The British Museum Excavations at Nineveh, 1931–32. Annals of Archaeology and Anthropology 20:71–186.

Van den Berghe, Louis
1982 Urartu. Ghent: Centrum.

Van Loon, Maurits N.
1966 Urartian Art. Istanbul: Nederlands Historisch-Archaeologisch Instituut.

Wartke, Ralf-Bernhard
1993 Urartu: Das Reich am Ararat. Mainz: Philipp von Zabern.

Winter, Irene J.
1983 The Program of the Throneroom of Assurnasirpal II. *In* Essays on Near Eastern Art and Archaeology in Honor of Charles Kyrle Wilkinson. Prudence O. Harper and H. Pittman, eds. Pp. 15–31. New York: Metropolitan Museum of Art.
1987 Legitimation of Authority through Image and Legend: Seals Belonging to Officials in the Administrative Bureaucracy of the Ur III State. *In* The Organization of Power: Aspects of Bureaucracy in the Ancient Near East. McGuire Gibson and Robert D. Biggs, eds. Pp. 69–116. Chicago: Oriental Institute.
1995 Aesthetics in Ancient Mesopotamian Art. *In* Civilizations of the Ancient Near East. Jack M. Sasson, J. Baines, G. Beckman, and K. S. Rubinson, eds. Pp. 2569–2580. New York: Scribner.

1997 Art in Empire: The Royal Image and the Visual Dimensions of Assyrian Ideology. *In* Assyria 1995. Simo Parpola and Robert M. Whiting, eds. Pp. 359–381. Helsinki: Neo-Assyrian Text Corpus Project.

Zimansky, Paul
1995 An Urartian Ozymandias. *Expedition* 58(2):94–100.

SCENE 5

IMPERSONATION, DANCE, AND THE PROBLEM OF SPECTACLE AMONG THE CLASSIC MAYA

Stephen D. Houston

Spectacle ≠ Performance ≠ Ritual?

Spectacle should induce large reactions: awe, delight, wonder, desire, sorrow, intoxication, even fear and revulsion. It does many other things: it demands attention, recruits an audience which becomes part of the performance, surprises but, paradoxically, dispenses the expected. It moves, exhausts, and bridles chaos. Yet it also agitates the cycles of everyday life. Above all, spectacle is flashy, loud, smelly or fragrant, long-winded, momentous. By definition, by its etyma—from the frequentative of Latin *specere*, "look"—spectacle privileges the act of seeing (Beeman 1993:380; cf. Gregor 1977). Nonetheless, it almost always involves sensory overload from other sources as well.

Somewhat in disagreement with other participants in this book, and in the session that generated it, the author cannot accept the view that "spectacle" is a bankrupt concept. He persists in using the term but not with the shadings proposed by others. For example, the "scopic" definition, in which "spectacle" pertains merely to acts of seeing and looking, as explained by Ian Hodder in a session paper, explains little. It bypasses the quality of performance that so clearly operates in these effusions of human energy. If taken literally, a "scopic" definition applies equally to any showy, natural production, such as a volcanic explosion or tsunami. Krakatoa was thus a "spectacle" and Hilo too. Purely scopic events would not necessarily require human authorship. By the same scopic definition, "performance" describes the mechanical operation of a crashing glacier or ice flow. Though impressive to viewers, even awe-inspiring, yet there must be more than "motion" or things that move. "Actions," the acts of human beings, belong too (Burke 1969). There is another shade of inappropriate meaning: the slightly voyeuristic quality of "scopic" as an adjective recalls the practice of "scopophilia," an eroticized looking described by psychoanalysts (Olin 1996:211). Hodder cannot intend this meaning, yet it filters to the surface.

A second claim made at the session, that scale is irrelevant and that the number of participants and observers counts for little, cannot be conceded from a sociological or anthropological perspective. Depending on scale, the preparation, intensity, and ability to influence must vary, in the same way that Desert Storm differs qualitatively from a bar scuffle or marital spat. A spectacle, whether of a Barberini festival in baroque Rome (Hammond 1994:117) or the officially sponsored and housed theater of imperial Rome (Beacham 1999:61–74), aims for "magnificence" and, to quote Maecenas advising Octavian, "disregard for expense" (Beacham 1999:xi), or at least the illusion of that boundlessness. Spectacle can project an expansive view over the Land of Cockaigne or the Rock Candy Mountain, a place of bounty, excess, indulgence, as seen from places and lives that, in antiquity, were nearly always crimped by want. Nor is it crucial that the more esoteric messages broadcast by spectacle be widely understood. It was mostly important that the spectacle impress and entertain (Anglo 1997:xi). All the while, spectacle should stir emotion, as in the raw empathy commanded of those witnessing the *via dolorum* of Christ's suffering in early modern Spain (Flynn 1994:153).

For these reasons, spectacle has, within the snug harbor of this chapter, all of the effervescent properties above. It works; it does analytical service. In a sociological sense, spectacle inherently involves suprahousehold groupings, some constituted into self-identified collectivities that we might call "communities." These communities participate in and observe the spectacle; they are re-formed and energized by performances and gatherings of this scale and energy (Handelman 1990:116–35; see also Beeman 1993:380–381). As Inomata suggests (this volume), spectacle reaches out to bridge, unify, and demarcate different levels of society.[1] It can also, much like all human activity, work at cross-purposes. Even the partly excavated site of Çatalhöyük, which Hodder discusses in his chapter, may well have had its spectacular proscenia in the form of plazas or courtyards viewed from rooftops. Puebloan festivities in the American Southwest show how congested apartment compounds might be reconciled with flamboyant theatricality (Fewkes 1892; see Triadan, this volume).

The issue before us is whether loose definitions are better than tight ones. For example, Ian Hodder's definition, in his conference paper, of spectacle "performance as a dimension of action that bridges to meaning and communication" would also pertain to ordering a hamburger at the nearest fast-food outlet. To use the Foucaultian jargon of our day: the Body has entered the restaurant, been disciplined by the need to wait in lines, communicated its hunger, trafficked in meaning by proffering symbolic specie in the form of small slips of paper and valueless metals, and made a political statement by consuming the products of agro-industry. And if spectacle is simply a "showing" and a "looking," as Hodder claims, then a greeting wave of the hand, responded to friendly-like, must be spectacle. It is difficult to understand how an inexact definition that includes all behavioral displays helps describe events that are usefully understood as outsized and public. This is a failure of typology. As Adam Smith points out in his chapter, images of spectacle may be small and intimately perused, but they elicit memories of awesome, staged public events. A culturally understood sense of "splashiness" and *éclat* must play a role. By depiction, those events have been idealized into generality but linked by recollection to specific moments in the viewer's experience. The Urartian belts and plaques studied by Smith are not spectacles but synesthetic evocations of them. They were not meant for us to see. To modern gaze, they yield an affective flatness that would have differed greatly from Urartian perception.

Erving Goffman is ultimately to blame for such disarray of terminology and, perhaps, for the imprecisions in Hodder's approach as articulated in his session paper. Goffman's metaphor of social life as theater is compelling because it seems so intuitively true, yet the metaphor is, as one critic has put it, "literally absurd" (Manning 1992:54). It rests on a view of sociality that is rather like "ping-pong in masks," games of human interaction that involve hidden motives and ruthless, unknowable agents (Geertz 1983:24; Geertz also makes the point that Goffman's idea of dramaturgy is like no form of theater he has ever seen). Humans may play roles, work in "teams," manage impressions of each other, manipulating all the while (Goffman 1959:32). Perhaps interaction really is like a game in that it has problematic outcomes—no foregone conclusions—and affords the opportunity to display valued attributes such as dexterity, strength, and self-control (Goffman 1961). But, in contrast to these maneuvers, true performance is above all a "marked" behavior of restricted occurrence (e.g., Beeman 1993:377). It deliberately contrasts with, and is bounded from, the neutral hum of quotidian existence. The Japanese tea ceremony is a performance; eating noodles at a bar in Tokyo (or San Francisco)—which may follow accustomed habits of behavior—is not. Nonetheless, Hodder is correct in his paper when he suggests that content is equally important (see also Bell 1992:43–45). No spectacle can be understood without probing and stripping its tissues of meaning.[2]

A definition of performance based on markedness raises two sets of questions. Is markedness dichotomous, as implied by its original, paradigmatic formulation in linguistics (Lyons 1968:59), or does it exist on a continuum of low to high levels of special comportment (Wolfowitz 1991:9–10)? And what is the relation between spectacle, ritual, and performance, the latter a preferred term in this volume? The answer to the first question would seem to be that spectacle is inherently staged and achieves greater intensity by including a welter of central and marginal activities and central and marginal people. Margins are the places of experimentation and "ludic disruption" where new forms are devised and tested against the acid of public acceptance or rejection (Camille 1992:26, 145). In medieval thought, they could also be dangerous but necessary to the center. They were not intended to subvert so much as stand in necessary, antithetical relation to curial or religious decorum (Camille 1992:16). Yet, by definition, even these charivaric irruptions would have been marked *within their context and in relation to the inventory of conventional behaviors of the time*. Spectacle belonged to the same, exclusive category of marked behaviors.

The second question is best understood in terms of overlapping labels. Catherine Bell views ritual as inherently marked, a "way of acting that sets itself off"; it both establishes and confirms "certain types of power relationships" (Bell 1992:140, 197). Roy Rappaport also interprets ritual as an act that involves invariant sequences of statements and movements, but with ambitious aims: the sealing of social contracts, the encoding of morality, and their joint sanctification by the numinous and divine (Rappaport 1999:27). Depending on whether one wishes to extend ritual to secular activities, as Maurice Bloch, David Kertzer, and Bruce Lincoln have done, spectacle would represent a kind of ritual (Bloch 1977:281–285; Kertzer 1988:9–12; Lincoln 1989:4). Moreover, most of the societies discussed in this volume would have devised very different ideas about the sacred and the profane. In Mesoamerica, the planting, harvesting, and consumption of corn is, and was, as sacramental as the feeding of spirits with incense (Monaghan 2000:30–31). Yet ritual is the larger term and would logically include, by its repetition and marking, both spectacle and small-scale, ordered acts such as the enigmatic ones undertaken near the bucrania of Çatalhöyük. This leaves performance, another marked activity that is fully typologized by Richard Schechner (1990: fig. 2.1). Spectacle can do positive service as a label that applies to performances of great scale and, one presumes, rarity. Not all performances, however, would be spectacles, nor are all performances rituals. Thus ritual ≠ spectacle ≠ performance, although the categories do overlap, sometimes to differing degrees during their execution. The Classic Maya may have been a congeries of societies in which the overlap was greater than elsewhere. Civic spectacle, theatrical "mummery," and ritual were as close here as any Balinese theater state, not least because of the need for competitive displays of wealth, sacrality, and gestures of generosity to courtiers (cf. Geertz 1980:125).

The Problem of Spectacle

In his session paper, Jerry Moore questions whether, to quote Houston and Taube (2000), archaeologists can ever experience what the ancients did. One suspects that no amount of optical science, as marshaled cleverly and well in Moore's original paper, will ever refute one basic point: human experience is never literally replicable nor, barring unsettling inventions, are we in a position to buy tickets to Pastland. Yet Moore's more general suggestions are promising. The social and cultural construction of emotions, illness, sundry body parts, gender, sex, knowledge, and so forth, started as a useful approach and even represented a safety line to the splintering components of anthropology. It could combine meaning with the physicality of the body, and thereby to representations from antiquity. That aim is still tenable. Many of us pursue it with alacrity.

However, like all good ideas, it has the potential to arrive at a position that is at once pure yet empty—the proposition that nothing comes from the nature of things or is inevitable in its conceptualization (Hacking 1999:6). Instead, things or categories are defined within Kant's mentalist panorama, or according to the many species of constructionism that trundle along in Kant's expansive shadow. Constructionism as it exists today relates only tangentially to the past or others. A skeptic might conjecture that the real target is a reflection in the mirror, the academic self at the cusp of the millennium (Houston and McAnany 2003). Neither can that same skeptic relish terms like "power." In much the same way as "beauty," "power" appears to be self-explanatory but is not. There can be only two viable understandings of power, as a cultural notion of immanent force and strength (Maya languages have many such labels, especially *'ip*), and as a historically unique, discursive application of force or suasion. Moore suggests an intermediate point of view, one lying between constructionism (rooted in mind) and experientialism (rooted in human senses), the latter an approach he has long advocated (e.g., Moore 1996:98–101): one can commit to the theory that ideas exist in a social, cultural, historical or any other *-al* matrix yet also claim that humans occupy bodies with a finite suite of detectable attributes. Neurological wiring has been set by evolutionary process and, after much debate, does not differ perceptibly across human populations. The rock kicked by Dr. Johnson hurt his foot and leapt through the air—can it only have been a Kantian figment?

Classic Maya concepts of sight show that Moore's compromise is valid. Sight was clearly understood as a perceptual field that included peripheral vision and more direct sight lines in intermediate arcs (Houston and Taube 2000). This accords with pan-cultural understandings of what the human eye can see, an optical architecture that, aside from melanin content and idiosyncratic pathologies, occurs in all humans around the world. To the Maya, this field was the *-ichnal*, an obligatorily possessed particle that, to some extent, explained the Maya concern with architecture forms such as courtyards: such configurations can be scanned from a single *-ichnal* point. The physiological feature of peripheral vision would occur anywhere. But then society and culture intervene in relation to biological apparatus. The glyph for "see" was read *ILA*, a transitive root depicted as a single eyeball from which two looping lines emanate. As in much of the world, the indigenous theory of sight was *projective* rather than *receptive* or "extramission" versus "intromission" (Lindberg 1976:136). The eye was understood not as an organ with retinal receptors—as a receiver—but as something that reached out, projected, to engage and absorb external shape and color. Enough was known of anatomy to focus on the optical stalk, which the Maya appear to have recognized as a crucial conduit of sight. (A particularly brutal game among the Maya involved a stone "knuckle duster" or *manopla*, not a few of which show the effects to the orbit of a robust blow: faces carved on the surfaces of *manopla* show an eye dangling out, still attached to the stalk; Karl Taube, personal communication, 1999). The Classic Maya had a deft means of displaying the invisible and rendering it concrete, as, indeed, they may well have visualized it: the lines represent projection but also, one suspects, the two edges of peripheral sight, which appear to be liquid and wavering. (Speech was also shown by sinuous lines, perhaps as an aesthetic comment on graceful and mannered language or as a way of showing the oscillating volume of speech.)

The meaning of "seeing" and the visual field, *-ichnal*, were invested with more than optical properties. "Seeing" was done in three contexts: (1) as an act of witnessing by illustrious visitors to foreign courts; (2) as comparable acts of witnessing by local lords, sometimes known as the twenty-eight *ajawtaak*, the "twenty-eight lords" (although it remains unclear whether these lords were alive or deceased; the decipherment of the plural suffix is by Alfonso Lacadena and David Stuart); and (3) as apparent acts of revelatory *ekstasis* in pilgrimage locations such as caves, where one rather obscure text records the couplet *il-b'i(h), il-way*, "see the road, see an aspect of the soul" (Stone 1995: fig. 7-9). In this cave, Naj Tunich, seeing was always specified as to place and may have involved "spectacles" that no one else could see or what was meant to see. The *-ichnal* always involved someone of higher status, either a lord or a set of tutelary gods. That is, what is known ethnographically to be linked to all people was, in the classic texts, heavily hierarchical (cf. Hanks 1990:90–91). In this respect, the only sight that seemed to have mattered officially to the Maya was royal and godly, with implications for the understanding of spectacle among these peoples. Some deities appear to have been born out of the excrescence of deity eyes, and, in a singular kind of elite solipsism, no formal event existed without, apparently, it having been seen by people or beings who mattered; the projective theory of sight had thus become nearly procreative as well. The theory did not just apply to the flesh and blood: Mayan portraits too were often mutilated by having their eyes pecked out in Terminal Classic times or when a stela or other monument was ritually buried.

Yet, despite the official rhetoric, spectacle requires spectators. In some ways, Classic Maya ideas about seeing and perceptual fields are slyly misleading. Imagery and texts stress the centrality of the royal person and its never quite clear relation to the divine—Maya kings fit into the category of sacred rulers, not god kings (Houston and Stuart 1996). But, aside from those rare interactive monuments where the texts and iconography interact with the implied presence of the ruler (Houston and Stuart 1998), most situate the viewer in a decidedly subordinate position. Courtly scenes on pots are beheld from the vantage of a lowly supplicant; even the texts on the vessels can only be read by holding up the pot at eye level, as though offering drinks to others in elevated toasts. That is, Mayan text and image require spectators of lower rank and, at the same time, seldom acknowledge those viewers by the courtesy of frontal address. In most cases (the exceptions need study) the royal gaze resolutely faces to the side, in studied disattention to the viewer. There is an implicit comment: although the spectator benefits from the grace of royal presence, the king maintains a posture of insouciance and unemotional decorum (Houston 2001).

Finally, there are spectators that, at times (see below), no one can see. A common trope in Early Classic sculpture is that of the floating ancestor, usually the direct predecessor of a ruler. The ancestor has the eyes of the sun god (a conventional linkage with deceased male rulers, just as females relate to the moon), only an arm, no body, the whole manifestation wreathed in smoke and mist. In even more abbreviated form, this trope goes back to the images at sites like El Mirador and Uaxactun from the Late Preclassic period, when scholars can just begin, barely, to speak about the particulars of Maya kingship. Ancestors are also embodied in wind jewels worn as pectorals, or as stately, fuller figures on jade celts worn around waists or suspended from belts (the clinking of thin slats of jade probably rang musically to Mayan ears, the very voices of the prestigious dead, Stuart et al. 1999). One text from Caracol, Belize, makes this explicit, by saying that a deceased ruler "sees" *(yi-ILA-IL/li-'a)* a censing event by his successor (Stela 6:B20; Beetz and Satterthwaite 1981: fig. 7b; the possibility remains that what we take to be a deceased ruler may simply be an abdicant). In later stelae, many from the Terminal Classic period, deities hover in clouds, looking downward. This evidence suggests that spectators could include an unseen contingent of supernaturals or, at least, such beings made immanent in ornaments and effigies.

Types of Classic Maya Spectacle

In spectacle, meant to overwhelm, the sensorium of the Classic Maya would have included objects of sight, but also sound and smell. Smell came from the ambient odor of ordure, rotting waste, burning fields, and, cloaking them all, the deliberate incineration of tree resins, principally copal or *pom*, and paper. Resinous fire appears to have fascinated the Maya. It transformed solids to insubstantial smoke; its wispy products could, in the eye of the faithful, be made to take shapes; and it took a substantive role in the feeding of buildings and communications with the deceased (Stuart 1998). The principal memorials to nonroyal elites at the site of Palenque, Chiapas, were in the form of supports for incense burners (Schele and Mathews 1979: pl. 281, 282, 303, 391). Voluminous smoke would have had the added effect of heightening a sense of disconnection with performers, who could appear suddenly, then flit away. Some deities were shown floating in clouds, and the same image could have struck those looking at Classic dance.

Sound was equally important. Instruments consisted of rasps, gourd rattles, and trumpets—shape could be teased into a variety of forms by the cunning gardener—open and split drums, whistles, ocarinas, flutes, ceramic drums known as *lajab'*, "things for hand-clapping," as attested on surviving examples from Piedras Negras, Guatemala, conches (with tone modulated by shoving a fist into the opening, K1453; the K numbers used here correspond to a catalogue system of rollout photographs by Justin Kerr; see www.famsi.org), turtle shells struck with antlers, and human song, performed by *k'ayoom*, "singers" (Houston 2002). One Mayan ruler, a king of Tikal, employs this epithet as one of his principal titles, so the accomplishment obviously generated some pride. At sites like Piedras Negras, whistles slathered with Mayan blue and shaped into various beasts, birds, warriors, women, and gods occur commonly across the site. These hint that spectacle could also have involved performances from, and collaborations with, the entire community. When whistles are held up to the lips, the face of the performer is obscured by the visage on the instrument (Charles Golden, personal communication, 1998). The Spaniards described much later performances of the early Colonial Maya as cacophonous and distempered, even doleful, but one wonders what they would have made of Debussy or Shostakovich. Spanish descriptions of dance as highly orderly, involving as many as eight hundred (a rather suspiciously round number in their vigesimal system), make it unlikely that music would have been performed willy-nilly, like so many snapping party favors (Tozzer 1941:94). Some of the song was mimetic, amazing the Spaniards by its ability, with dance, to emulate bird calls and flight (Tozzer 1941:79).

Above all there was mannered movement, often involving the shuffling of legs. Not surprisingly, "dance" references are common in Classic Maya texts (Grube 1992). In Mesoamerica, the customary attitude of prayer was not clasped hands but rapid movements of the feet, a form of motion very much present in present-day ethnographic communities (John Monaghan, personal communication, 1992). Calls to the supernatural were thus facilitated by vigorous movement of the body rather than contemplative immobility. To judge from extant iconography, the upper body does not appear to have played a central part in this, only a slight bending of the knees and graceful scuffling of the feet. Although we have only images to go on, virtually all movement at the court was highly stylized, or, at the least, artists chose a very narrow repertoire of motions and gestures for their canon of acceptable display. This also extended to ball playing, invariably shown in a small number of poses, either ready to strike or in the process of doing so. It is striking that ball play could be undertaken by all ages, as could dance: nonetheless, some sites, such as Bonampak, assign this dancing role to youths or *ch'ok*. There may well have been age-grade dances and, according to Yucatec sources, "erotic" or "courtship" ones (i.e., male and female), such as are occasionally depicted in Maya art (Tozzer 1941:93–94, 128; e.g., K4356). One vessel shows a figure with a decidedly phallic nose being pawed by a female (K1549).

The remainder of this chapter will focus on a subset of spectacle—deity "impersonation" and prayerful dance—but there is nonetheless a broad array of ostentatious, ordered display that needs to be categorized. All probably employed dance and music and, perhaps, "impersonation" or even puppetry (Karl Taube, personal communication, 2002). The underlying impulse here is to divide spectacle into two gross categories, those that have no secure outcome and those that do. What they can do is permit a division into spectacles of certain and uncertain outcomes: (1) uncertain: war, boxing, ball play with balls of sundry size; (2a) certain, directional: "arrival" processions, parading of deity effigies, interment of caches and bodies, enthronement and accession, temple ascent, descent, and censing, temple sacrifice on stairways; (2b) certain, nondirectional: weddings, deity summoning, puberty rituals, feasts of drunken abandon, stelae and monument erection, postpuberty bloodletting *(yax ch'ahb')*.

To explain further: certain outcomes can be distinguished by the nature of their movement, whether they take place within a fixed locale visible from one vantage (nondirectional), or whether they involve processions on Mayan causeways *(sakb'ih)* or climbing up and down precipitous stairways (directional). Both could merge into a single spectacle, depending on the context. Other kinds of variation can also be considered: length of celebration, time and date of celebration, number of participants, number of audience, gender of same, setting, spatial extent, costuming and accouterments, and episodic structuring and staging. Regrettably, available data do not allow most of these variables to be evaluated. Moreover, in all of these, "private" is not the same as "secret" and "nonpublic." A key component of spectacle could be the flux of appearance and disappearance, rather like the pope on the front balcony of St. Peter's or British royalty waving with spurious bonhomie from Buckingham Palace. Mayan temples too are ideally configured for such episodes of closeting and emergence, as are other features of Mayan architecture, including passageways beneath stairways at sites like Edzna, Campeche, and Early Classic buildings in Quintana Roo (Karl Taube, personal communication, 1997). The expectant public cannot see, but they can sense the concealed presence of personages out of view.

Concurrence

One feature of physicality needs further thought. Theater, spectacle, and performance are often seen today in terms of "method acting," the Stanislavskian fusion of the actor and the role, or an English mode of craft and superficial artifice. Sociologically, Goffman would liken the second to human interaction; a less cynical perspective might prefer the first and its pretense of self-integrity and authentic projection. Nonetheless, when applied to antiquity, both run the risk of anachronism. For the classic Maya, *who* dances and sings and processes? Are they performers in any current sense of the world or something else entirely? The problem is that the Maya had their own concept of self that consisted, at the least, of multiple vitalizing energies. In marked performance, other beings could be invited within the body as intermittent guests, in adjunct to dance and music.

Houston and Stuart call this "deity impersonation," with the proviso that it appears to involve a *concurrence* rather than a displacement of identities (Houston and Stuart 1996:297–300). The dancer is always specified, as is the deity he or, far more rarely, she, "impersonates." The glyphic expression of this action includes a statement that an image or "self" is present *(u-b'aah)* along with a specialized suffix that usually pertains to supernaturals or the deceased *(-il)*—in one context the term for "god" *(k'uh)*—followed by a title *(a-nu)* of uncertain meaning, the names of a deity, and, finally, the names and titles of a ruler or noble. The important point is that nothing is dissembling, feigned, or concealed. There is no evident "fiction," but there is, apparently, a belief in godly immanence and transubstantiation, of specific people who become, in special moments, figures from sacred legend and the Mayan pantheon.[3] Inomata cites Thomas Gage to indicate the resilience of these beliefs into the colonial period (Gage 1958:247): "they seem almost to believe that they have actually done what they only performed for the dance," whether it be in the benign guise of John the Baptist or the malevolent pose of Herod.

The concurrence of human and divine essence is emphasized by the iconographic counterpart to these texts. These images show costumes with what has been termed "X-ray" views (Coe 1978: pl. 20), a narrow space left exposed around the face of the dancer or performer to underscore their historical identity. Strangely, many of these images come from only one part of the Mayan lowlands, somewhere around and to the northwest of Lake Peten Itza, Guatemala: some lords dress as great bloated toads holding rattles (and, as toads do today, probably making a right hellish racket), others as horrific jaguar beings with overbites beyond any dentist's skill, and composite birds with sharp bills. One vessel (K1439), now in the Art Institute of Chicago, shows lords dressed as other humans (Fig. 5.1; see also K1439, K4606, K6888). The texts on the vessel are difficult to read, but it may be that this represented a historical reenactment in which temporal frames blurred and later actors replicated actions of earlier ones (Schele and Miller 1986: pl. 92b). The historical nature of some dances is explicitly mentioned in the Rabinal Achi of the Alta Verapaz (Akkeren 1999, 2000) and, in Classic times, on Hieroglyphic Stairway 4 of Dos Pilas (Houston and Inomata In press). The risers of the stairway were positioned at two different times. The bottom four, the first to be put into place, commemorated a civil war between the local cadet and the

Figure 5.1. A Possible Historical Impersonation. © Justin Kerr (K1439)

progenitor dynasty at Tikal, the top riser a dance on what may have been the anniversary of the cadet branch's first important ruler (Houston 1993: Fig. 4-11, 102, 107). The overall impression is that this dance reviewed and celebrated the events mentioned on the bottom risers.

The archaeological residue of such impersonations have been found in the form of light-weight masks fortuitously preserved, against all odds, at the site of Aguateca, Guatemala (Inomata et al. 1998: fig. 7). The material is of unprecedented type, being composed of textiles soaked in clay, fashioned into the heads of deities, and then dried and painted red. The storage of such masks within the most formal buildings of the royal palace at Aguateca demonstrates their importance. A vessel excavated from the Mundo Perdido sector of Tikal (Fig. 5.2; K2695) shows a ruler being dressed for just such an impersonation (see also K764, K1454, K1524). A courtier holds a mirror so that the dancer can make adjustments, and two females, both identified by the same titles *(IX-'i-sa),* respectively offer a mask and a shield to the dancer, who already grasps a rattle. The dressing takes place within a building called the "house of writing *(tz'ib'alnaah),* the home of the *b'akab'*," this last being an exalted honorific. The scene evokes history in that the impersonation is of a male with highly detailed facial features that do not appear to be supernatural. Often the Maya place names in headdresses (Houston and Stuart 1998), and the name of the impersonated personage is strikingly similar to that of early rulers of the Tikal dynasty.

Figure 5.2. A Dressing Scene, Prelude to a Dance of Historical Concurrence. © Justin Kerr (K2695)

Approximately fifty separate references occur in the Maya corpus of texts to "deity concurrence." They show a great range of supernaturals: wind gods (*ik' k'uh*), an enigmatic god known as *9 yokte' k'uh*, a watery serpent (once "concurrent" with a royal lady), gods of incense burning, the sun god, underworld gods who exercise dominion over (pre-Hawking) "black holes," supernaturals connected to the Mexican site of Teotihuacan *(18 u-b'aah k'awiil),* gods of ball playing, moon goddesses, hunting gods, stony gods, fire drilling jaguar deities, and the major god known as Itzamnaaj. It is extremely difficult to detect any systematic patterns in this luxuriance of prancing gods. The most obvious are the wind gods who, for the Classic Maya, operated as atlantean figures. They were often "concurrent" with nobles who, by analogy, did not support the world so much as the throne. The event describing the "arrival" of a lady dressed as the moon goddess almost certainly originated in a term for the new crescent moon, which the Maya regarded as quintessentially female and fecund. (Even today in Peten, Guatemala, campesinos think that germinating rains correlate with changes in the moon, and that this is when sap flows freely in the veins of trees. Did this also signal some understanding of monthly cycles of fertility in women?) People drilling sacred fire often adopted the guise of a distinctive deity known as the jaguar god of the underworld.

What this evidence suggests is that, with deeper knowledge, scholars should be able to sort out specific motivations for "impersonation." There are hints that the motivations reflect a theory of dual action, in that actions or roles (the two are scarcely distinguishable) in one frame parallel those in another. The injection of the divine brings those frames, one human, the other supernatural, into contact and congruence; a timeless action was made timely and vested with all of the resonances of a particular court and its personalities. The more sociological features of such impersonation, urged on the author by the editors, are not easily contemplated: one suspects that these matters are best addressed by determining who could dance, much as, in the Pueblos of the Rio Grande valley today, only certain moieties or subgroups inherit the right to perform. Unfortunately, our sources of Maya evidence do not speak to this issue.

Conclusion

Spectacle is large performance at the outer limits of markedness. (The only more embracing concept might be "festival," which comprises many such spectacles.) To describe small moments of jocularity, contemplation, and action, or episodes of seeing and looking, as "spectacle" weakens the entire classification of marked behaviors, to no clear benefit. The Classic Maya complicate definitions by suggesting that, in their minds, spectacle could also involve nonhuman actors and audience. On some occasions, the experience would have vibrated with the paradox of transubstantiation, a paradox that brought different beings and world frames into concurrence. "Transcendence" would be precisely the wrong word to describe this experience. The spectator and performer were not taken anywhere else; they did not lose themselves in their roles. Rather, divine essences came to visit, briefly, and were made animate by human flesh and motion. Practiced movement, especially of the feet, may have summoned these essences. Choreography was a way to replicate other frames, place them in the present, and fashion narrative structure to shape the whole. Actors evinced a control over supernatural forces that went beyond the unmarked activities of the everyday world. If cadence and pacing are at the heart of any great performance, such moments of concurrence may have materialized only at the peak or crescendo of sacred theater. The smaller episodes of spectacle, the dancing, whistling, drumming set the stage for the time when gods descended to dance with humans.

Notes

My gratitude goes to Takeshi Inomata and Larry Coben for inviting me to attend the working group that generated this volume. The discussion was, to say the least, lively and heated. Takeshi and Larry also provided substantive comments on an earlier draft of this chapter, which I have tried to follow in part. The ever generous Justin Kerr allowed his images to be used in this volume. This work parallels collaborative work with good friends and colleagues David Stuart and Karl Taube.

1. A chapter on spectacle can hardly avoid the work of Guy Debord (1995, 1998). He argued that spectacle is engineered by capitalists and their bureaucratic lackeys to dull and mystify workers through a projection of false, organized "appearances" (Debord 1995:153, 1998:8). This theory reflects a conspiratorial vision of the world that can only be described as paranoid and, to this writer, tenuous. Moreover, Debord's ideas, all of unpersuasive cynicism, target the modern world and do not serve as a useful template for events in the premodern past.
2. Still, in his position paper, it seems imprudent of Hodder to illustrate his point with megalithic monuments, surely among the most opaque semantic productions from the ancient world. To say that Stonehenge relates to solar movements is like observing that Mormon temples face east. Is this the kind of detail Hodder means, and is it sufficient, as seems doubtful, for any deliberation of intended and received meaning? As an undergraduate attending the University of Edinburgh, the author dug at a henge site in Scotland. From firsthand knowledge, therefore, he is perplexed why the scholars most intrigued by paleo-phenomenology work on periods where independent controls on speculation are nearly nonexistent (Bradley 1998; Tilley 1994).
3. "Pantheon" is used deliberately as it underscores the courtly nature of godly society, the finite, general categories of deities (albeit with innumerable avatars), and their involvement in legendary narratives; "myth" implies limited credibility and may not be appropriate to Classic belief and practice (see Veyne 1988, for similar problems in classical studies).

References Cited

Akkeren, Ruud W. van
1999 Sacrifice at the Maize Tree: Rab'inal Achí in Its Historical and Symbolic Context. Ancient Mesoamerica 10(2):281–295.

2000 El baile-drama Rab'inal Achí: sus custodios y linajes de poder. Mésoamerica 21:1–39.

Anglo, Sydney
1997 Spectacle, Pageantry, and Early Tudor Policy. 2nd edition. Oxford: Clarendon.

Beacham, Richard C.
1999 Spectacle Entertainments of Early Imperial Rome. New Haven: Yale University Press.

Beeman, William O.
1993 The Anthropology of Theater and Spectacle. Annual Review of Anthropology 22:369–393.

Beetz, Carl P., and Linton Satterthwaite
1981 The Monuments and Inscriptions of Caracol, Belize. University Museum Monographs 45. Philadelphia: University Museum, University of Pennsylvania.

Bell, Catherine
1992 Ritual Theory, Ritual Practice. Oxford: Oxford University Press.

Bloch, Maurice
1977 The Past and the Present in the Present. Man 18:278–292.

Bradley, Richard
1998 The Significance of Monuments: On the Shaping of Human Experience in Neolithic and Bronze Age Europe. London: Routledge.

Burke, Kenneth
1969 A Rhetoric of Motives. Berkeley: University of California Press.

Camille, Michael
1992 Image on the Edge: The Margins of Medieval Art. London: Reaktion.

Coe, Michael D.
1978 Lords of the Underworld: Masterpieces of Classic Maya Ceramics. Princeton: Art Museum, Princeton University.

Debord, Guy
1995 The Society of the Spectacle. New York: Zone.
1998 Comments on the Society of Spectacle. London: Verso.

Fewkes, J. Walter
1892 The Ceremonial Circuit among the Village Indians of Northeastern Arizona. Journal of American Folk-Lore 5(16):33–42.

Flynn, Maureen

1994 The Spectacle of Suffering on Spanish Streets. *In* City and Spectacle in Medieval Europe. Barbara A. Hanawalt and Kathryn L. Reyerson, eds. Pp. 153–168. Minneapolis: University of Minnesota Press.

Gage, Thomas

1958 Thomas Gage's Travels in the New World. J. Eric S. Thompson, ed. Norman: University of Oklahoma Press.

Geertz, Clifford

1980 Negara: The Theatre State in Nineteenth-Century Bali. Princeton: Princeton University Press.

1983 Local Knowledge. New York: Basic.

Goffman, Erving

1959 The Presentation of Self in Everyday Life. Harmondsworth, U.K.: Penguin.

1961 Encounters: Two Studies in the Sociology of Interaction. Indianapolis: Bobbs-Merrill.

Gregor, Thomas.

1977 Mehinaku: The Drama of Daily Life in a Brazilian Indian Village. Chicago: University of Chicago Press.

Grube, Nikolai

1992 Classic Maya Dance: Evidence from Hieroglyphs and Iconography. Ancient Mesoamerica 3:201–218.

Hacking, Ian

1999 The Social Construction of What? Cambridge: Harvard University Press.

Hammond, Frederick

1994 Music and Spectacle in Baroque Rome: Barberini Patronage under Urban VIII. New Haven: Yale University Press.

Hanks, William F.

1990 Referential Practice: Language and Lived Space among the Maya. Chicago: University of Chicago Press.

Handelman, Don

1990 Models and Mirrors: Towards an Anthropology of Public Events. Cambridge: Cambridge University Press.

Houston, Stephen
1993 Hieroglyphs and History at Dos Pilas, Guatemala: Dynastic Politics of the Classic Maya. Austin: University of Texas Press.
2001 Decorous Bodies and Disordered Passions: Representations of Emotion among the Classic Maya. World Archaeology 33(2):206–219.
2002 Cantantes y danzantes de Bonampak. Arqueología Mexicana 10(55):54–55.

Houston, Stephen, and Takeshi Inomata
In press The Classic Maya. Cambridge: Cambridge University Press.

Houston, Stephen, and Patricia McAnany
2003 Bodies and Blood: Critiquing Social Construction in Maya Archaeology. Journal of Anthropological Archaeology 22:26–41.

Houston, Stephen, and David Stuart
1996 Of Gods, Glyphs, and Kings: Divinity and Rulership among the Classic Maya. Antiquity 70:289–312.
1998 The Ancient Maya Self: Personhood and Portraiture in the Classic period. RES 33:73–101.

Houston, Stephen, and Karl A. Taube
2000 An Archaeology of the Senses: Perception and Cultural Expression in Ancient Mesoamerica. Cambridge Archaeological Journal 10(2):261–294.

Inomata, Takeshi, Daniela Triadan, Erick Ponciano, Richard E. Terry, Harriet F. Beaubien, Estela Pinto, and Shannon Coyston
1998 Residencias de la familia real y de la élite en Aguateca, Guatemala. Mayab 11:23–39.

Kertzer, David I.
1988 Ritual, Politics and Power. New Haven: Yale University Press.

Lincoln, Bruce
1989 Discourse and the Construction of Society: Comparative Studies in Myth, Ritual, and Classification. Oxford: Oxford University Press.

Lindberg, David C.
1976 Theories of Vision from Al-Kindi to Kepler. Chicago: University of Chicago Press.

Lyons, John
1968 Introduction to Theoretical Linguistics. Cambridge: Cambridge University Press.

Manning, Philip
1992 Erving Goffman and Modern Sociology. Stanford: Stanford University Press.

Monaghan, John D.
2000 Theology and History in the Study of Mesoamerican Religions. *In* Handbook of Middle American Indians, Supplement 6: Ethnology. John D. Monaghan, ed., and Victoria R. Bricker, gen. ed. Pp. 24–49. Austin: University of Texas Press.

Moore, Jerry D.
1996 Architecture and Power in the Ancient Andes: The Archaeology of Public Buildings. Cambridge: Cambridge University Press.

Olin, Margaret
1996 Gaze. *In* Critical Terms for Art History. Robert S. Nelson and Richard Shiff, eds. Pp. 208–219. Chicago: University of Chicago Press.

Rappaport, Roy A.
1999 Ritual and Religion in the Making of Humanity. Cambridge: Cambridge University Press.

Schechner, Richard
1990 Magnitudes of Performance. *In* By Means of Performance: Intercultural Studies of Theatre and Ritual. Richard Schechner and Willa Appel, eds. Pp. 19–49. Cambridge: Cambridge University Press.

Schele, Linda, and Peter Mathews
1979 The Bodega of Palenque, Chiapas, Mexico. Washington, D.C.: Dumbarton Oaks.

Schele, Linda, and Mary E. Miller
1986 The Blood of Kings: Dynasty and Ritual in Maya Art. Forth Worth: Kimbell Art Museum.

Stone, Andrea J.
1995 Images from the Underworld: Naj Tunich and the Tradition of Maya Cave Painting. Austin: University of Texas Press.

Stuart, David
1998 "The Fire Enters His House": Architecture and Ritual in Classic Maya Texts. *In* Function and Meaning in Classic Maya Architecture. Stephen D. Houston, ed. Pp. 373–425. Washington, D.C.: Dumbarton Oaks.

Stuart, David, Stephen Houston, and John Robertson
1999 Recovering the Past: Classic Maya Language and Classic Maya Gods. *In* Notebook for the XXIIIrd Maya Hieroglyphic Forum at Texas, Part 2, Maya Workshop Foundation, Austin, pp. 1–96.

Tilley, Christopher
1994 A Phenomenology of Landscape: Places, Paths and Monuments. London: Berg.

Tozzer, Alfred M.
1941 Landa's Relación de las Cosas de Yucatan. Papers of the Peabody Museum of American Archaeology and Ethnology, no. 18. Cambridge: Harvard University Press.

Veyne, Paul
1988 Did the Greeks Believe in Their Myths? An Essay in the Constitutive Imagination. Chicago: University of Chicago Press.

Wolfowitz, Clare
1991 Language Style and Social Space: Stylistic Choice in Suriname Javanese. Urbana: University of Illinois Press.

Act III

PUBLIC PERFORMANCE OF POWER AND COMMUNITY

SCENE 6

DANCING GODS: RITUAL, PERFORMANCE, AND POLITICAL ORGANIZATION IN THE PREHISTORIC SOUTHWEST

Daniela Triadan

> After dusk, the giant figures which had been left on the plain across the river came in one by one. They were, by all odds, the most monstrous conceptions I had seen among the Zuñi dances. They were at least twelve feet high. Their gigantic heads were shocks of long black hair with great horns at the sides, green masks with huge, protruding eyeballs, and long, pointed square-ended, wooden beaks; and their bodies were draped with embroidered and tasseled cotton blankets, underneath which only the tiny, bare, painted feet of the actor could be seen. The spasmodic rolling of the great eyeballs and the sharp snapping of the beak as it rapidly opened and closed, together with a fan-shaped arrangement of eagle feathers at the back of the head, gave these figures the appearance of angry monster-birds.
>
> —Cushing 1979:86

A fascinating and "exotic" (to Euro-Americans) aspect of the Pueblo people of the Southwest are the rich and colorful dance dramas, which are part of their religious ceremonies (Bourke 1884; Hough 1900; Stephen 1940 for early accounts of the Hopi snake dance). Anthropologists have interpreted these rituals as a major force of political integration for these village-dwelling agriculturalists, because they involve the participation of the whole community and their staging and enactment is usually the responsibility of clans and/or religious societies whose membership crosscuts kinship ties (Eggan 1950; Kroeber 1917; Parsons 1933; Stevenson 1904; Titiev 1944).

Similarly (and not incidentally due to a heavy reliance on ethnographic and ethnohistorical accounts), archaeologists have long seen ritual as an integral component of social organization and power, as well as a potent agent of cultural change in prehistoric Southwestern societies (Adams 1991; Crown 1994; Fewkes 1896, 1919; Potter and Perry 2000; Walker 1995). Most researchers have concentrated on the spatial manifestations of ritual defined by architecture and artifact assemblages, and on iconography (i.e., depictions of potential ritual performers) and regional distributions of certain ceramic styles. For example, settlement patterns and ceremonial to domestic room ratios provide arguments for the level of political integration and the social structure and cohesion of prehistoric Puebloan groups (Lipe and Hegmon 1989). Adams (1991) interprets changes in settlements to plaza-focused villages and the appearance of masked personages on pottery and walls of ceremonial structures as the beginnings of the Pueblo katsina[1] cult and the rituals associated with this cult as a major social integrative force of late prehistoric communities. Crown (1994) suggests that the emergence of a supraregional pottery style that appears on several different ceramic wares indicates a pan-Southwestern ritual cult that had similar integrative functions. Ritual practices and accompanying performances have generally not been the focus of these studies (but see Potter and Perry 2000).

Given the emphasis that Southwestern archeologists place on the social integrative function of ritual, the question is how and why does ritual integrate people socially and, if indeed it does so, what role do the performance aspects of pueblo ritual play in this process? In the broadest sense rituals are participatory and inclusive because indoctrinated people can identify with the ritual acts performed within their cultural framework. Participants, be it ritual specialists, actively involved participants, or spectators, know or recognize the message conveyed by the ritual performed and understand and interpret the ritual acts as well as the symbols displayed. Thus a sense of belonging may be created (Bell 1997:160). Clearly exposure (such as repeated participation) and some form of indoctrination are needed to learn and understand what is going on. The level or depth of knowledge, however, often depends on age (and concomitant experience) and the role or responsibility the participant has in the ritual. For example, ritual specialists (such as ordained priests) often have specialized and esoteric knowledge as well as the authority to conduct ritual ceremonies. On this level ritual knowledge is *exclusive* and held only by a select group of people. Some might argue that this lends itself naturally to assuming positions of power and control and ultimately social stratification (Plog 1995; Plog and Solometo 1996). There is thus a dichotomy or ambivalence inherent in ritual acts: participation fosters community cohesion through identification with the group, while specialized ritual knowledge by specific individuals bestows power that could be exploited for political gain.

Many scholars have emphasized the performance aspects of ritual from different perspectives (Bloch 1974; Burke 1973; Goffman 1959, 1967; Tambiah 1985; Turner 1969; see also Bell 1997:72–76). Specialists conduct ritual acts frequently in a setting that resembles a stage (e.g., the central altar in a basilica or the temple on top of a Maya pyramid), and in these settings their actions can be observed and heard by a large number of people. Often they wear elaborate costumes (be it the chasuble and mitre of the pope or the impressive headdress of a Maya ruler). Music and dance are also often a component of ritual. All of these visual and auditory aspects may instill awe, joy, fear, and other strong emotions and a profound communal experience in the participants. (This may be true whether ritual is performed on a grand scale or in a more intimate setting).

Performance and theatricality are an integral part of pueblo ritual. "With their great love of theatrical effects, the Hopi have based their Tribal Initiation drama on the libretto of the Emergence myth, keeping the rites close to the details of the 'script'" (Titiev 1944:138; see also Fewkes 1894, 1900). "The sacred dance court of the Zuñi is not only their temple where they invoke their god, but is their theater where they gratify their love for the spectacular" (Stevenson 1904:148). Every ceremony involves public dance dramas that are performed by costumed (and sometimes masked) members of religious societies in public as well as not so public spaces (see discussion below). Participation in these rituals, as performers or spectators, ensures the well-being and survival of the community. Because membership in the religious societies crosscuts kinship ties, it is a means to counter tendencies of clan segmentation and thus helps to keep communities together (Titiev 1944; but see Whiteley 1988). The performers are ritual specialists who have secret esoteric knowledge and are charged with conducting the ceremonies in the correct way. They may thus wield considerable influence and power over the rest of the community. From this perspective, looking at who and what is involved in ritual performances may give important information on how ritual performance creates and maintains social order, and it may provide information on the mechanisms involved in prehistoric changes in Pueblo social and political organization.

Obviously it is not easy to project ritual performances into the prehistoric past. Because of the nature of the archaeological record, it is important to analyze the material aspects of ritual performance in this context, such as the space where performances take place, features that may hint at the function of and access to performances, and objects used in performances, to be able to draw any meaningful inferences.

In this chapter I focus on the northwestern part of the American Southwest, the homeland of contemporary Western Puebloan peoples such as the Zuni and Hopi and their prehistoric ancestors, mainly because my research interests lie in this area. In my attempt to interpret prehistoric data of ritual behavior with respect to performance, I will "set the stage" by describing ritual performance and theatricality among the historic Hopi and Zuni.

Ethnohistoric sources provide probably the most detailed and extensive information on Pueblo ritual and performance. Using ethnohistoric data in archaeological interpretation is clearly not unproblematic because we cannot disregard the impact Spanish colonization had on Puebloan social and political organization (Upham 1982, 1987). However, because contact with the Spanish authorities was much less intense in the Western Pueblos, religious syncretism is much weaker (or nonexistent in the case of Hopi) and their ceremonies were not forced underground; they probably represent a more direct development from prehistoric times than those of the Rio Grande Pueblos. Despite the potential shortcomings of ethnographic analogy, I believe that ethnohistoric accounts can give some vital glimpses of how ritual and performance may have operated in the past, especially when combined with contextual and spatial analyses of archaeological data.

Pueblo Ritual Performance

In this description of historic and current Pueblo ritual, I will look at specific components of ritual performance as a theatrical event to demonstrate who is involved and how performance affects different parts of pueblo society socially and politically. However, Pueblo religion is very complex and this chapter hardly exhausts the subject. I have divided the components of ritual performance into actors (performers), audience, stage (space where the ritual is performed), mechanisms (script) of the drama, and the political implications of these enactments. I believe these units of analysis may also be useful when discussing the archaeological evidence. I would like to draw the reader's attention specifically to the material aspects of these performances as they are the type of evidence that may be found in archaeological contexts.

The Actors/Performers

The actors in Western Pueblo rituals are members of various religious societies, some of which are clan-based while others crosscut clans. During half of the ceremonial year the *dramatis personae* are masked performers or *katsinas*. During the other half, the performers are costumed and painted (which identifies them as members of specific religious societies) but unmasked.

The katsinas are probably the best known and most conspicuous protagonists of Pueblo rituals. Katsinas are supernatural beings, ancestors that become spirits and often come to visit in the form of clouds. The word "katsina" also connotes the mask itself, the performer, spirits of other beings, as well as wooden figures.[2] In katsina (masked) dances, the characters can be manifold, but often only a few groups of specific katsinas appear (e.g., Wright et al. 1986: pl. 13). There are hundreds of katsinas and different ones appear in different dances. A specific katsina can usually be identified by the attributes, colors, and symbols of its mask and its identity determines its role and behavior (e.g., whether it is an ogre who threatens people if they behave badly or if it is benevolent and brings food and presents). The material attributes and symbols of the masks are especially interesting with regard to the archaeological record, as I discuss below. Female katsinas exist and are impersonated by males dressed in the costume and mask characteristic of the particular female katsina. The pantheon of katsinas is not static; through time new katsinas have been added (e.g., cow katsina, Navajo katsina), and katsinas from other pueblo groups have been incorporated (Wright 1994:142, pl. 17–33). Katsinas are part of the ceremonial system at all Pueblos, Western or Eastern.

The performers in both masked and unmasked dances are invariably *initiated* members of religious societies or kiva groups because performing in these dances requires ritual and often secret knowledge. Some of these societies are exclusive, and the role of women varies among Pueblo groups. At Zuni all youths are initiated into the katsina society, but women are generally not members of the kiva groups or other religious societies. Women perform in unmasked dances, like the Basket Dance (Parsons 1933; Stevenson 1904). At Hopi both boys and girls are initiated into the katsina cult and women can belong to religious societies. In fact, there are women societies. Women perform in the dances sponsored by these societies and in other unmasked dances (Parsons 1933; Titiev 1944).

Moral and ritual obligation motivates the performers to act in these dance dramas because the ceremonies are performed to ensure the continuity of the community. They are vital for the proper conduct of Pueblo rituals. There is also an aspect of pride in the art of performing (Sanner 1995:13).

The Audience

Pueblo rituals are performed to ensure the benevolence of the gods (such as sun and earth) and supernatural beings (ancestor spirits) to benefit the entire society.[3] The audience in these ritual performances varies depending on the part (or act if you will) of the ceremony. Some parts of the ceremony are all-inclusive and open to complete outsiders, some parts are open only to people of the same group (e.g., Hopis or Zunis), but include all members of that group—men, women and children—and some parts of the performance are open only to a select and restricted audience, the initiates of *secret societies.*[4]

> I stealthily followed the retiring *Keó-yi-mo-shis* [Koyemsi] to a large room on the south side of the pueblo. A sentinel stood at the door, and no one but these clowns was permitted to enter. Nor could I catch more than a glimpse of the fire-lit interior, as the windows were heavily curtained with blankets. I learned that the group had been confined in this room four days and nights, engaged in fasting, prayer, and sacred incantations; so I determined to visit them. (Cushing 1979:81; modern transcription added)

After having been allowed to enter the kiva of the Koyemsi, Cushing (1979:83) states, "This little glimpse revealed to me a mysterious life by which I had little dreamed I was surrounded, and I looked forward with curious anxiety to the coming ceremonials."

The difference between *initiated* (adults) and *uninitiated* spectators (children) is also important in the public parts of the ceremonies in which children are allowed to participate. During the masked dances adults are careful with their language in front of the uninitiated to not let them in on the secret of the katsinas. For instance, they refer to katsina masks as "friend" and do not use the word "katsina" (Sanner 1995:9). Until children are initiated into the katsina society, they do *not* know that their fathers and uncles are impersonating the katsinas, and the masks are *never* taken off in public.[5] Children are an important part of the audience because part of the katsinas' role is as educators; they admonish the children to adhere to proper behavior and bring them presents (Parsons 1939:49–54).

For the audience the rituals provide theatrical drama that may cause excitement, a feeling of well-being and belonging, and a profound communal experience. Because of the dramatic effects, these emotions may be especially strong for uninitiated spectators. The communal experience of the rituals is bolstered by food sharing. Feasting is an important part of all ceremonies, and days are spent to prepare special foods. However, the spectators may also evaluate the performance critically. Based on their knowledge of the ritual and traditional expectations, as well as the results (did it rain?), they may judge whether the performance was done right.

The Stage

Pueblo ritual dramas are generally performed in two spaces: *plazas* and *kivas*. These spaces affect who participates in the ritual, as well as the size and makeup of the audience. Plazas are the place for public performances. They serve the whole community or several communities. The audience usually sits or stands around the plaza and on rooftops of surrounding houses to watch the spectacle, in an amphitheater-like setting (Fig. 6.1; Cushing 1979:71, fig.9; Wright et al. 1986: pl. 5).

Kivas are semisubterranean or subterranean ceremonial rooms or chambers.[6] Specific architectural features are present that give these rooms their ritual function. They have a restricted entry through the rooftop, via a ladder (Wright et al. 1986: pl. 2); a fire pit directly under the hatchway; a *sipapu*, which is an opening in the floor that symbolizes the place of

Figure 6.1. Spectators and Performers during a *Niman* Ceremony. Reproduced with Permission from Wright et al. 1986: pl. 43

emergence of the first people; benches along the walls; and an elevated chamber (Fig. 6.2; Hieb 1979:579, Fig. 3; Stephen 1940:23; Titiev 1944:103–104). The spectators sit on the benches and the elevated platform. In the Western Pueblo villages, kivas are rectangular.

Compared to the plaza, a kiva represents a smaller, restricted space, and activities are not visible from the outside (though they may be heard). Even though some parts of the ceremonies that are conducted in the kivas are open to the community (such as night dances at Hopi), fewer spectators can participate. The kivas are also the place where rituals occur that are only open to members of the respective religious society. Thus kivas have a dual role: they can be exclusive or inclusive spaces, depending on what part of the ceremony is going on.[7]

Dramatic Elements

Ceremonies normally take place over several days, most parts of which are not public performances. The public dances in the plazas occur toward

Figure 6.2. Layout of a Hopi Kiva. Reproduced with Permission from the Smithsonian Institution from *Hopi World View*, by L. A. Hieb, fig. 3, p. 579, in Handbook of North American Indians, vol. 9 of *Southwest*, edited by A. Ortiz, 1979. Original Drawing by Jo Ann Moore

the end of the ceremony (Titiev 1944:104–105). They are rich in visual and auditory drama. For instance, following oral traditions, the katsinas emerge from the symbolic underworld. The masked dancers are initially hidden from view and then suddenly arrive out in the open. Often one can first hear only drums, rattles, and chanting from far away, and then the dancers burst on the scene; the visual and auditory impact is awesome. Once the dancers are in the plaza, this effect is heightened by the costumes, the synchronized rhythmic movements, the music, and the chants. Some of the performers also directly engage the audience, such as the clowns, and in some ceremonies the katsinas interact with the spectators.

Rituals performed in the kiva have a very different dramatic ambiance than the dances performed in the plaza. The dramatic effects are enhanced by the restricted space and the dark, cavelike atmosphere that is only illuminated by the flicker of a fire. Noise, smoke, and smell are amplified.

> The blazes of the splinter-lit fire on the stone altar, sometimes licking the very ladder-poles in their flight upward toward the sky-hole, which served at once as door-way, chimney, and window; the painted tablets in one end, with priests and musicians grouped around; the spectators opposite and along the sides; the thin, upward streams of blue smoke from hundreds of cigarettes; the shrill calls of the rapidly coming and departing dancers, their wild songs, and the din of the great drum, which fairly jarred the ancient, smoke-blackened rafters; the less distinguishable but terribly thrilling "swirr-r" of the yucca-whips, when brought down on some luckless sleeper's head and shoulders; the odors of the burning sacrifices, the tobacco, and of evergreen. (Cushing 1979:112–113)

They also often involve ritual paraphernalia that are distinct for each ceremony.

> At the western end stood an altar, composed of various heights and widths, strangely carved and painted in representation of gods, and set up in the form of a square. At the back were larger tablets, on and through which figures of the sun, moon, and stars were painted and cut. Within the square stood a number of sacred wands of long macaw feathers inserted into beautiful wicker-work handles. Overhead hung the figure of a winged god, a little in front and below which was suspended horizontally an elaborate cross. It was composed of two tablets, carved to zigzag points at

> the ends, and joined at the center, so as to resemble a wind-mill with four arms. Numerous eagle-plumes depended from the lower edges of the four arms, on each of which was perched the effigy of a swallow. Underneath this stood a large medicine-bowl with terraced edges. It was covered with figures of frogs, tadpoles, and dragon-flies, and contained a clear yellowish fluid. Over this two of the priests were crouching and muttering encantations. Behind the altar, partly covered, with little embroidered cotton kilts, were the warty masks and the neck-cloths of these priestly clowns. Almost immediately on entering, my guide had uttered prayers and scattered medicine flour over them. All along the walls of the great room, now vivid in the fire-light, now indistinct in the flickering shadows, were painted in red, green, blue and yellow, the figures of animals, birds, human monsters, demons, and significant pictographs. (Cushing 1979:82–83)

This ritual paraphernalia is kept in the kivas and clan houses.

Ritual Performance and Power

One of the questions that has long been a focus of archaeological and anthropological research is if rituals were and are performed to assert and exert political power (e.g., Whiteley 1988). They served to integrate a population that lived in very close quarters. Pueblos are virtual apartment buildings with hundreds of people living on top of each other.

Among the Pueblo people, who are agriculturalists living in the arid, marginal environments of the Southwest, religious ceremonies are enacted to ask for the goodwill and benevolence of the ancestral spirits (the katsinas) and the gods, who bring rain. The rituals have a long history of importance for Pueblo social and political organization. For instance, oral histories record that when new clans arrived at a village, they had to demonstrate what ritual knowledge they could contribute to rainmaking in order to be incorporated into the community (Fewkes 1902; Titiev, 1944:44).

The rituals foster cooperation because there is an obligation to serve in the religious societies for the greater good of all. Virtually every adult is initiated into the katsina cult (gaining insider knowledge about the masked performers) and then assumes ritual responsibilities. In addition, there are usually several other religious societies of which adults (excluding women in Zuni) become members through subsequent initiations.

These societies do not lend themselves to hereditary hierarchies because they are not based on familial ties (though at Hopi some positions in these societies can be clan-based), and often officials charged with specific responsibilities in these societies are elected every year (Stevenson 1904:128–129). Because the religious societies (as well as clans and other social groups) crosscut kinship ties, they hinder stratification (Eggan 1994; Kroeber 1917:186).

On the other hand, people who are initiated into the exclusive secret societies have power that can best be described as (secret) ritual knowledge.[8] They are able to communicate with and command specific supernatural forces (they also have the obligation and authority to do so). Ritual knowledge is used to harness nature (rain) to guarantee the growing of crops. "Ritual action, because of its intent to affect instrumentally the conditions of existence, is simultaneously political action" (Whiteley 1988:68). This knowledge may compute itself into real political power (Whiteley 1988), and there may be a potential for political manipulation by individuals, but there are mechanisms that hold the rampant abuse of power in check. If ritual knowledge is abused, or ceremonies are not performed correctly, or the results of the ceremonies are disappointing (no rain), ritual specialists are in danger of being accused of witchcraft (in earlier times this meant that if they were convicted of this crime they were killed). Also, because communal obligations are stressed in all aspects of Pueblo society, the system discourages obvious display of material wealth and power (there are no emblematic clothes or other objects, in contrast, for instance, to the Classic Maya, where nobles and kings had clear items of status, such as dress, headdresses, and jewelry, and were publicly displaying them).

Even though the hereditary ascent of individuals is discouraged in Pueblo society, there seems to exist some hierarchy within the religious societies (Cushing 1979; Titiev 1944), and some were politically more powerful than others. For example, at Zuni the Priesthood of the Bow, a warrior society, was the most powerful. Members of the Priesthood of the Bow were the keepers of the Zuni war gods (Cushing 1979:96–97), and they were charged with maintaining law and order and its enforcement, often using witch trials to punish social transgressors (Cushing 1979:123–127). Also, most villages have a founding clan (the clan that arrived first at the location of the village), and male members of this clan often occupy important positions.[9] Thus political power is principally group based, with checks and balances keeping individuals from gaining extraordinarily powerful positions.

Ritual Performance in Prehistory

Two sets of archaeological data lend themselves to investigate ritual performance and its sociopolitical implications during prehistoric times: ritual architecture and iconography. Ritual architecture represents the space (or stage) where ritual performances took place. It may indirectly inform on the audience if viewed from the perspective of access and exclusion. Iconography provides information on ritual symbols and performers. The interpretation of these data relies partly on ethnohistorical data, but spatial analysis of ritual architecture (such as accessibility, visibility, and organization of space) provides independent information to draw inferences about performers and spectators in the past.

Pueblo Ritual Architecture

Ritual architecture provided the stage for prehistoric performers and the space for the spectators. Round subterranean or semisubterranean structures that are interpreted as ritual and communal structures occur as early as about A.D. 300 (Haury 1985:287–367) in Mogollon pithouse villages. Walker and Lucero (2000) argue that they developed from house rituals that were originally performed inside the residences. In most cases, Southwestern archaeologists call these great kivas, based on specific attributes that are interpreted analogous to historic kivas (Haury 1950; but see Anyon and LeBlanc 1980). They usually have one or several of the following features: benches, a fire pit with a stone deflector, a ventilator shaft, and a hole in the floor that is interpreted as the *sipapu*. Sometimes they have an elevated antechamber. In later times (around A.D. 1000–1100) these great kivas often have a pair of trenches that may have functioned as foot drums (Fig. 6.3; Vivian and Reiter 1960). Most of these structures were roofed.

Most researchers agree that great kivas served the whole community or several communities. They are interpreted as cooperative community facilities where people gathered for feasts and rituals. The presence of at least one of these structures in early villages is seen as evidence for community integration through shared ritual activities. On a more fundamental level,

Figure 6.3. Casa Rinconada, Chaco Canyon. Photograph by Paul Logsdou. Reproduced with Permission from Paul Logsdou Photography

building a great kiva required a significant amount of labor, and the whole village may have been involved. Thus participation in the construction of these buildings in itself may have formed and shaped communities.

In A.D. 700–900 Anasazi and around A.D. 1000 Mogollon settlements changed from pithouses to above-ground rooms organized in room blocks. Settlement patterns were usually dispersed, small villages, with a detached great kiva that served as ceremonial center. During this time there occurred also smaller round structures, sometimes with benches and usually some typical kiva features, in these settlements. The ratio of these rooms to rectangular habitation rooms prompted many archaeologists to argue that these small kivas served several households or suprahousehold groups, and that the great kivas in turn served the whole community or several communities (Lipe 1989; Reid and Whittlesey 1982). Following Kroeber's (1917) model, Ferguson (1989) suggests that at that time religious membership may have coincided with residential kinship groups, meaning that kin group A belonged to kiva A, which belonged to religious society A. Although most people agree that the large structures called great kivas probably had a ritual/communal function that socially integrated the community, there is considerable debate about the function of the smaller kivas and if they were indeed predominantly ritual structures (Lekson 1989; Smith 1990).

Great kivas occur most frequently from about A.D. 700 until the late 1200s. As mentioned above, they were originally large, round, subterranean structures entered through a hatch in the roof (Fig. 6.3).[10] Many have a bench along the wall that probably seated the spectators. In some cases there was an antechamber connected to the main room by an underground passage (Fig. 6.3). These passages could have been used to considerable dramatic effect by the performers. They would literally rise from the underworld. Large trenches that may have been covered by wooden logs and may have served as foot drums and platforms on which performers danced may also have been used to considerable dramatic effect. If this was the case, then the enclosed cavernous space of these structures must have provided incredible resonance for these drums. These scenes were usually illuminated by a large fireplace in the center of the structure.

Though the function of great kivas was probably integrative and they could accommodate a large number of people, their architectural layout shows that access to the interior of the structure was restricted. The ritual performances that took place in these buildings could not be observed from the outside; thus the spectators had literally to be *insiders.* Maybe inclusiveness pertained only to one's own community and other communities were deliberately excluded from participation. Perhaps only certain segments of a community took part in the ritual activities, and these activities were exclusive and shielded from outsiders within the same community.

In the late 1200s large-scale population movements took place in the northern Southwest. Whole areas on the northern Colorado Plateau and in the Four Corners region that had been occupied for over a thousand years were permanently abandoned. To the south of these areas massive settlement aggregation occurred, and ultimately these events led to wholesale social reorganization (Spielmann 1998). Interestingly, at the same time villages started to be constructed around plazas, enclosed but accessible communal spaces, and great kivas almost disappeared (Fig. 6.4; Adams 1989, 1991; Adams and Duff 2004:157–182; Potter 1996). Smaller kivas continued to exist and became rectangular in the western parts of the Pueblo area. It should be emphasized, however, that most of these large aggregated fourteenth-century villages lasted only for a short period of time and were abandoned around A.D. 1400. Only villages in the Hopi and Zuni areas survived into historic times.

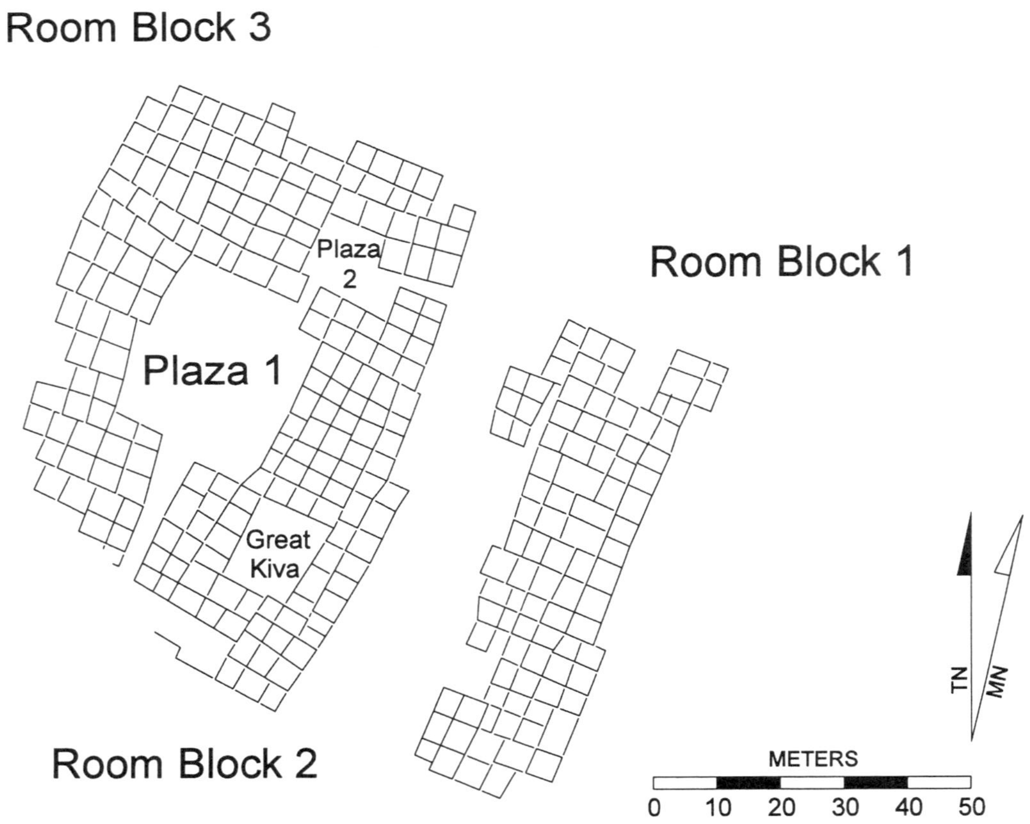

Figure 6.4. Map of Main Room Blocks at Grasshopper Pueblo

It is intriguing to speculate that at this time the nature of ritual performance changed. As I have discussed above, plazas are the forum where the public parts of ritual performances take place and can be observed by a large audience (much larger than the audience that would have fit into a great kiva). The intent may have been to give larger and diverse groups of the community access to ritual performances.

Prehistoric Ritual Performers

Coinciding with the shifts in settlement patterns and village layouts to large aggregated communities organized around plazas, the first depictions of *masked* figures occur (Adams 1991, 1994; Hays 1994). They appear on pottery as well as on painted kiva murals that date to about A.D. 1300, and in rare cases as painted figures on stone tablets (Cummings 1940: pl. 34; Di Peso 1950; Kidder 1932). Depictions on pottery are predominantly human heads that wear masks (Fig. 6.5), but there are some vessels that actually portray scenes of a variety of masked characters including some performers who seem to dance in line (Fig. 6.6), similar to katsinas in

Figure 6.5. Paayu Polychrome Bowl from Homol'ovi II (AZ J:14:15). Courtesy of K. A. Hays

Figure 6.6. Unprovenienced Sikyatki Polychrome Bowl, Showing Performers Dancing in Line and a Person inside a Shalako Figure Manipulating Its Mask. Courtesy of K. A. Hays

modern ceremonies (cf. Wright et al. 1986: pl. 13). A couple of vessels are especially interesting because they show a figure that resembles the Zuni Shalako and inside one can see its human impersonator (Fig. 6.6 shows one of these vessels). Hays (1994) argues that some of the masked characters can be clearly identified as Hopi katsinas, based on the attributes of their masks, which are similar to those of specific modern katsinas.

Polychrome murals appear in prehistoric kivas that date to the same time and show scenes that involve persons as well as animals (Smith 1952; Vivian 1994). The painted scenes show masked persons as well as warriors and women (Schafsmaa 1994, pl. 9), and some may depict the insides of a kiva with the attendant ritual paraphernalia. In most cases these scenes were repeatedly painted over (Smith 1952; Vivian 1994:83), indicating that the painting and repainting of kivas formed an integral part of ritual ceremonies.[11] Large open plazas as well as the appearance of individuals who may have been performers in ritual ceremonies indicate that the nature of ritual performance began to change drastically around A.D. 1300 in the northwestern parts of the Southwest.

Conclusion

The development and spatial distribution of distinctively public architecture such as plazas in the northern Southwest during late prehistoric times suggests a growing importance of rituals that involve the participation of a large number of people at some prehistoric villages. At about the same time depictions of masked performers occur for the first time on ceramics and murals in kivas. Though there seems to be an increasing emphasis on public performances, small kivas with restricted access continue to be in use, hinting that more exclusive groups of performers and spectators also played a role.

The settlement and architectural changes during the 1300s indicate that there occurred a change in ritual performances. Adams (1991, 1994) argues that this time saw the beginnings of the katsina cult or religion. The large aggregated villages probably housed people from different areas and different ethnic backgrounds; thus rituals that involved groups or institutions that crosscut kinship ties may have developed to integrate these heterogeneous communities.

However, more than anything the thirteenth and fourteenth centuries were times of social upheaval and experimentation (LeBlanc 1999; Rice and LeBlanc 2001). In general villages were not occupied for long time periods, some for only fifty years, and by A.D. 1400 most of the region was completely abandoned except for villages in the Hopi and Zuni areas. Analysis of the circulation of fourteenth-century polychrome ceramics in the Mogollon mountains has shown that this pottery moved with people and that people probably moved as family groups or households at this time (Triadan 1997; Triadan et al. 2002). These data suggest that political (and ritual) integration in most of these communities was rather weak.

Another interesting example for this experimentation is that at three large fourteenth-century villages in the Mogollon highlands (Kinishba, Grasshopper Pueblo, and Point of Pines), a plaza was converted into a rectangular great kiva later in its occupation (Cummings 1940; Gerald 1957; Reid and Shimada 1982:17; Riggs 2001:107–111, Fig. 3.40). It almost looks like a reversal of older ritual practices. All three communities were abandoned in A.D. 1400.

In the cases where sociopolitical reorganization was successful and villages survived (such as Zuni and Hopi), it may have been because the people devised rituals that entailed the participation of the whole community and fostered relationships that connected every individual living in the community with everybody else (Kroeber 1917:186). This restructuring may not have completely prevented fissioning within villages (Dockstader 1979:526–529; Titiev 1944:69–95; Whiteley 1988 on the historic Oraibi Split), but groups that moved out may have been composed of several kinship groups, connected through clan and ritual society membership. Thus there was a shift from lineage-based groups that may have moved independently (as seems to have been the case in the Mogollon mountains), to larger community segments that moved as a group. With the latter, the general social and ceremonial structure could have been transferred to another location and remained more or less intact. Ultimately the success of large, late, prehistoric, aggregated villages depended on adopting or developing social strategies that helped keep these communities together and functional. Changes in ritual practices and performance seem to have played an integral part in their survival.

Notes

1. The spelling follows the convention of the *Hopi Dictionary* (1998:134).
2. When the performer dons the mask, he becomes the katsina and transforms himself into a supernatural being (e.g., Sekaquaptewa 1976:39; Stephen 1940:17; Titiev 1944:109).
3. The Hopi actually pray for all human beings.
4. In historic times, Navajo, Hopi, and people from the Rio Grande Pueblos regularly visited Zuni to participate as spectators in the Shalako, for example (Cushing 1979:83). Later more and more Europeans came to watch the Pueblo dances (e.g., Udall 1996:56, fig. 21).
5. Gill (1977) describes the shock and disillusion, when the initiates learn the truth about the katsinas (see also Simmons 1942:84; Titiev 1944:119).
6. The number of kivas per village varies; for example, Zuni has six kivas that correspond to the six kiva societies (Tedlock 1979:503, fig. 3), Walpi, a Hopi Pueblo on First Mesa has five, and Sichomovi, another First Mesa village, has two (Connelly 1979:540, fig.3).
7. Kivas were and are also used for secular activities of members of kiva societies, such as weaving (which at Hopi and Zuni is done by men).

8. Secrecy is so important that people (including women) are forcibly initiated if they accidentally stumble upon closed proceedings of a secret society (Parsons 1933:10; 1939:113; Stevenson 1904:416).

9. Clans are matrilineal and thus the inheritance of these positions is prevented.

10. In the Mogollon mountains *rectangular* great kivas appear around A.D. 1240 (Lowell 1991), and rectangular ceremonial structures occur even earlier in the Mimbres region (Anyon and LeBlanc 1980).

11. Titiev (1944:115) describes whitewashing of kivas before the Powamu ceremony at Oraibi.

References Cited

Adams, E. Charles

1989 Changing Form and Function in Western Pueblo Ceremonial Architecture from A.D. 1000 to A.D. 1500. *In* The Architecture of Social Integration. William. D. Lipe and Michelle Hegmon, eds. Pp. 155–160. Occasional Paper of the Crow Canyon Archaeological Center, 1. Cortez: Crow Canyon Archaeological Center.

1991 The Emergence of the Katsina Cult. Tucson: University of Arizona Press.

1994 The Katsina Cult: A Western Pueblo Perspective. *In* Kachinas in the Pueblo World. Polly Schafsmaa, ed. Pp. 35–46. Albuquerque: University of New Mexico Press.

Adams, E. Charles, and Andrew I. Duff

2004 The Protohistoric Pueblo World, A.D. 1275–1600. Tucson: University of Arizona Press.

Anyon, Roger, and Steven A. LeBlanc

1980 The Architectural Evolution of Mogollon-Mimbres Communal Structures. The Kiva 45(3):253–277.

Bell, Catherine

1997 Ritual: Perspectives and Dimensions. New York: Oxford University Press.

Bloch, Maurice

1974 Symbols, Song, Dance, and Features of Articulation. Archives Europeénes de Sociologie 15:55–81.

Bourke, J. G.
1884 The Snake Dance of the Moquis of Arizona. New York: Scribner.

Burke, Kenneth
1973 The Philosophy of Literary Form. 3rd edition. Berkeley: University of California Press.

Connelly, John C.
1979 Hopi Social Organization. *In* Southwest. Alfonso Ortiz, ed. Pp. 539–553. Handbook of North American Indians, vol. 9. William C. Sturtevant, gen. ed. Washington, D.C: Smithsonian Institution.

Crown, Patricia L.
1994 Ceramics and Ideology: Salado Polychrome Pottery. Albuquerque: University of New Mexico Press.

Cummings, Byron
1940 Kinishba: A Prehistoric Pueblo of the Great Pueblo Period. Tucson: Hohokam Museums Association and University of Arizona.

Cushing, Frank Hamilton
1979 My Adventures in Zuñi. *In* Zuñi: Selected Writings by Frank Hamilton Cushing. Jesse Green, ed. Pp. 46–134. Lincoln: University of Nebraska Press.

Di Peso, Charles C.
1950 Painted Stone Slabs of Point of Pines, Arizona. American Antiquity 16(1):57–65.

Dockstader, Frederick J.
1979 Hopi History, 1850–1940. In *Southwest.* Alfonso Ortiz, ed. Pp. 524–532. Handbook of North American Indians, vol. 9. William C. Sturtevant, gen. ed. Washington, D.C: Smithsonian Institution.

Eggan, Fred
1950 Social Organization of the Western Pueblos. Chicago: University of Chicago Press.
1994 The Hopi Cosmology or World-View. *In* Kachinas in the Pueblo World. Polly Schafsmaa, ed. Pp. 7–16. Albuquerque: University of New Mexico Press.

Ferguson, T. J.
1989 Comment on Social Integration and Anasazi Architecture. *In* The Architecture of Social Integration. William D. Lipe and Michelle Hegmon, eds.

Pp.169–173. Occasional Paper of the Crow Canyon Archaeological Center, 1. Cortez: Crow Canyon Archaeological Center.

Fewkes, Jesse W.

1894 The Walpi Flute Observance: A Study of Primitive Dramatization. Journal of American Folklore 7(27):265–288.

1896 The Prehistoric Culture of Tusayan. American Anthropologist 9:151–173.

1900 A Theatrical Performance at Walpi. Washington Academy of Sciences Proceedings, vol. 2, no. 33. Washington, D.C: Academy of Sciences.

1902 Tusayan Migration Traditions. Annual Report of the Bureau of Ethnology, 19. Washington, D.C.: Smithsonian Institution.

1919 Prehistoric Villages, Castles, and Towers of Southwestern Colorado. Bureau of American Ethnology Bulletin, 70. Washington, D.C.: Smithsonian Institution.

Gerald, M. Virginia

1957 Two Great Kivas at Point of Pines Ruin. M.A. thesis, Department of Anthropology, University of Arizona.

Gill, Sam D.

1977 Hopi Kachina Cult Initiation: The Shocking Beginning to the Hopi's Religious Life. Journal of the American Academy of Religion, Supplement 2:447–464.

Goffman, Erving

1959 The Presentation of Self in Everyday Life. Garden City, N.Y.: Doubleday.

1967 Interaction Ritual. Garden City, N.Y.: Doubleday.

Haury, Emil W.

1950 A Sequence of Great Kivas in the Forestdale Valley. *In* For the Dean: Essays in Anthropology in Honor of Byron Cummings on his Eighty-Ninth Birthday, September 20, 1950. Erik K. Reed and Dale S. King, eds. Pp. 29–39. Tucson: Hohokam Museums Association.

1985 Mogollon Culture in the Forestdale Valley, East-Central Arizona. Tucson: University of Arizona Press.

Hays, Kelly A.

1994 Kachina Depictions on Prehistoric Pueblo Pottery. *In* Kachinas in the Pueblo World. Polly Schafsmaa, ed. Pp. 47–62. Albuquerque: University of New Mexico Press.

Hieb, Louis A.

1979 Hopi World View. *In* Southwest. Alfonso Ortiz, ed. Pp. 577–580. Handbook of North American Indians, vol. 9. William C. Sturtevant, gen. ed. Washington, D.C.: Smithsonian Institution.

Hopi Dictionary

1998 Hopi Dictionary = Hopìikwa Lavàytutuveni: A Hopi-English Dictionary of the Third Mesa Dialect. Compiled by the Hopi Dictionary Project, Bureau of Applied Research in Anthropology, University of Arizona. Tucson: University of Arizona Press.

Hough, Walter

1900 The Moki Snake Dance. Passenger Department, the Santa Fe Route.

Kidder, Alfred V.

1932 The Artifacts of Pecos. Papers of the Phillips Academy Southwestern Expedition, 6. New Haven: Yale University Press.

Kroeber, Alfred L.

1917 Zuni Kin and Clan. Anthropological Papers of the American Museum of Natural History, vol. 18, pt. 2. Pp. 41–204. New York: American Museum of Natural History.

LeBlanc, Steven A.

1999 Prehistoric Warfare in the American Southwest. Salt Lake City: University of Utah Press.

Lekson, Stephen H.

1989 Kivas? *In* The Architecture of Social Integration. William D. Lipe and Michelle Hegmon, eds. Pp. 161–167. Occasional Papers of the Crow Canyon Archaeological Center, 1. Cortez: Crow Canyon Archaeological Center.

Lipe, William D.

1989 Social Scale of Mesa Verde Anasazi Kivas. *In* The Architecture of Social Integration. William D. Lipe and Michelle Hegmon, eds. Pp. 53–71. Occasional Paper of the Crow Canyon Archaeological Center, 1. Cortez: Crow Canyon Archaeological Center.

Lipe, William D., and Michelle Hegmon, eds.

1989 The Architecture of Social Integration. Occasional Papers of the Crow Canyon Archaeological Center, 1. Cortez: Crow Canyon Archaeological Center.

Lowell, Julie C.
1991 Prehistoric Households at Turkey Creek Pueblo, Arizona. Anthropological Papers of the University of Arizona, 54. Tucson: University of Arizona Press.

Parsons, Elsie Clews
1933 Hopi and Zuñi Ceremonialism. Memoirs of the American Anthropological Association, 39. Menasha: American Anthropological Association.
1939 Pueblo Indian Religion. Chicago: University of Chicago Press.

Plog, Stephen
1995 Equality and Hierarchy: Holistic Approaches to Understanding Social Dynamics in the Pueblo Southwest. *In* Foundations of Social Inequality. T. Douglas Price and Gary M. Feinman, eds. Pp. 189–206. New York: Plenum.

Plog, Stephen, and Julie Solometo
1996 Alternative Pathways in the Evaluation of Western Pueblo Ritual. *In* Debating Complexity: Proceedings of the 26th Annual Chacmool Conference. Daniel A. Mayer, Peter C. Dawson, and Donald T. Hanna, eds. Pp. 326–332. Calgary: Archaeological Association and the Department of Anthropology, University of Calgary.

Potter, James M.
1996 The Structure of Open Space in Late Prehistoric Settlements in the Southwest. *In* Migration and Reorganization: The Pueblo IV Period in the American Southwest. Katherine A. Spielmann, ed. Pp. 137–164. Arizona State University Anthropological Research Papers, 15. Tempe: Arizona State University.

Potter, James M., and Elizabeth M. Perry
2000 Ritual as a Power Resource in the American Southwest. *In* Alternative Leadership Strategies in the Prehispanic Southwest. Barbara J. Mills, ed. Pp. 60–78. Tucson: University of Arizona Press.

Reid, J. Jefferson, and Izumi Shimada
1982 Pueblo Growth at Grasshopper: Methods and Models. *In* Multidisciplinary Research at Grasshopper Pueblo, Arizona. William A. Longacre, Sally J. Holbrook, and Michael W. Graves, eds. Pp. 12–18. Anthropological Papers of the University of Arizona, 40. Tucson: University of Arizona Press.

Reid, J. Jefferson, and Stephanie M. Whittlesey
1982 Households at Grasshopper Pueblo. American Behavioral Scientist 25(6):687–703.

Rice, Glenn E., and Steven A. LeBlanc, eds.
2001 Deadly Landscapes: Case Studies in Prehistoric Southwestern Warfare. Tucson: University of Arizona Press.

Riggs, Charles R.
2001 The Architecture of Grasshopper Pueblo. Salt Lake City: University of Utah Press.

Sanner, Hans-Ulrich
1995 Kachina Coding: Ritual Humor as Ritual Metacommunication. European Review of Native American Studies 9(1):9–14.

Schafsmaa, Polly, ed.
1994 Kachinas in the Pueblo World. Albuquerque: University of New Mexico Press.

Sekaquaptewa, Emory
1976 Hopi Indian Ceremonies. *In* Seeing with a Native Eye: Essays on Native American Religion. Walter H. Capps and Åke Hultkrantz, eds. Pp. 35–43. New York: Harper & Row.

Simmons, Leo W., ed.
1942 Sun Chief: The Autobiography of a Hopi Indian. New Haven: Yale University Press.

Smith, Watson
1952 Kiva Mural Decorations at Awatowi and Kawaika-a. Papers of the Peabody Museum of Archaeology and Ethnology, 38. Cambridge: Harvard University.

Smith, Watson
1990 When Is a Kiva? *In* When Is a Kiva? And Other Questions about Southwestern Archaeology. Raymond H. Thompson, ed. Pp. 59–75. Tucson: University of Arizona Press.

Spielmann, Katherine A., ed.
1998 Migration and Reorganization: The Pueblo IV Period in the American Southwest. Arizona State University Anthropological Research Papers, 15. Tempe: Arizona State University.

Stephen, Alexander M.
1940 Hopi Indians of Arizona. Southwest Museum Leaflets, 14. Los Angeles: Southwest Museum.

Stevenson, Matilda C.
1904 The Zuñi Indians: Their Mythology, Esoteric Fraternities, and Ceremonies. Annual Report of the Bureau of American Ethnology, 23. Washington, D.C.: Smithsonian Institution.

Tambiah, Stanley J.
1985 Culture, Thought, and Social Action: An Anthropological Perspective. Cambridge: Harvard University Press.

Tedlock, Dennis
1979 Zuni Religion and World View. *In* Southwest. Alfonso Ortiz, ed. Pp. 499–508. Handbook of North American Indians, vol. 9. William C. Sturtevant, gen. ed. Washington, D.C.: Smithsonian Institution.

Titiev, Mischa
1944 Old Oraibi: A Study of the Hopi Indians of Third Mesa. Papers of the Peabody Museum of American Archaeology and Ethnology, vol. 22, no. 1. Cambridge: Harvard University.

Triadan, Daniela
1997 Ceramic Commodities and Common Containers: Production and Distribution of White Mountain Red Ware in the Grasshopper Region, Arizona. Anthropological Papers of the University of Arizona, 61. Tucson: University of Arizona Press.

Triadan, Daniela, Barbara J. Mills, and Andrew I. Duff
2002 From Compositional to Anthropological: 14th Century Red Ware Circulation and Its Implications for Pueblo Reorganization. *In* Ceramic Production and Circulations in the Greater Southwest: Source Determination by INAA and Complementary Mineralogical Investigations. Donna M. Glowacki and Hector Neff, eds. Pp. 85–97. The Cotsen Institute of Archaeology, Monograph 44. Los Angeles: University of California.

Turner, Victor
1969 The Ritual Process: Structure and Anti-Structure. Ithaca, N.Y.: Cornell University Press.

Udall, Sharyn R.
1996 The Irresistible Other: Hopi Ritual Drama and Euro-American Audiences. *In* Contested Terrain: Myth and Meaning in Southwestern Art. Pp. 43–67. Albuquerque: University of New Mexico Press.

Upham, Steadman
1982 Polities and Power: An Economic and Political History of the Western Pueblo. New York: Academic.
1987 The Tyranny of Ethnographic Analogy in Southwestern Archaeology. *In* Coasts, Plains, and Deserts: Papers in Honor of Reynold J. Ruppé. Sylvia W. Gaines, ed. Pp. 265–281. Arizona State University Anthropological Research Papers, 18. Tempe: Arizona State University.

Vivian, Gordon, and Paul Reiter
1960 The Great Kivas of Chaco Canyon and Their Relationships. School of American Research Monographs, 22. Santa Fe: School of American Research.

Vivian, Patricia
1994 Anthropomorphic Figures in the Pottery Mound Murals. *In* Kachinas in the Pueblo World. Polly Schafsmaa, ed. Pp. 81–91. Albuquerque: University of New Mexico Press.

Walker, William H.
1995 Ritual Prehistory: A Pueblo Case Study. Ph.D. dissertation, Department of Anthropology, University of Arizona, Tucson.

Walker, William H., and Lisa J. Lucero
2000 The Depositional History of Ritual and Power. *In* Agency in Archaeology. Marcia-Anne Dobres and John Robb, eds. Pp. 130–147. New York: Routledge.

Whiteley, Peter M.
1988 Deliberate Acts: Changing Hopi Culture through the Oraibi Split. Tucson: University of Arizona Press.

Wright, Barton
1994 The Changing Kachina. *In* Kachinas in the Pueblo World. Polly Schafsmaa, ed. Pp. 139–145. Albuquerque: University of New Mexico Press.

Wright, Barton, Marnie Gaede, and Marc Gaede
1986 The Hopi Photographs: Kate Cory, 1905–1912. La Cañada, California: Chaco.

SCENE 7

POLITICS AND THEATRICALITY IN MAYAN SOCIETY

Takeshi Inomata

In this chapter I examine political implications of theatrical events in Classic Maya society, particularly in relation to the integration of a community and to the creation, maintenance, and subversion of political power. Although there probably coexisted multiple types of communities in Classic Maya society, including small local groups and those based on kinship relations, the main concern of this chapter is a community consisting of the ruler, the royal court, and their subject population, which may have corresponded roughly to a polity. However, I am not assuming that there existed well-integrated polities with which individual members strongly identified. The degree and mode of integration and the configurations of identities should be examined through the analysis of data. In this regard, the question of community integration at this level leads directly to the other theme of this chapter: power relations among community members. A community involved schisms, conflicts, and negotiations among individuals and groups in different dispositions and with different resources.

This chapter primarily focuses on the Classic period (A.D. 250–950), though there is evidence that theatrical performance was a critical element of Maya lives throughout its history from Preclassic (1000 B.C.–A.D. 205) to Classic, Postclassic (A.D. 950–1520), and postconquest times. The analysis of theatrical space and images of performance provide important data for this inquiry. The use of spaces, however, could have been highly flexible, and spatial settings alone do not determine the specifics of theatrical performance. To remedy such uncertainties in archaeological data, I also examine historical documents from the colonial period that offer vivid descriptions of theatrical events. One must be cautious in using textual data in this manner because the nature and social contexts of theatrical events certainly changed through time. Admittedly, the understanding of this diachronic aspect remains highly challenging because of differences in the nature and quality of data available from those periods. Although colonial documents describe certain specifics of performance not available in Classic period data, spatial settings in the colonial period were rapidly transforming through the construction of churches facing plazas and through the Spanish policy of *congregación,* which forced indigenous populations to aggregate in towns. Despite this problem, I believe that a sensible comparison of Classic and colonial data helps us set a stepping-stone for the promising field of Maya spectacles and performance.

Theater, Power, and Meaning

My focus on the community and power relations at the polity level does not imply that public performance is unique to large-scale societies or that power relations do not operate at the level of intimate, daily practices, as Hodder (this volume) criticizes. On the contrary, our argument in the introductory chapter (Inomata and Coben, this volume) is that the imposition, maintenance, and subversion of power through performance take place on every scale and in diverse contexts. A starting assumption that we had in mind as we planned this edited volume was that public events that commonly occur in small-scale societies also play critical roles in various other societies, including modern nation-states.

Hodder also criticizes our focus on community-wide power relations by claiming that disciplinary mechanisms operated on small scales. Again, our intention is not to negate such processes in daily practice. In any society, "disciplining" prevalently occurs in interactions at home, school, and workplace, both through conscious discursive processes and through less conscious bodily practices. A critical insight of Michel Foucault (1977), nonetheless, is that an analogous yet different process of discipline may take place even on a society-wide scale exceeding circles of daily, personal interactions. Some archaeologists have emphasized new "inventions" of states and complex societies, such as bureaucracy and other forms of administrative institution. By focusing on the nexus of theater and power, I wish to explore the operation of the state rooted in more fundamental aspects of human existence that are found in both small- and large-scale societies and both in daily lives and on special occasions. Such basic aspects include bodily practices and direct interactions through performing, viewing, and hearing.

Still, the nature of power that operates at the level of the state is different from that found among a small number of individuals sustaining constant face-to-face interactions. Living in a state or other forms of large community is something our Paleolithic ancestors never experienced. The creation and maintenance of such communities, even at the level of Çatalhöyük, cannot be taken for granted. Claiming the existence of disciplinary mechanism on a small scale does not explain the persistence of cohesion and order on a broader scale. Our effort in addressing this issue is always burdened by our experience of living in modern nation-states. The shared identity and order of a modern state are maintained partly through the development in communication systems, such as printed media, as Benedict Anderson (1991) has suggested, and in society-wide disciplinary mechanisms, as Foucault (1977) has argued. In many premodern states, such technologies and devices did not exist or were not fully developed.

This observation leads us to inquire about the potential of such events as feasts, rituals, and construction projects that physically bring people together beyond the daily circles of interactions. In this chapter, I argue that in Classic Maya society, in particular, mass spectacles constituted a key mechanism for the cohesion of polities and for the imposition and subversion of power. However, I do not mean to indicate a clear division between premodern states and modern ones. Such events and performance continue to have critical social implications and consequences today (Handelman 1990; Kertzer 1988).

Nor do I privilege what we may call the public over the domestic or the extraordinary over the ordinary, as Hodder criticizes. The division between the public and the domestic is often problematic (see Inomata and Houston 2001; Inomata et al. 2002 for discussion of intersections of so-called public and domestic spheres). Yet certain forms of interactions, such as mass rituals and festivals, do have qualities different from household-level affairs. We still need to use the terms "public" and "domestic" in a heuristic manner to explore these issues. A similar argument applies to the question of the extraordinary and the ordinary. Human life, as perceived and experienced by each agent, whether in small societies or large ones, is filled with drastically different qualities of time, space, and events (Bradley 1998:85–100). We will not understand human culture and society without examining both constant rhythms of daily life and unique moments in which routine practices are disrupted and subverted.

Hodder also misunderstands our discussion on meaning and action in the introductory chapter. Our main intention is to criticize the approach that dichotomizes meaning and action and that assumes the preexistence of meaning leading to subsequent acts. We argue that in theatrical events, as well as in any social processes, the ideational domain of thought, meaning, and ideology is inseparably intertwined with the physical domain of behavior and of the materiality of human bodies, objects, and the environment. Not only is performance shaped by thoughts of individuals and meanings shared among participants, but such acts, through interactions with other participants, objects, and the surrounding settings, define and impose meanings and values (Bell 1992, 1997:72–83; Tambiah 1981).

Our intention, then, is not to ignore or underestimate the meaning of events and performance. On the contrary, we argue that one needs to confront the complex nature of meaning seriously. Archaeologists often have to rely on similarities or associations in shapes, orientations, and locations in extracting meaning, including the example of Stonehenge that Hodder mentions. We cannot assume that such superficial meanings always have important political implications. Does the shape of the Washington Monument, which invokes a relation to Egyptian obelisks, matter to most Americans who visit there? Certainly the importance of the Washington Monument derives partly from the historical narratives attached to it. We, however, cannot assume that historical narratives associated with places, objects, and events are always shared by most members of the society. For example, millions of Japanese visit Shinto shrines, which encompass various sacred places, buildings, objects, as well as historical narratives accumulated, in some cases, over a thousand years. Yet significant numbers of Japanese who visit these places are ignorant of much of their intricate symbolism and dense narratives.

More importantly, there exist numerous layers of meaning. Recently there has been much criticism of the tyranny of "culture," which gives us an illusion that a homogeneous, consistent system of meaning is shared by all members of a society (Abu-Lughod 1991; Appadurai 1996:12; Friedman 1994:207). At deeper levels underneath collectively held superficial meaning, symbolic acts and objects never signify the same thing to people of different social backgrounds (Turner 1967:50). Such meaning at deeper levels is often closely tied to the identity and emotions, such as joy, sadness, admiration, and hatred, of each individual, and may sometimes be more important than collectively held meaning in terms of political dynamics. Giving primacy to archaeologically recoverable, superficial meaning may be at times as misleading as ignoring the importance of meaning.

Whereas collectively held meaning, such as the association of Stonehenge with the summer solstice, may exist apart from people's acts, deeper meanings held by different individuals are always tied to their actions and experience. Such meanings are constantly generated and reworked by each individual through his or her actions. It is overly optimistic to try to recover a full account of diverse meanings. Some of them are so vague, inconsistent, and fleeting that even a member of the society may not be able to articulate them. Search for deep meanings sometimes results in impositions of the researcher's own preconceived narratives.

Also related is the performative aspect of ritual and other theatrical events. Ritual with strict protocol holds participants in a formalized situation that allows no options to challenge authority except by its total refusal. In this sense, ritual imposes a certain type of power relations among participants not by transmitting specific messages but by the formalism of its acts (Bloch 1974:59–60; see Inomata and Coben, this volume, for more detailed discussion). Given this defining force of the form of performance, as opposed to the ambiguity in its symbolic contents, a productive approach may be to examine how theatrical events shape social relations among participants, in what contexts such symbolic acts become meaningful, and how dominant ideologies are imposed, resisted, and subverted, rather than asking what performance specifically means (see Wuthnow 1987:332–344). This approach compels us to pay closer attention to the forms and physical qualities of theatrical events, including the problems of who participated and how they interacted.

Theatrical Events during the Colonial Period

> Here comes the important *holpop*. . . .
> Also the Lord Ahau Can Pech. . . .
> The drum and conch shell horn sound . . .
> Then they go dancing to the *popol nah* where the Lord Ahau Can is.
> There also is the *holpop* . . .
> The musicians, singers, comedians, dancers, contortionists, hunchbacks, and spectators have come.
> All the people have come following the Lord Ahau Can for the festivity that will take place in the middle of the plaza of our town. . . .
> Let's gather in the town.

This extract from the Songs of Dzitbalché (Barrera Vásquez 1965) from the colonial period Campeche in the northern Maya lowlands touches on the important themes of this chapter.[1] Spectacles were important events for a community, involving various performers and numerous spectators; they were viewed not only as religious duties but as entertainments; the ruler and other elites, particularly the officer called *holpop*, played central roles on those occasions; and performances took place in the plaza of the town, as well as in front of a council house called *popol nah*.

Other documentary sources also point to the importance of community festivals. Bishop Landa (Tozzer 1941:147), who recorded Maya practices in the northern lowlands during the early sixteenth century before significant Spanish influence was introduced, suggested that festivals and ceremonies were the primary concerns and obligations of all community members. The Relación de Campocolche (Relaciones de Yucatán, 1900:2:185) notes that for the Maya public dances were extremely important.[2] Ciudad Real (1976:2:314–371), who traveled Mexico and Central America accompanying the commissary Alonso Ponce in the late sixteenth century, mentioned festive receptions with music and dances that they received at various towns during their tour, but such descriptions are particularly notable in their visit to Yucatán. These documents show that theatrical events were important for the colonial period Maya.

Participants and Spatial Settings

Many colonial period theatrical events were religious ceremonies and rites scheduled for various times of the year according to their calendars, but others took place on special occasions, such as visits of foreign dignitaries, as experienced by Ciudad Real. Dances and music were central elements in many public events. Performers were often elaborately dressed, and some events involved dancers dressed as animals (Gage 1958:243–245). Many dances may have represented mythical themes, such as the dance of Xibalba (underworld) (Tozzer 1941:147) and the acts of the Hero Twins that paralleled descriptions in the K'iche' myth of Popol Vuh (Estrada Monroy 1979:168–174). In addition, there were probably events that enacted historical tales, as seen in Rabinal Achí.[3]

Some theatrical events involved a large number of participants. According to Bishop Landa (Tozzer 1941:94), eight hundred men danced together with everybody keeping the rhythm, and food and drink were brought to performers, who kept dancing the whole day. This description suggests that the event involved a large number of people beyond the dancers, including those who prepared food and viewed the performance. Landa (Tozzer 1941:152) wrote that for the new year ceremony all men and old women—but not younger women—assembled in the plaza. Another remarkable event described by him (Tozzer 1941:158–159) is a ceremony that took place in the month of Mol, in which all boys and girls of the town were assembled. The Relación de Campocolche (Relaciones de Yucatán, 1900:2:185) tells us that for some dances more than 1,500 people gathered with some participants coming from places as far as thirty leagues away. In the Guatemalan highlands, for the foundation ceremony of the town of San Juan Chamelco, the plaza was filled with thousands of people (Estrada Monroy 1979:168–174). Although it is impossible to tell how accurate these figures mentioned in the documents are, they at least show that a large number of people, in some cases a significant portion of a community and beyond, participated in such events. Some dances, however, involved only certain sections of the population, such as men and old women.

Certain ceremonies and festivals were not only important events for a community but also diplomatic occasions that involved visitors from other towns. For example, in Yucatán all priests and lords, as well as large numbers of people from various towns, assembled in Mani for a ceremony in the month of Xul (Tozzer 1941:158). Diego Lopéz de Cogolludo (1971:1:296), who stayed in Yucatán during the early seventeenth century, wrote that chiefs from various towns gathered and exchanged hospitality and gifts for the festival of the patron saint of a town.

Many large theatrical events took place in public plazas, as indicated by the Songs of Dzitbalché (see also Ringle and Bey 2001:275; Restall 2001:344–345). Landa (Tozzer 1941:152) described the fire ceremony conducted in the new year in the plaza in front of temples. There were also large ceremonies held outside of the core areas of settlements. According to Landa (Tozzer 1941:147), before the beginning of a year that started with the day Kawak, people danced on a causeway, or plaza connected by a causeway, outside of the town center. The festive reception that Ciudad Real (1976:2:314–371) and the commissary Alonso Ponce enjoyed at each Yucatán town appears to have taken place first outside of the town and then was moved to the plaza.

Although most documents do not describe theatrical settings of such events, certain information can be gleaned. In the dances and ceremonies described by Landa and in the Songs of Dzitbalché, performers appear to have occupied the floor of the plaza. For a new year's ceremony, Landa (Tozzer 1941:152) specifically noted that the priest sat in the middle of the plaza. The location of the audience is in most cases unclear, but for certain ceremonies seats for elite spectators were constructed in the plaza. In the foundation ceremony of San Juan Chamelco, the lord sat on a throne surrounded by ceramic vessels filled with flowers, and some spectators appear to have occupied wooden platforms or structures built specifically for this event, surrounding the dance space in the middle of the plaza (Estrada Monroy 1979:168–174). In some events, high temples facing the plaza probably served as theatrical stages. Landa (Tozzer 1941:119) described sacrificial ceremonies, in which victims were killed on top of temples and their bodies were thrown down the steps. In these cases, a large audience probably occupied the plaza floor below.

Many theatrical events involved the construction of temporary structures as parts of theatrical settings. For the fire-walking ceremony of the new year, for example, a large arch of wood was constructed in the plaza (Tozzer 1941:148–149). Ciudad Real (1976:2:314–371) noted that at each town the residents constructed ramadas for the reception of the commissary. Although it is not clear whether the construction of such temporary structures reflects pre-Hispanic practices or followed instructions from Spanish friars, some constructions at least appear to show some indigenous elements.[4] Ciudad Real made particular mention of one ramada, on which a large figure of a monster was placed, and of other structures providing high stages for singers.

Some stage sets gave unique theatrical effects. In the foundation ceremony of San Juan Chamelco, after a large amount of wood was burned in the plaza during a dramatic dance, performers appeared from the ground to the amazement of Spanish friars (Estrada Monroy 1979:168–174).[5] Ciudad Real (1976:2:327; Tozzer 1941:94) was impressed with the litters used in the reception at the town of Kantunil. On top of each litter was an elaborately dressed performer standing in a tower-like frame decorated with painted cotton and flags.

Politics of Theatrical Performance

The social, political, and economic importance of theatrical events derived from, and was reflected in, the significant investment of time and effort for their preparation. Thomas Gage (1958:243), who stayed in the Guatemalan highlands in the early seventeenth century, noted that the highland Maya prepared for dances for two or three months and during this period the silence of the night was broken with their practices of songs, instruments, and dances. Moreover, theatrical events usually involved feasts, in which a large amount of food, including turkeys grown over a year with much care, was consumed in one day (Cogolludo 1971:1:243, 295). Comparable investments of time, energy, and materials for the preparation of important fiestas can also be seen among the modern highland Maya (Gossen 1986; Vogt 1969:520–567).

The rehearsal and logistical organization of theatrical events appear to have been important work of elites. Gage (1958:243) wrote that for each kind of dance several houses and masters were appointed for practice. In Yucatán the preparation of such events was primarily the responsibility of an officer called *holpop*. According to Cogolludo (1971:1:243), the *holpop* was a principal singer who set the key, taught others, was entrusted with various musical instruments, and was a venerated figure who had important roles in religious affairs, at feasts, and in assemblies. Ethnohistorian Ralph Roys (1939, 1943:63) has noted that the *holpop* was not only in charge of ceremonial affairs but also an important administrative officer, through whom the ruler—*halach uinic*—and chiefs—*batab*—governed the people of a town and through whom the people negotiated with the lord. The Motul dictionary (Martínez Hernández 1929) from the colonial period listed *holpop* as the head of the banquet and the master of the *popol nah.* The *popol nah*, which means a mat house in a direct translation, was a council house where political matters were discussed and dances were prepared. As the Songs of Dzitbalché describe, areas in front of these buildings were also stages for certain dances and festivals, which may have been more exclusive ones than those held in public plazas. These functions of the *holpop* and the *popol nah* suggest that festivity and administration merged inseparably in the Maya concept and practice. The convergence of theatrical performance and administration can also be reflected by the roles of the ruler and elites, who were central figures in many theatrical events. Gage (1958:245), for example, wrote that the important dance called *toncontin* was danced only by the chief and principals of the town.

Although theatrical events were often marked with joyous entertainment, the preparation for such occasions heavily comprised spiritual elements, and the participants needed to maintain purity through fast and abstinence before the ceremonies (Tozzer 1941:158). Although there must have been individuals who were disinterested or opposed to collectively defined ritual practices, these ceremonies involved a certain level of social control that demanded the compliance of most community members. Bernardo de Lizana (1988:59), who stayed in Yucatán in the early seventeenth century, wrote that the Maya were highly observant of their rituals and ceremonies, and those who did not follow them were severely punished by priests of their indigenous religion. Interestingly, Bernardo de Lizana commented that those priests were crueler than rulers. The devotion of the Maya to their traditional rituals probably appeared particularly strong in the eyes of the Spaniards who met the resistance of the Maya as they attempted to abolish pagan practices. Even when their performances took the appearance of Christian dramas, the serious commitment of the Maya to whatever ceremonies they engaged in impressed some European friars. Gage (1958:246–247) wrote about the dramas of the execution of Christian saints played by the Maya, which appears to have reflected their pre-Columbian sacrificial practices. According to Gage, "Most of the Indians who take part in this dance are superstitious about what they have done, and they seem almost to believe that they have actually done what they only performed for the dance." Thus those who acted St. Peter or

John the Baptist said that they must remain holy and pure like the saints and must prepare themselves to die. Those who acted Herod or Herodias desired absolution from the blood guilt they played in the dramas.

Ceremonies and festivals were the time in which diversions from the normal codes of conduct were allowed. Various historical sources, including Relación de Campocolche (Relación de Yucatán 1900:2:185), Gage (1958:243), Cogolludo (1971:1:243) and Landa (Tozzer 1941:91), noted that ceremonies often involved heavy drinking and the town was full of drunks. The Songs of Dzitbalché and Landa's (Tozzer 1941:158; see also Acuña 1978) descriptions suggest that comedians who played in farces and historical tales were important parts of festivals. These figures were not only entertainers but also critical social commentators. Cogolludo (1971:1:243; see also Miller and Taube 1993:63) noted that comedians called *baldzam* criticized officials in their faces. Like modern Maya ritual humors discussed by Bricker (1973), colonial period farces and comedians may also have functioned as a way of social control by ridiculing those who diverge from social codes.

Although theatrical events during the colonial period appear to have maintained significant continuity from pre-Hispanic times, practices of the postconquest Maya, however, cannot be understood in a broader political context of the colonial regime. Gage (1958:242) wrote that despite their suffering under Spanish rule the Maya remained cheerful and dedicated to feasting, sporting, and dancing. It is probable that theatrical events were occasions on which the Maya reaffirmed their cultural identity. As ethnohistorian Nancy Farriss (1984:339) has noted, festivals that brought everyone together were crucial for the social and cultural survival of the Maya under the Spanish oppression.

Theatrical Events during the Classic Period

Mass Spectacle

Like their colonial period descendants, the Classic Maya engaged in diverse types of performance in various spatial contexts, including large, open areas for mass spectacles and more restricted spaces for elite interactions. Stelae and other stone monuments in plazas commonly depict dances and other theatrical performances of rulers and other elites, suggesting that

Figure 7.1. View of the Plaza of Copán, which Contains Numerous Stelas

these spaces were used for theatrical performance (Fig. 7.1) (Grube 1992; Looper 2001). William Ringle and George Bey (2001:279) have argued that "rather than being the by-product of building placement, the plaza instead may be seen as a socially and ritually charged field *about which* buildings were built. In other words, such spaces are owed primacy in understanding site layouts."

Large plazas were probably used flexibly, and various permanent and temporary settings enhanced theatrical effects. On many occasions, the central part of a plaza appears to have served as a stage for performance by a large number of actors and dancers, as in colonial period events. Spectators probably occupied the surrounding areas, including the terraces and steps along the edges of the plaza. At the northern centers of Chichén Itzá and Uxmal, among others, low square platforms were placed in large plazas. The association of thrones with these platforms suggests that leaders sat on the platforms to address large audiences who filled the plazas (Ringle and Bey 2001:277; see also Kowalski 1987). A potential problem of theatrical events using the center of a plaza as a stage is that performers may not have been clearly visible if the flat area was filled with a large audience. The use of temporary stages and sets may have mitigated this difficulty. Some images from the Classic period depict wooden scaffolds with sacrificial victims (Taube 1988). Charles Suhler and David Freidel (2000) suggest that the postholes found in the Great Plaza of Tikal in front of structure 5D-33-2nd resulted from the construction of a wooden scaffold (Coe 1990:518–521, fig. 168B). The use of these temporary settings parallels those of the colonial period. Sacrificial victims tied to wooden scaffolds and performers occupying elevated stages were clearly visible to spectators standing or sitting in the plaza. Another way to enhance the visibility of actors was the use of litters. Lintels of Tikal, as well as some graffiti, show rulers or other elites carried on palanquins (Chase and Chase 2001b: fig. 4.12; Harrison 1999:133, 153, figs. 77, 94; Trik and Kampen 1983: figs. 71–73). These images remind us of descriptions by Ciudad Real, but some Classic period litters were even more impressive than colonial versions, with large statues of deities and jaguars towering behind the rulers.

On other occasions, the peripheral areas of a plaza or surrounding buildings served as primary stages, and audiences occupied the central part of the plaza. High temples that faced plazas, like those in colonial times, were also important theatrical stages. Rulers and other performers who climbed up the stairs of temples would have been highly visible. Even more important theatrical stages were wide stairways flanking plazas, which were common features at many Maya centers. Joyce Marcus (1974) has indicated that some stairways, including those at Dos Pilas and Tamarindito, exhibit sculptures of bound captives. Stela 12 of Piedras Negras depicts war captives placed on a stairway in front of the triumphant king and warriors. The murals of Bonampak clearly show that some wide stairways were used as stages for the presentation and torture of war captives, as well as for subsequent dances. Mary Miller (1986:115; Schele and Miller 1986:218) has identified the stairway depicted in the mural as the one on the southern end of the plaza of Bonampak, and has suggested that the use of stairway for captive presentations was common at other Maya centers as well. Similar scenes with captives placed in front of rulers and elites who occupied higher positions on stairways are also found in ceramic vase paintings (Fig. 7.2) (Reents-Budet 2001). Thus ample stairways were designed not only for access to the buildings but also for theatrical effects. They provided effective stages for presentations and performance, on which actors were highly visible to a large audience occupying the plazas in front of them. In other cases, they may have been used as seating areas for spectators.

Figure 7.2. Ceramic Vase Painting Depicting a Presentation of Captives in Front of a Wide Stairway. © Justin Kerr, File no. 767

The ways plazas and associated features were used imply that these theatrical events were indeed mass spectacles with numerous participants. Although spectators are not depicted in pictorial media, theatrical performance appears to have been designed as presentations to a large audience. At small centers with populations of 5,000 to 15,000, such as Quirigua and Aguateca, plazas were usually large enough to accommodate the entire population. As in colonial period ceremonies, a significant number of community members probably gathered in such plazas for important theatrical events. At larger centers, the situation may have been somewhat different. The larger the population of a center, the more difficult it was for the entire community to gather in one place. This problem must have been particularly serious at such centers as Tikal and Caracol that possessed populations of over 50,000 people. The Maya of these large centers appear to have made a serious effort to deal with this problem by building a series of plazas. Causeways connecting these plazas and other complexes may also have provided additional theatrical spaces (cf. Chase and Chase 2001a). Since streets serve as primary theatrical spaces in carnivals or other events in modern cities (Da Matta 1984), a large number of Classic Maya spectators may have lined the causeways to watch processions of performers.

Performance at Royal Courts

The Classic Maya engaged in theatrical performance in more exclusive courtly settings as well. At Copán, the East and West Courts located on the Acropolis built over the residences of Early Classic rulers (Sharer et al. 1999) were smaller and had more restricted access than the great plazas and the adjacent open spaces. Fash and others (1992) have identified Structure 10L-22A located northwest of the East Court as a *popol nah*, based on its association with mat motifs and stone carvings of possible toponyms referring to places in the Copán polity (see also Stomper 1996). They have also suggested that a low platform, Structure 10L-25, next to this building, was used as a dancing platform. Although the identification of this building as a *popol nah* needs to be further examined, the presence of a probable dancing platform in the courtly core of this center is highly significant, and is analogous to the references to dances at *popol nah* in various colonial documents.

At Aguateca, the patio of the Palace Group was most likely an important space for theatrical performance, although it was smaller and had

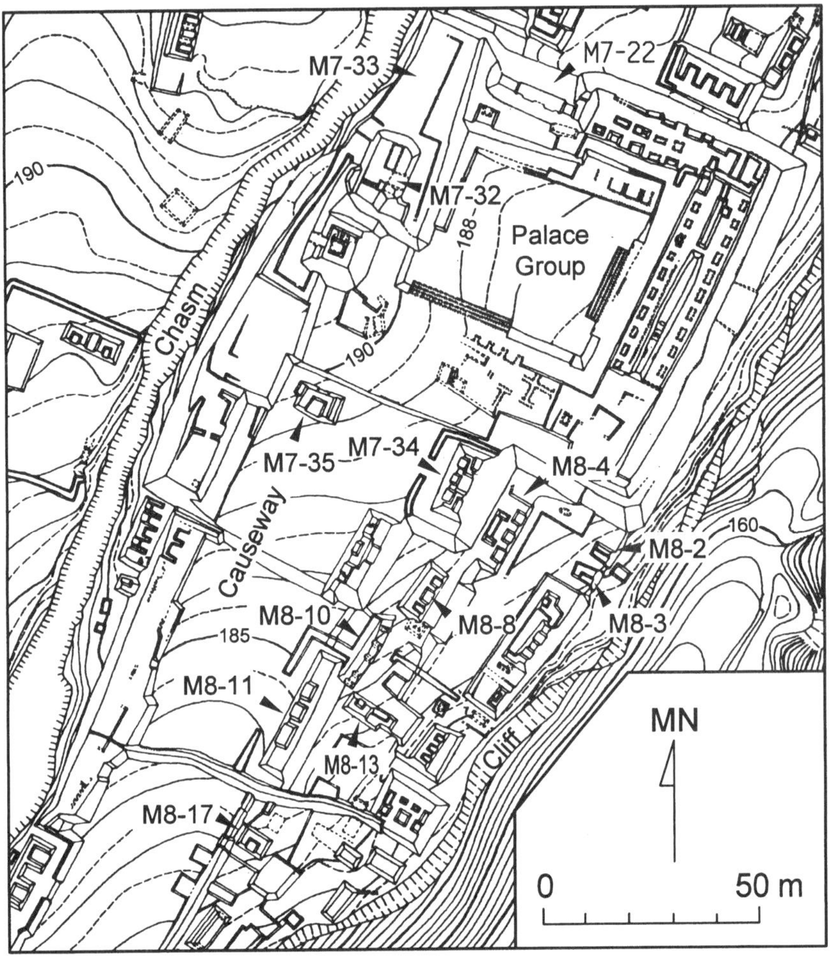

Figure 7.3. The Palace Group and the Elite Residential Area of Aguateca

more limited access than the Main Plaza (Fig. 7.3). Excavation results indicate that Structures M7-22 and M7-32 were primary living quarters of the royal family (Inomata et al. 2002). Unique finds of excavation were two benches without evidence of permanent roofs over them, one attached to the western exterior wall of Structure M7-22 and the other built against the northern exterior wall of Structure M7-32. The area in front of these outdoor benches was Structure M7-33. Although this low platform has not been excavated, a careful examination of its surface did not reveal any evidence of superstructures. Structure M7-33 may have been an open platform used for dancing, which could have been seen by individuals sitting on the outdoor benches of Structures M7-22 and M7-32. The possible dancing platforms at Copán and Aguateca attest to the importance of theatrical performance in courtly settings.

In addition to explicit theatrical performance of dances, various other courtly events, including diplomatic meetings and royal audiences, exhibited strong theatricality. Numerous ceramic paintings depict scenes of courtly gatherings, which most likely took place in royal palaces and elite residences (Fig. 7.4) (Reents-Budet 2001; Inomata 2001a, b; Inomata et al. 2002). These images were rendered from the point of view of an audience occupying areas in front of the meeting rooms. Maya residential buildings typically faced a patio that could house a moderate-size audience. The fact that many of these gatherings were depicted in ceramic paintings suggests that such diplomatic and political meetings needed to be witnessed.

Although these royal palaces and elite residences were substantially smaller than main plazas and their access was more limited, it remains unclear how exclusive such performances were. The descriptions in the Songs of Dzitbalché give an impression that a substantial number of people had access to the event that took place at the *popol nah*. In addition, the probable throne room at the center of Structure M7-22 of Aguateca was placed along the axis of the causeway, and those who stood in the northern part of the causeway could see the ruler sitting on this throne if there was enough light in the room (Inomata 2001a; Inomata et al. 2001). Thus the audiences and meetings that the ruler held in front of this throne room may have been visible to those who were not allowed into the Palace Group. At larger centers, however, the visibility of and access to courtly meetings in royal palaces were more limited. For example, the Central Acropolis of Tikal, which was probably the royal residential compound of this center, consisted of a complex arrangement of multiple patio groups, and its inner core was shielded from outside view (Harrison 1999). Meetings held in the royal quarters were exclusive, involving only the highest echelon of this community. Thus there appears to have been varying degrees of exclusivity for gatherings in courtly settings of different centers.

Figure 7.4. Painting on a Cylinder Vase Excavated at Aguateca. It Shows a Scene of a Meeting Held in a Room of an Elite Residence

Integration and Division through Performance in Classic Maya Society

The Integration of a Community

The Classic Maya polity was probably a relatively loose, fluid entity. Like their colonial counterparts documented in historical sources, Classic Maya farmers may have been highly mobile and may have changed their residences and political affiliations with relative ease (Inomata 2004). In addition, many goods, such as utilitarian ceramics, appear to have been exchanged through social networks between producers and consumers without significant political interventions from the central authority. Within a polity, there appear to have existed multiple production sources of utilitarian ceramics, each of which supplied materials for a fairly small area (Fry 1979; Rands and Bishop 1980; Rice 1987), though important goods such as obsidian may have been regulated by the elite within their spheres of control (Aoyama 1999; Inomata and Aoyama 1996). Thus the bureaucratic administrative system appears to have been relatively undeveloped, which may indicate that the territorial control by the central authority was relatively weak (Demarest 1992; Inomata 2001b; Sanders and Webster 1988; Tambiah 1976).

These data suggest that the Maya community at the polity level had a strong characteristic of a centripetal organization focused on the rulership rather than of a corporate group with clear boundaries. During the contact period, there existed patronymic groups that provided social networks crosscutting polities (Tozzer 1941:99). During the Classic period, when some polities were significantly larger than those of the contact period, kin groups and relatively small local groups may have been more important parts of identities of most Maya than the political affiliation to the polity imposed by the elite. Such kin and local groups, as well as informal social networks, may have worked as centrifugal forces that threatened the cohesion of a polity. The Classic Maya polity as an imagined community, then, may have occupied a relatively small place in the mind of each individual (Anderson 1991).

Although the Maya may have conducted daily life without considerable intervention from the central authorities, there existed various processes in which individuals were involved in polity-wide affairs, possibly including taxation by elites, the distribution of certain goods, the supply of water during dry seasons through centralized reservoirs, and service in military campaigns. I emphasize the importance of two types of occasions on which individuals directly sensed and witnessed the presence and operation of the polity-wide community—large-scale spectacles and grand construction projects. On those occasions, a significant part of a community congregated and worked together under the organization and supervision of elites. These events held according to the ritual calendars or between busy agricultural seasons gave regulating rhythm to the lives of the Classic Maya. It appears that securing effective theatrical spaces for mass spectacles was an important motivation for many construction projects. Laborers were probably well aware of the prospects of future theatrical pageants that would take place in these places. Such prospects of theatrical events, in addition to religious beliefs, may even have justified the enormous investment of labor and materials in these constructions.

Theatrical events in which the ruler and other elites were primary performers and sponsors may have served as centripetal forces that counteracted centrifugal tendencies of Maya polities. Mass spectacles gave the physical reality to a community through the bodily copresence of their members and helped ground precarious community identities on sensible physical forms through the use of symbolic acts and objects. Such theatrical events probably defined the boundary of a community, at least temporarily; those who gathered for spectacles made a community. Thus the cohesion of a Maya polity may have been rooted deeply in its aspect of a real, albeit temporal, community with its physical qualities. This implies that the continuation of its imagined moral unity required constant physical gatherings of its members.

Roles of Elites

The importance of public events for the integration of a community implies that the preparation, organization, and execution of such events were primary concerns for Classic Maya elites. The association of the *popol nah* with a dancing platform at Copán, as well as the presence of a probable dance platform in the royal palace complex of Aguateca, indicates the conceptual, practical, and spatial convergence of theatrical and administrative affairs. In addition, Ringle (1990:236–240) identifies the title of *holpop* in the inscription of Chichén Itzá, which suggests the presence of officers simultaneously responsible for festivals and administration, comparable to their colonial period counterparts.

The convergence of administrative and ceremonial functions can also be seen in archaeological evidence from Aguateca. Excavations have demonstrated that residences located along the causeway were burned and abandoned rapidly. The occupants of these buildings were courtiers of the highest rank, who were probably responsible for political affairs of the polity. Remarkable finds from these structures were abundant implements for scribal and artistic production (Inomata 2001c). Thus a significant portion of high courtiers was also scribe-artists who enjoyed both political power and cultural prestige (see also Coe 1977; Coe and Kerr 1997). Some ornaments elaborated by these scribe-artists were probably used by themselves or other elites. The most conspicuous evidence came from structure M8-4, which we nicknamed "the House of Mirrors." The residents of this structure were manufacturing pieces of pyrite ornaments recycled from mosaic pieces of pyrite mirrors, probably for the production of elaborate ceremonial attire. Adjacent to the worked pieces of pyrite, Daniela Triadan unearthed an alabaster ornament representing an image of the jester god. Diadems with images of the jester god were the symbols of rulership, although they may also have been used by other elites. It is probable that the high courtier who lived in the House of Mirrors was producing or refurbishing ceremonial attires for the ruler of Aguateca.

These elite residences contained numerous musical instruments, such as conch horns, ceramic flutes, ceramic whistles, ceramic drums, and bone rasps, suggesting that these political elites engaged in musical performances on various occasions. The multiple activities indicated by objects recovered from Aguateca elite residences parallel depictions of Hun Butz and Hun Choven in Popol Vuh. These simian figures were brothers of mythical cultural heroes and were at once scribes, artists, jewelers, and musicians. The prominence of theatrical and musical paraphernalia is also evident in royal residences. The sealed room of Structure M7-22 of the Palace Group contained such theatrical objects as ceramic drums and ceramic masks (Figs. 7.5 and 7.6). The ruler of Aguateca probably wore these masks on ceremonial occasions and played musical instruments. These Aguateca data remind us of the murals of Bonampak that vividly depict elites dancing in elaborate costumes and playing music (Miller 1986).

Figure 7.5. Ceramic Drums Found in the Storage Room of the Royal Palace of Aguateca

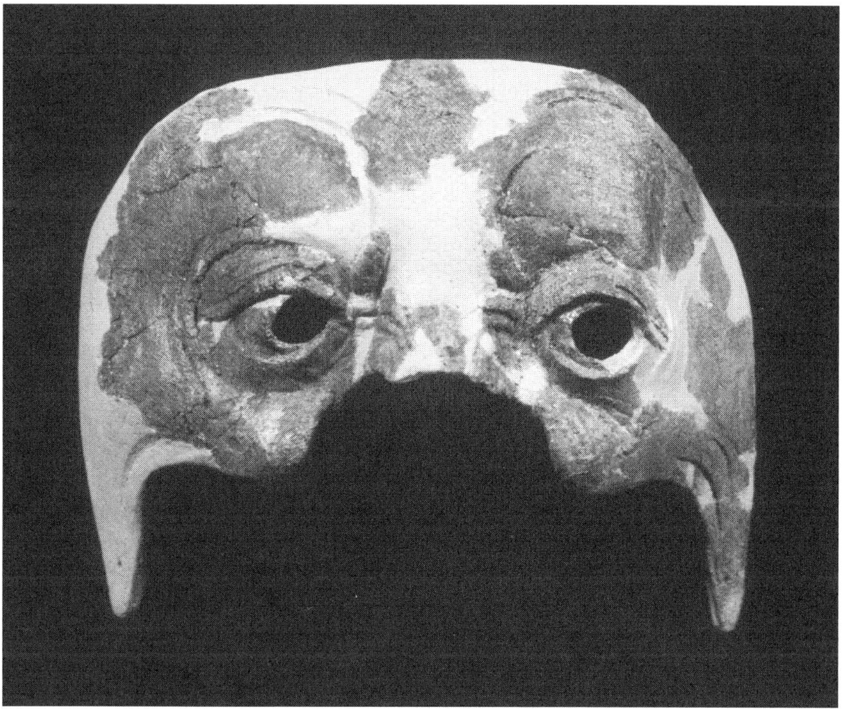

Figure 7.6. Ceramic Mask Found in the Storage Room of the Royal Palace of Aguateca (Conservation Work by Harriet Beaubien)

In Classic Maya society theatrical performance was not mere embellishment of underlying political mechanisms, but a critical part of politics in terms of the reality of social process and of the native perceptions (Geertz 1980). In addition, the organization of mass theatrical events probably ranked among the most important administrative work for Classic Maya elites. Administrative work associated with community rituals was not limited to dramaturgical supervision because mass spectacles involved the consumption of a large amount of food in feasts, the acquisition and elaboration of ceremonial gears, and the construction and preparation of theatrical spaces. In other words, theatrical events were among the most significant economic events in Maya society.

The Maintenance and Subversion of Power Relations

As in any societies, community rituals in Classic Maya society served, among other social functions, to define and maintain asymmetrical power relations. The sponsoring of major public events and performance on those occasions were opportunities for elites to assert their images as moral leaders of the community and the embodiments of community integration. They were opportunities for elites to take credit for the success of the community and the continuation of the cosmic order. Impersonation of deities and Hero Twins by rulers was a straightforward way to stress their divine status (Houston and Stuart 1996). Thus the display of the bodies of rulers and other elites, as well as their performance in front of many spectators, was the basis of their power (Foucault 1977:187). In addition, rituals taking place in spaces surrounded by dynastic monuments, such as stelae and funerary pyramids of former rulers, were constant remainders of the direct association of each community member with the dynastic regime, whether or not nonelite individuals were committed to the dominant ideologies.

Theatrical events, ranging from the most inclusive ceremonies held in public plazas to more exclusive events that took place in royal residential complexes, served to define various social categories and ranks through the right and duty of participation. It is common in many societies of the world that individuals' right to be in the spatial proximity of the ruler directly corresponds with their rank in the courtly order (Inomata 2001b). Social differentiation through varying access to theatrical events was probably not limited to the distinction between elites and nonelites. Colonial period examples show that public performance was primarily a male domain. Iconographic data suggests that Classic Maya women may have more actively taken central roles in theatrical events. Still, the right of participating in certain ceremonies and taking specific theatrical roles was probably defined through the divisions of gender and age groups.

As various colonial documents suggest, theatrical events were probably entertainments for many participants, which involved positive emotional elevation. The use of theatrical attractions for ideological campaigns may have been an effective strategy for elites. This, however, does not deny the presence of those who were disinterested in, reluctant to, or opposed to participating in community events. Nor is it likely that all community members blindly subscribed to the elite version of ideology (Scott 1990). As noted by Lizana for the colonial period, Classic Maya elites may have wielded coercive force to ensure the compliance of commoners. Yet more importantly, once such rituals had been institutionalized, they probably made deviations from prescribed patterns difficult (Bloch 1974:59–60).

Individuals do not have many choices but to comply with the protocols or to deny them totally and risk social rejection from peers or punishments from elites. When asked why they invest so much time, energy, and money in the festival, modern Chamula informants simply answered, "It is the custom. If we don't do it and do it properly, we will die" (Gossen 1986:247). While comprising potentials for the subversion of existing orders, this tendency of collective rituals toward conservatism possibly contributed significantly to the maintenance of the power structure of the Classic Maya polity.

The same restrictive force applied, probably even more strongly, to the ruler and other elites. Although elites had power to create ceremonial spaces and to impose specific forms of performance, at the very basic level they did not have other choices but to perform publicly and to sponsor theatrical events. Such acts were not only their right but also their duty. In this sense, elites were prisoners of their own tradition, which strongly emphasized ceremonialism. Important elements in certain public events were bloodletting rituals conducted by the ruler and other elites, as well as the sacrifice of elites captured from other polities. Although there is no evidence of regicide as seen in some African kingdoms (see the introductory chapter), these forms of sacrifice and mutilation of elites represent a related theme. Bloodletting was probably widely conducted by various segments of Classic Maya society, and the performance of bloodletting in public ritual, which involved severe pain and the risk of serious infection, was not so much the right of elites as their duty. Common practices of elite sacrifice meant that even the ruler of the most powerful center was not free from the risk of being captured and sacrificed by enemies. The strong emphasis on such practices implies the primacy of kingship as an institution over kings as individuals. The tradition of dynastic ceremonialism simultaneously enhanced and restricted the power of elites.

Theatrical events thus cannot be viewed simply as tools of elites for their ideological propaganda; rather, they were arenas of negotiation and conflict of power. The strong emphasis on public performance by the ruler and other elites implied that they were under constant check by their peers and subjects. The level of visibility that can be observed in the Aguateca Palace Group hints that the ruler was not completely shielded from public view even in his residence. Although royal residential complexes of larger centers, such as Tikal and Caracol, had more restricted access than that of Aguateca, most of the Maya palace complexes were not as closed and shielded as those of some other parts of the world, such as the Labyrinth of Knossos, the Forbidden City of China, and the compounds at Chan Chan, Peru. The prominence of gathering scenes in Classic Maya ceramic paintings also implies that political and diplomatic meetings in courtly settings were in a sense theatrical performance that was meant to be witnessed. Such publicly visible meetings imply that political acts required certain forms of approval by the viewers.

Resistance to and criticism of the dominant may also have been expressed in a more direct manner in theatrical events. Taube (1989) has demonstrated that during the Classic period there existed clowns who may have been critical social commentators comparable to those in colonial and modern times (Acuña 1978; Cogolludo 1971:1:243; Bricker 1973). Colonial period informants told Bishop Landa that two small platforms in the plaza of Chichén Itzá were stages on which farces were presented for the pleasure of the public (Tozzer 1941:179). Their association with a jaguar throne and *chacmools*—stone figures probably used for human sacrifice—pointed out by Ringle and Bey (2001:277–279), however, may mean that these platforms were used for royal audience and sacrificial rituals, and thus the interpretation given by colonial period informants was not reliable. Another possibility is that the presence of the ruler and the performance of farces by clowns were not mutually exclusive. Probably Classic period clowns were not only entertainers but also social critics who may have publicly commented on the ruler and other powerful figures, representing dissident voices of the masses.

Conclusion

Important information on ancient theatrical events can be gleaned from archaeological data, particularly from the settings of theatrical spaces, though spatial data alone do not determine the specific forms of performance. This gap can be narrowed with the use of iconographic and historic sources. A problem still remains in determining diachronic changes of theatrical practices as I examined archaeological data from the Classic period and documentary sources from colonial times. Importantly, colonial period events were shaped and given meaning under Spanish rule. Many colonial period Maya may have participated in theatrical events to consciously assert their cultural identity against Spanish oppression, whereas for most nonelite

Maya during the Classic period, mass spectacles may have been occasions to adore or resent their relationships with the ruler. Despite these differences, we can see continuity between the two periods in terms of the forms and spatial settings of theatrical events, as well as in the way they were embedded in political organizations. The overwhelming concern of elites in theatrical performance is obvious, both in Classic period iconographic and epigraphic data and in colonial period accounts. The prominence of rulers' performance as themes of stone monuments suggests that Classic period kings as the central performers in mass spectacles were even more prominent than colonial period rulers. In particular, rulers of small Classic period centers, such as Aguateca, appear to have maintained a certain level of visibility even in their residences. This, along with common depictions of gathering scenes in ceramic paintings, indicates that political meetings held there had a strong aspect of theatrical performance that was meant to be witnessed.

In Classic Maya society, theatrical events were critical arenas where communities were reconstituted and asymmetrical power relations were imposed, negotiated, and resisted. They provided moments of a "real" community where individuals could sense the physical presence and acts of other members. This quality of public events counteracted the divisive tendency of a Maya polity consisting of smaller kin and local groups that may have weighed more in individual identities than their polity affiliation. While comprising diverse meanings held by different individuals, the fact that community members gathered and acted together posed a strong force that defined social relations among participants. The power of the ruler and other elites was also constituted and restricted in the defining framework of public events. It is probable that theatrical performance merged inseparably with polity administration in the perception and practice of the Classic Maya. The preparation and organization of theatrical events, along with the acquisition of related materials and the construction of theatrical spaces, were probably a significant part of work of court officials.

Notes

1. The orthography of this document suggests to Barrera Vásquez (1965:14) that it is an eighteenth-century copy of an earlier material. Although it shows some Christian elements, it retains strong pre-Hispanic contents such as political offices

and sacrificial rituals. The preface of the document also claims that it describes old customs prior to the arrival of the Spaniards.

2. Relaciones are reports sent to the Spanish Crown that described the local environment and customs of specific parts of the conquered areas.

3. The musical drama of Rabinal Achí, first recorded by Brasseur de Bourbourg (1862) in the nineteenth century, shows remarkably little Spanish influence and enacts conflicts between Postclassic highland Maya rulers.

4. Ciudad Real often noted that receptions involved dances in indigenous traditions, but he also mentioned Spanish-style dances.

5. Freidel and Suhler (1999) suggest that the Late Classic platform with subterranean passages that they excavated at Yaxuná, Yucatán, served for similar theatrical effects.

References Cited

Abu-Lughod, Lila
1991 Writing against Culture. *In* Recapturing Anthropology. Richard G. Fox, ed. Pp. 137–162. Santa Fe: School of American Research Press.

Acuña, René
1978 Farsas y representaciones escénicas de los mayas antiguos. Centro de Estudios Mayas, vol. 15. Mexico: Universidad Nacional Autónoma de México.

Anderson, Benedict
1991 Imagined Communities: Reflections on the Origin and Spread of Nationalism. 2nd edition. London: Verso.

Aoyama, Kazuo
1999 Ancient Maya State, Urbanism, Exchange, and Craft Specialization. University of Pittsburgh Memoirs in Latin American Archaeology, no. 12. Pittsburgh: Department of Anthropology, University of Pittsburgh.

Appadurai, Arjun
1996 Modernity at Large: Cultural Dimensions of Globalization. Minneapolis: University of Minnesota Press.

Barrera Vásquez, Alfredo
1965 El libro de los Cantares de Dzitbalché. Mexico: Instituto Nacional de Antropología e Historia.

Bell, Catherine
1992 Ritual Theory, Ritual Practice. Oxford: Oxford University Press.

1997 Ritual: Perspectives and Dimensions. Oxford: Oxford University Press.

Bloch, Maurice
1974 Symbols, Song, Dance, and Features of Articulation. Archives européenes de sociologie 15:55–81.

Bradley, Richard
1998 The Significance of Monuments: On the Shaping of Human Experience in Neolithic and Bronze Age Europe. London: Routledge.

Brasseur de Bourbourg, Charles E.
1862 Rabinal-Achi ou le drame-ballet de tun. Paris: Arthus Bertrand.

Bricker, Victoria
1973 Ritual Humor in Highland Chiapas. Austin: University of Texas Press.

Carr, Robert F., and James E. Hazard
1961 Tikal Report no. 11: Map of the Ruins of Tikal, El Peten, Guatemala. Philadelphia: University Museum, University of Pennsylvania.

Chase, Arlen F., and Diane Z. Chase
2001a Ancient Maya Causeways and Site Organization at Caracol, Belize. Ancient Mesoamerica 12:273–281.
2001b The Royal Court of Caracol, Belize: Its Palaces and People. *In* Royal Courts of the Ancient Maya, vol. 2: Data and Case Studies. Takeshi Inomata and Stephen D. Houston, eds. Pp. 102–137. Boulder: Westview.

Ciudad Real, Antonio de
1976 Tratado cuioso y docto de las grandezas de la Nueva España: Relación breve y verdadera de algunas cosas de las muchas que sucedieron al padre fray Alonso Ponce en las provincias de la Nueva España siendo comisario general de aquellas partes. 2 vols. Mexico: Instituto de Investigaciones Históricas, Universidad Nacional Autónoma de México.

Coe, Michael D.
1975 Classic Maya Pottery at Dumbarton Oaks. Washington, D.C. Dumbarton Oaks Research Library and Collection.
1977 Supernatural Patrons of Maya Scribes and Artists. *In* Social Process in Maya Prehistory: Essays in Honor of Sir Eric Thompson. Norman Hammond, ed. Pp. 327–347. London: Academic.

Coe, Michael D., and Justin Kerr
1997 The Art of the Maya Scribe. New York: Abrams.

Coe, William R.
1990 Tikal Report no. 14: Excavations in the Great Plaza, North Terrace, and North Acropolis of Tikal. Philadelphia: University Museum, University of Pennsylvania.

Cogolludo, Diego López de
1971[1654] Los tres siglos de la dominación española en Yucatán o sea historia de esta provincia. 2 vols. Graz: Akademische Druck- und Verlangsanstalt.

Da Matta, Roberto
1984 Carnival in Multiple Planes. *In* Rite, Drama, Festival, Spectacle: Rehearsals Toward a Theory of Cultural Performance. John J. MacAloon, ed. Pp. 208–240. Philadelphia: Institute for the Study of Human Issues.

Demarest, Arthur A.
1992 Ideology in Ancient Maya Cultural Evolution: The Dynamics of Galactic Polities. In Ideology and Pre-Colombian Civilizations. Arthur A. Demarest and Geoffrey W. Conrad, eds. Pp. 135–158. Santa Fe: School of American Research Press.

Estrada Monroy, Agustín
1979 El mundo K'ekchi' de la Vera-Paz. Guatemala: Editorial del Ejército.

Farriss, Nancy M.
1984 Maya Society under Colonial Rule: The Collective Enterprise of Survival. Princeton, N.J.: Princeton University Press.

Fash, Barbara, William Fash, Sheree Lane, Rudy Larios, Linda Schele, Jeffrey Stomper, and David Stuart
1992 Investigations of a Classic Maya Council House at Copán, Honduras. Journal of Field Archaeology 19:419–442.

Fash, William L.
2001 Scribes, Warriors and Kings: The City of Copán and the Ancient Maya. Rev. edition. London: Thames & Hudson.

Foucault, Michel
1977 Discipline and Punish: The Birth of the Prison. A. Sheridan, trans. New York: Pantheon.

Freidel, David, and Charles Suhler
1999 The Path of Life: Toward a Functional Analysis of Ancient Maya Architecture. *In* Mesoamerican Architecture as a Cultural Symbol. Jeff K. Kowalski, ed. Pp. 250–273. Oxford: Oxford University Press.

Friedman, Jonathan
1994 Cultural Identity and Global Process. London: Sage.

Fry, Robert E.
1979 The Economics of Pottery at Tikal, Guatemala: Models of Exchange for Serving Vessels. American Antiquity 44(3):494–512.

Gage, Thomas
1958 Travels in the New World. Norman: University of Oklahoma Press.

Geertz, Clifford
1980 Negara: The Theatre State in Nineteenth-Century Bali. Princeton, N.J.: Princeton University Press.

Gossen, Gary H.
1986 The Chamula Festival of Games: Native Macroanalysis and Social Commentary in a Maya Carnival. *In* Symbol and Meaning Beyond the Closed Community: Essays in Mesoamerican Ideas. Gary H. Gossen, ed. Pp. 227–254. Studies on Culture and Society, vol. 1. Albany: Institute for Mesoamerican Studies, State University of New York, Albany.

Grube, Nikolai
1992 Classic Maya Dance: Evidence from Hieroglyphs and Iconography. Ancient Mesoamerica 3:201–218.

Handelman, Don
1990 Models and Mirrors: Toward an Anthropology of Public Events. Cambridge University Press, Cambridge.

Harrison, Peter D.
1999 The Lords of Tikal: Rulers of an Ancient Maya City. London: Thames & Hudson.

Houston, Stephen D., and David Stuart
1996 Of Gods, Glyphs, and Kings: Divinity and Rulership among the Classic Maya. Antiquity 70:289–312.

Inomata, Takeshi
2001a The Classic Maya Royal Palace as a Political Theater. *In* Reconstruyendo la ciudad maya: El urbanismo en la sociedades antigua. Andrés Ciudad Ruiz, María J. Iglesias Ponce de León, and María de Carmen Martínez Martínez, eds. Pp. 341–362. Madrid: Sociedad Española de Estudios Mayas.
2001b King's People: Classic Maya Royal Courtiers in a Comparative Perspective. *In* Royal Courts of the Ancient Maya, vol. 1: Theory, Comparison,

and Synthesis. Takeshi Inomata and Stephen D. Houston, eds. Pp. 27–53. Boulder: Westview.

2001c The Power and Ideology of Artistic Creation: Elite Craft Specialists in Classic Maya Society. Current Anthropology 42(3):321–333.

2004 The Spatial Mobility of Non-Elite Populations in Classic Maya Society and Its Political Implications. *In* Ancient Maya Commoners. Jon Lohse and Fred Valez Jr., eds. Pp. 175–196. Austin: University of Texas Press.

Inomata, Takeshi, and Kazuo Aoyama

1996 Central Place Analyses in the La Entrada Region, Honduras: Implications for Understanding the Classic Maya Political and Economic Systems. Latin American Antiquity 7(4):291–312.

Inomata, Takeshi, and Stephen Houston

2001 Opening the Royal Court. *In* Royal Courts of the Ancient Maya, vol. 1: Theory, Comparison, and Synthesis. Takeshi Inomata and Stephen Houston, eds. Pp. 3–23. Boulder: Westview.

Inomata, Takeshi, Daniela Triadan, Erick Ponciano, Richard Terry, and Harriet F. Beaubien

2001 In the Palace of the Fallen King: The Royal Residential Complex at the Classic Maya Center of Aguateca, Guatemala. Journal of Field Archaeology 28:287–306.

Inomata, Takeshi, Daniela Triadan, Erick Ponciano, Estela Pinto, Richard E. Terry, and Markus Eberl

2002 Domestic and Political Lives of Classic Maya Elites: The Excavation of Rapidly Abandoned Structures at Aguateca, Guatemala. Latin American Antiquity 13(3): 305–330.

Kertzer, David I.

1988 Ritual, Politics, and Power. New Haven: Yale University Press.

Kowalski, Jeff K.

1987 The House of the Governor: A Maya Palace at Uxmal, Yucatan, Mexico. Norman: University of Oklahoma Press.

Lizana, Bernardo de

1988 Historia de Yucatán. Félix Jiménez Villalba, ed. Crónicas de América, vol. 43. Madrid: Historia 16.

Looper, Matthew G.

2001 Dance Performances at Quiriguá. *In* Landscape and Power in Ancient Mesoamerica. Rex Koontz, Kathryn Reese-Taylor, and Annabeth Headrick, eds. Pp. 113–136. Boulder: Westview.

López de Cogolludo, Diego
1971 Historia de Yucatán: los tres siglos de la dominación española en Yucatán, o sea historia de esta provincia (desde la conquista hasta la independencia). Graz, Austria: Akadem. Druck- u. Verlangsanst.

Marcus, Joyce P.
1974 The Iconography of Power among the Classic Maya. World Archaeology 6:83–94.

Martínez Hernández, Juan, ed.
1929 Diccionario de Motul maya-español, atribuído a Fray Antonio de Ciudad Real y Arte de lengua maya por Fray Juan Coronel. Mérida: Talleres de la Compañía Tipográfica Yucateca.

Miller, Mary Ellen
1986 The Murals of Bonampak. Princeton, N.J.: Princeton University Press.

Miller, Mary Ellen, and Karl A. Taube
1993 The Gods and Symbols of Ancient Mexico and the Maya: An Illustrated Dictionary of Mesoamerican Religion. New York: Thames & Hudson.

Rands, Robert L., and Ronald L. Bishop
1980 Resource Procurement Zones and Patterns of Ceramic Exchange in the Palenque Region, Mexico. *In* Models and Methods in Regional Exchange. Robert E. Fry, ed. Pp. 19–46. Washington, D.C.: Society for American Archaeology.

Reents-Budet, Dorie
2001 Classic Maya Concepts of the Royal Court: An Analysis of Renderings on Pictorial Ceramics. *In* Royal Courts of the Ancient Maya, vol. 1: Theory, Comparison, and Synthesis. Takeshi Inomata and Stephen D. Houston, eds. Pp. 195–236. Boulder: Westview.

Relaciones de Yucatán
1900 Relaciones de Yucatán. Colección de documentos inéditos relativos al descubrimiento, conquista y organización de las antiguas posesiones españolas de ultramar. Segunda serie. Tomo 13. Madrid: Real Academia de la Historia.

Restall, Matthew
2001 The People of the Patio: Ethnohistorical Evidence of Yucatec Maya Royal Courts. *In* Royal Courts of the Ancient Maya, vol. 2: Data and Case Studies. Takeshi Inomata and Stephen D. Houston, eds. Pp. 335–90. Boulder: Westview.

Rice, Prudence M.
1987 Economic Change in the Lowland Maya Late Classic Period. *In* Specialization, Exchange, and Complex Societies. Elizabeth M. Brumfiel and Timothy K. Earle, eds. Pp. 76–85. Cambridge: Cambridge University Press.

Ringle, William M.
1990 Who Was Who in Ninth-Century Chichen Itza. Ancient Mesoamerica 1:233–243.

Ringle, William M., and George J. Bey III
2001 Post-Classic and Terminal Classic Courts of the Northern Maya Lowlands. *In* Royal Courts of the Ancient Maya, vol. 2: Data and Case Studies. Takeshi Inomata and Stephen D. Houston, eds. Pp. 266–307. Boulder: Westview.

Roys, Ralph L.
1939 The Titles of Ebtun. Carnegie Institution of Washington Publication 505. Washington, D.C.
1943 The Indian Background of Colonial Yucatan. Carnegie Institution of Washington Publication 548. Washington, D.C.

Sanders, William T., and David Webster
1988 Mesoamerican Urban Tradition. American Anthropologist 90(3): 521–546.

Schele, Linda, and Mary Ellen Miller
1986 The Blood of Kings: Dynasty and Ritual in Maya Art. Fort Worth, Tex.: Kimbell Art Museum.

Scott, James C.
1990 Domination and the Arts of Resistance: Hidden Transcript. New Haven: Yale University Press.

Sharer, Robert J., Loa P. Traxler, David W. Sedat, Ellen E. Bell, Marcello A. Canuto, and Christopher Powell
1999 Early Classic Architecture Beneath the Copan Acropolis: A Research Update. Ancient Mesoamerica 10(1):3–23.

Stomper, Jeffrey A.
1996 The Popol Na: A Model for Ancient Maya Community Structure at Copan, Honduras. Ph.D. dissertation, Yale University.

Suhler, Charles, and David Freidel
2000 Rituales de terminación: Implicaciones de la guerra maya. *In* La guerra entre los antiguos mayas: Memoria de la Primera Mesa Redonda de Palenque.

Silvia Trejo, ed. Pp. 73–104. Mexico: Instituto Nacional de Antropología e Historia.

Tambiah, Stanley J.
1976 World Conqueror and World Renouncer: A Study of Buddhism and Polity in Thailand against a Historical Background. Cambridge: Cambridge University Press.
1981 A Performative Approach to Ritual. London: British Academy.

Taube, Karl
1988 A Study of Classic Maya Scaffold Sacrifice. *In* Maya Iconography. Elizabeth Benson and Gillett Griffin, eds. Pp. 331–351. Princeton, N.J.: Princeton University Press.
1989 Ritual Humor in Classic Maya Religion. *In* Word and Image in Maya Culture: Explorations in Language, Writing, and Representation. William F. Hanks and Don S. Rice, eds. Pp. 351–382. Salt Lake City: University of Utah Press.

Tozzer, Alfred M.
1941 Landa's Relación de las cosas de Yucatan. Papers of the Peabody Museum of American Archaeology and Ethnology, vol. 18. Cambridge: Harvard University.

Trik, Helen, and Michael E. Kampen
1983 Tikal Report no. 31: The Graffiti of Tikal. University Museum Monograph, vol. 57. Philadelphia: University of Pennsylvania.

Turner, Victor W.
1967 The Forest of Symbols: Aspects of Ndembu Ritual. Ithaca, N.Y.: Cornell University Press.

Vogt, Evon Z.
1969 Zinacantán: A Maya Community in the Highlands of Chiapas. Cambridge: Harvard University Press.

Wuthnow, Robert
1987 Meaning and Moral Order: Explorations in Cultural Analysis. Berkeley: University of California Press.

SCENE 8

OTHER CUZCOS: REPLICATED THEATERS OF INKA POWER

Lawrence S. Coben

This chapter examines the roles of ritual theater in constituting, extending, and manipulating political power in premodern complex societies, particularly states. By ritual theater, I refer to larger-scale nonquotidian performances that are organized and directed by political agents, occur generally at specified times and locations, and include elements of theatricality, cosmological invocation, and feasting. Drawing on data from my own research at such locations, my focus in this chapter will be the Inka empire of the central Andes in the fifteenth and sixteenth centuries. Analyzing religious and state constructions and spaces for their roles in and as the settings for spectacles and ceremonies and utilizing a performatic (see Taylor 2003:6) approach, I argue that ritual and secular performances were not epiphenomenal, but rather part of a political and ideological discourse to create, maintain, and subvert power relations.[1] The "power" of performance, its communicative and emotional import, is dramatic and not to be underestimated.

The effect of a dramatic presentation on an audience cannot be determined without consideration of the physical theater housing it. For purposes of this chapter, theater is any building, plaza, landscape, pilgrimage route, or other setting in which spectacles are performed and may include multiple locations and pathways. Consideration of a theater includes its performance characteristics or properties—size, shape, entrances and exits, location of the "stage," set, lighting, sound, costumes, orientation, changes in elevation, audience capacity, and viewing patterns of the spectators. Nor should analysis end at the theater door—its location within a settlement/city, the roads leading to it, and its relationship to other buildings and features are critical elements of the audience experience. Last, the examination must utilize such analysis and consideration to investigate the cultural meanings and roles generated by and associated with performance and its settings predicated upon historical context.

Utilizing theories of semiotics and pragmatics drawn from semiotic anthropology (see Parmentier 1994; Preucel and Bauer 2001), this chapter analyzes a particular set of Inka performance spaces and their role in imperial expansion and control: the capital of Cuzco and certain replicas of that city constructed in other parts of the empire. The Inka constructed their capital as a physical representation of their worldview. They then replicated important portions of this city in a particular manner in a limited number of strategic locations throughout their empire. I argue that a principal role of these sites was to serve as the setting for a calendar of ritual ceremonies and spectacles that referenced certain repeated material attributes of these sites and were performed by and for an audience of the Inka themselves, and did not, like other performances, involve the meaningful participation of other social groups within the empire. I also suggest that these Cuzco replicas were strategically placed in areas of war and rebellion where the utilization of ritual performance to maintain, reinforce, and manipulate Inka ideology and identity was a critical element of imperial strategy as the polity expanded from a single valley in highland modern Peru to encompass much of Peru and Bolivia, and significant parts of Ecuador, Argentina, and Chile (Fig. 8.1). My focus on intra-Inka performance is not designed to privilege large-scale elite spectacles or ignore the agency of those groups conquered by the Inka but rather to consider the practice, role, and importance of such internally directed performance as a critical element of imperial strategy during a period of rapid state expansion and strife.

My analysis will incorporate both archaeological and historical evidence, the latter from the rich early colonial chronicles of life in the Andes written by both Spaniards and natives. These chronicles are critical yet problematic sources of information on Inka life.[2] These text sources at times are at odds with data from the archaeological record. Many of the chronicles are focused on the Inka capital of Cuzco and its environs (Morris and Thompson 1985), and they provide less insight regarding

Figure 8.1. The Expansion of the Inka Empire and the Locations of the New Cuzcos

daily life or the exercise of imperial power in a particular region. This paper demonstrates how the descriptions in the texts, particularly the architecture, features, and rituals of Cuzco, may be combined with archaeological evidence to provide a richer interpretation of Inka life across the empire.

More particularly, this chapter utilizes historical and archaeological evidence to analyze the so-called other or new Cuzcos that according to some chroniclers were built by the Inka in certain locations of their empire. Utilizing Charles Sanders Peirce's concept of replication and the notion of hyperstructure developed by linguistic anthropologist Richard Parmentier and others, the chapter analyzes how and why Cuzco was replicated, and how changes in such replication over time and space represent ideological or political change.

Peircean Replication: Setting the Stage

In the past twenty-five years, "semiotic anthropology has been transformed by approaches that have moved beyond Saussure to explore the work of the American philosopher and semiotician Charles Sanders Peirce" (Preucel and Bauer 2001:88). Such exploration responded in part to the perceived shortcomings of anthropological analyses based on the semiology of Ferdinand de Saussure (Singer 1978; Hodder 1991). Milton Singer (1978) and Michael Silverstein (1976) both advocated Peircean frameworks, arguing that they allowed for more contextualized analyses of social action. More recently, Parmentier (1994, 1997) utilized a Peirce-based approach to study ritual performance and various aspects of material culture, discussed in greater detail below. Preucel and Bauer (2001:92) argued strongly for the use of a Peircean analytic framework in archaeology, suggesting it "allows us to acknowledge how meaning varies in social practice" and answered the criticisms of postprocessual archaeologists that Saussurean linguistic models were unable to account for multiple meanings.

In this chapter, I utilize such a framework to analyze certain Inka state-sponsored performances and the theaters in which they take place. I focus particularly on the concept of Peircean replication associated with the first trichotomy of signs (qualisign, sinsign, and legisign) described by Peirce (1931–1935). The qualisign is not relevant to my analysis and will not be discussed. A sinsign "is an actual existent thing or event which is a sign," while a legisign "is not a single object but a general type" (Peirce 1931–1935: 142–143). Sinsigns are actual material instantiations, while types/legisigns are archetypes or classes of objects and not tangible in Peirce's structure. Examples of legisigns include the noun "book" and the concept of architectural order, while sinsigns would include a particular book, diagram, or blueprint (Parmentier 1994:18).

Legisigns instantiate themselves through replicas; indeed, "to be a legisign is to be something that produces tokens of its type" (Parmentier

1994:18). A Peircean replica is the object through which a legisign, or "general type . . . signifies itself through an instance of its application" (Peirce 1931–1935:143). The replica is thus a sinsign, or token of the legisign, an actual manifestation, though one with particular and distinct characteristics.

Peircean replicas are not copies of some specified original, but rather are icons of their legisigns. Icons are "signs whose grounds involve formal resemblance" (Parmentier 1994:17); that is, there is a significant degree of likeness between the replica/sinsign and the type/legisign it instantiates. Each replica of a particular type will to some degree be iconic with every other replica of such type. For example, every materially manifested book is a replica of the type or legisign "book" and shares certain characteristics, yet every book is not identical nor a copy of some original. Peirce utilizes the linguistic example of the word "the," which may occur several times on a page (Peirce 1931–1935:143). In all of these occurrences, "the" is one and the same word, or the same type/legisign. Each single instantiation of "the" is both a sinsign and a replica.

As an instantiation, every Peircean replication is by definition contextualized—it occurs at a particular time and place and in an ideological and political setting. Replication is not an abstract notion of copying, but instead occurs on encounter or experience with a sign or signs by a person or persons. The word "the" only carries meaning and is a replication when seen, heard, or spoken. Meaning is generated and made manifest by contextualized encounters at a particular time and place.

Replication is thus a diachronic analytic framework, requiring that meaning be analyzed and determined in its historical context. An excellent example is the beginning of the U.S. Constitution, "We the people" (Urban 2001). The referent of this phrase in 1788 would be white male landowners. A replica of that phrase today for most Americans encompasses a broader class of people. Replication is not a static concept, and just as the meaning of a supposedly concrete phrase may change depending on context, so may the meaning of a supposedly concrete building, setting, sacred precinct, city, or landscape, or combination of any or all of them.

This chapter focuses on the replication of an idealized city and cosmological center across the Inka empire and the role of these replicas as sacral theaters.[3] With respect to a city, replication incorporates more than the architectural features, topography, and layout of an idealized legisign/type. Also subject to replication are the social actions and rituals performed in the city's designated spaces, including the various calendars that govern such performances and to varying degrees theatrical characteristics or "properties" such as movement, lighting, set, and sound. Replication may also be linguistic: the city's name, districts, streets, hills, and plazas may carry the same or similar names as their counterparts in the idealized city legisign. And if a city is imbued with ideological or religious significance or meaning, as in the case of a cosmological center, such significance may also be replicated to some degree. Iconicity (likeness or resemblance) of material culture potentially suggests iconicity of experience, action, and meaning, though the latter must be demonstrated rather than assumed.

The legisign of the idealized city is not constant. The idealized city type changes over time through ideological manipulation or historical circumstance, such as a change of ruler. Any physically embodied Peircean replica of this new type would reflect such change, and be an icon of the new legisign. Significant changes in the physical layout or major structures of a group's cosmological center should be reflected in any other replicas constructed thereafter. For example, post-Reformation, the idealized Protestant church and its physical manifestations differed from the Catholic church from which it evolved, though substantial iconicity remained both linguistically ("church" or its equivalent in other languages), in architectural form and related symbols such as the cross shape, and in ritual practice and belief.

Inka Spatial Design and Planning: Broadway

The Inka planned the locations and designs of their significant spaces and settlements in great detail. A specially trained class of experts was responsible for such planning (Cobo 1990). These experts decided the location, spatial allocation, and placement of buildings and compounds within a settlement (Hyslop 1990:27). Betanzos (1996) describes Cuzco as being rebuilt from a master plan, and Morris (1990:35) has described the "elaborate pre-conceived plan" of the Inka administrative center and other Cuzco of Huánuco Pampa.

These plans often followed certain structural principles. While all of these principles are not manifested at every Inka site, archaeological

Figure 8.2. The *Kallanka* and Upper Plaza of Incallajta. Photo by L. Coben

and ethnohistorical evidence confirms their presence at many Inka sites (Hyslop 1990). These principles, many of which are described more fully below, include the bi- and quadripartitioning of sites by roads, a radial partitioning scheme known as the *ceque* system, *ushnu* (ritual platform) complexes associated with main plazas, *kallankas* (large multidoored single room structures; see Fig. 8.2) on plazas, and waterworks and drains.

The application of many of these structural principles incorporated features of both the site and the landscape without distinguishing between them. Hyslop (1990:281) observed that "landscape modeling should be considered an integral part of an Inka space's architecture." The Inka made models of these spaces that included not just structures, but streets and "the countryside with high hills and low, flats and ravines, rivers and streams" (Garcilaso de la Vega 1987:124). Roads and plazas partitioned Inka spaces, and buildings were often oriented toward sacred rocks and mountains or aligned with astronomical phenomena. The flow of water in rivers and streams was often a critical element in Inka spatial design. Large stones, often in the shape of mountains, were often placed on or integrated into *ushnus* (ritual platforms) or otherwise incorporated into the planning and directional orientation of Inka ritual spaces (Hyslop 1990).

Cuzco: The Main Stage

Cuzco was the capital of the Inka empire and its political and cosmological center (Hyslop 1990; Rowe 1946; Betanzos 1996). One of the many definitions of Cuzco is "the navel of the world" (Garcilaso de la Vega 1987:93). The chroniclers report a variety of Inka origin myths, almost all of which conclude with the founding of Cuzco by the mythical first Inka ruler, Manco Capac (Cobo 1990:103–108). In many of these tales, Manco Capac strikes a gold staff into the ground to fix the capital's location.

Pachacuti, the ninth and likely the first historic Inka ruler (Rowe 1945), redesigned and rebuilt Cuzco during his reign (Betanzos 1996). Pachacuti ruled from approximately 1438–1471 (Rowe 1945), defeated with the help of mythical warriors the neighboring Chancas when they threatened Cuzco, and was the first Inka to conquer territory outside of the Cuzco valley. The Inka state or empire thus began during his rule.

According to Inka narratives, Pachacuti laid out Cuzco, its streets, plazas, roads, and buildings (Betanzos 1996).[4] He measured and constructed the *Coricancha*, the Temple of the Sun, at the southeast corner of the city's central district. He canalized the Tullumayo and Huatenay Rivers, which bound the central precinct of Cuzco and intersect near the Temple of the Sun.

Inka Cuzco was divided into two halves, or moieties, the upper (*hanansaya*) to the north and lower (*hurinsaya*) to the south. A road through the larger and more important of the city's two adjacent central plazas, Haukaypata, likely marked such division (Hyslop 1990:58). The Inka also divided the city and valley of Cuzco, as well as their empire, into four quadrants, or *suyus* (Bauer 1998:6). *Hanansaya* was divided into two parts, Chinchasuyu to the northwest and Antisuyu to the northeast. *Hurinsaya* was similarly divided, with the quarter of Cuntisuyu to the southwest and Collasuyu to the southeast. The Inka called their empire Tahuatinsuyu, the land of the four quarters. The center point of this system was the Haukaypata plaza. Four great roads emerged from this plaza, marking each of the *suyus* (Cieza de Leon 1959:144). Somewhere near the southern end of Haukaypata sat a sugarloaf-shaped stone covered with gold, either surrounded by or sitting on a stone basin or font (Betanzos 1996:47; Pizarro 1978:89–91). The Inka concept of *ushnu* was likely at least in part derived from this stone and font complex and its integral role in Inka spectacles performed in the Haukaypata plaza, though *ushnu* was represented as a stage or platform in many other Inka sites (Hyslop 1990:39; Zuidema 1980).

Later rulers constructed numerous other buildings and temples in the city. Most significantly, the massive Sacsayhuaman was constructed on the hill immediately north of the city. Three rows of zigzag walls mark the north side of this complex of several structures and other features. Interpretations of Sacsayhuaman include a fortress, temple, observatory, and storehouse, and the complex was likely some combination of all of these features. The construction of Sacsayhuaman has usually been attributed either to the end of the reign of Topa Inka, the tenth Inka ruler, or Huayna Capac, the eleventh Inka ruler. The complex was likely begun during the reign of the former and completed during the latter's rule (Hyslop 1990). A few chroniclers attribute Sacsayhuaman to the ruler Pachacuti, though this is a minority view among both chroniclers and archaeologists. Each ruler also constructed his own palace in Cuzco's center.

The Sun Temple of Cuzco was the center of the *ceque* system, a partitioning scheme radiating from such temples of 41 (Cobo 1990) or perhaps 42 (Bauer 1998:11) lines containing a total of 328 *huacas*, best glossed as sacred objects or shrines (van de Guchte 1999). Three of the *suyus* contain nine *ceques* each, while Cuntisuyu contains fourteen or fifteen. Cobo suggests that the *ceques* in each of the four *suyus* are found in groups of three, likely ranked by the social status *collana, payan,* and *cayao* (Zuidema 1964:2–5). These lines often pass through features of the built environment (Hyslop 1990:66). While Zuidema has suggested that the *ceques* were straight, field research such as Bauer's (1998:11) suggests that the *huacas* are not aligned linearly. Research by Susan Niles (1987:171–206) supports this conclusion. Bauer (1998:11) observes:

> In this model of the Cusco ceque system, it is the specific *locations* of the huacas that define the course of the lines and not vice versa. In other words, while the connotative model of the system by the Inca may have included the notions of ceques as straight lines, researchers cannot presume that the actual form of the system on the landscape reproduced this restrictive framework.

Cuzco-based kin groups were assigned to make offerings on specific *ceques* at particular *huacas* pursuant to a ritual calendar (Cobo 1990), establishing a schedule of performances at predetermined times and locations, discussed below. The worshiped *huacas* included mountains, rocks, springs, and other elements of the landscape (van de Guchte 1999). These *ceque/*huaca-based performances were linked to the social organization of the capital (Zuidema 1964: Bauer 1998) and to the location and ownership of water resources among social groups (Sherbondy 1982).

The Cuzco *ceque* system was dynamic rather than static, "a flexible expression of social and spatial relations" (Bauer 1998:161). Niles (1999:52) notes that "a number of places important to his ancestors or to his neighbors were organized into a system at the behest of Pachacuti." The ruler Huayna Capac later was said to have revised and expanded the system (Niles 1999:52; Rowe 1980, 1985). Special Inka experts could add or remove *huacas* from the system (Van de Guchte 1999). Certain chroniclers describe a system with more than 342 *huacas* in the latter part of the sixteenth century (Bauer 1998). The system "was able to adapt to social and territorial changes, and it was capable of incorporating those changes into *the continually developing ritual order of the region*" (Bauer 1998:161; emphasis added). The *ceque* system reflected, reaffirmed, manipulated, and created power relations at the core of the Inka empire through the continued yet changing schedule and locations of performances and offerings.

New and Other Cuzcos in the Province: Regional Theater

The significance of Cuzco and its layout extended well beyond the city itself. The late sixteenth-century chronicler Guaman Poma de Ayala (1980) describes other Cuzcos throughout the empire (Fig. 8.1), stating,

> There is another Cuzco in Quito, and another in Tumi [Tomebamba], and another in Guanoco [Huánuco Pampa], and another in Hatuncolla, another in Charcas [south central Bolivia].

Cieza de Leon (1959), a chronicler of the mid-sixteenth century, and Garcilaso de la Vega (1987) identify a new Cuzco at the head of the Huarco valley, likely the site of Inkawasi (Hyslop 1985).

> He [Topa Inka] came down with the *orejones* [noble warriors] of Cuzco . . . and built a new city, to which he gave the name of New Cuzco, the same as his main seat. . . . They also tell that he ordered that the districts of the city and the hills should have the same names as those of Cuzco. (Cieza de Leon 1959:338)

Cieza de Leon (1959:342) reiterates that the ruler Topa Inka ordered that the "streets and hills and plazas bore the same names as those of the real one [Cuzco]."

According to the chroniclers who recorded Inka narratives, new and other Cuzcos were founded by and closely associated with the Inka ruler. Tomebamba, located in Ecuador and also described as a "second capital" of the empire, was the birthplace of the ruler Huayna Capac, and designed and built by him on a settlement constructed by the ruler Topa Inka (Idrovo 2000:83; Cabello Balboa 1951). Similarly, Huayna Capac reconstructed Incallajta, located in central Bolivia, the likely other Cuzco of the Charcas (Ellefsen 1973; Ibarra Grasso 1982; Coben 2001, 2003), atop a site originally built by his father while Huayna Capac was visiting that region (Querejazu 1998; Sarmiento de Gamboa 1947). Topa Inka directed the construction of Inkawasi, located in central Peru (Cieza de Leon 1959:338, 342).

Archaeologists have conducted surveys, mapping, and excavations at most of the named new or other Cuzcos, including Hatuncolla (Julien 1983), Huánuco Pampa (Morris and Thompson 1985), Inkawasi (Hyslop 1985), Tomebamba (Uhle 1923; Idrovo 2000), and Incallajta (Nordenskiold 1957; Coben 2001, 2003).[5] Most of these studies have identified strong similarities and connections between the design of Cuzco and the sites under study, predicated on the possible presence of structural principles such as dual organization or moiety, quadripartition and the *ceque* system, and similarities in layout, building materials, structures, spaces, and directional orientation. Replication may also have been linguistic. As discussed above, these sites are referred to as new or other Cuzcos, and both Cieza de Leon and Garcilaso de la Vega suggest that the districts, streets, hills, and plazas of the site of Inkawasi carried the same names as their counterparts in the capital. Many of Tomebamba's toponyms similarly replicate those of Cuzco (Idrovo 2000). Although varying degrees

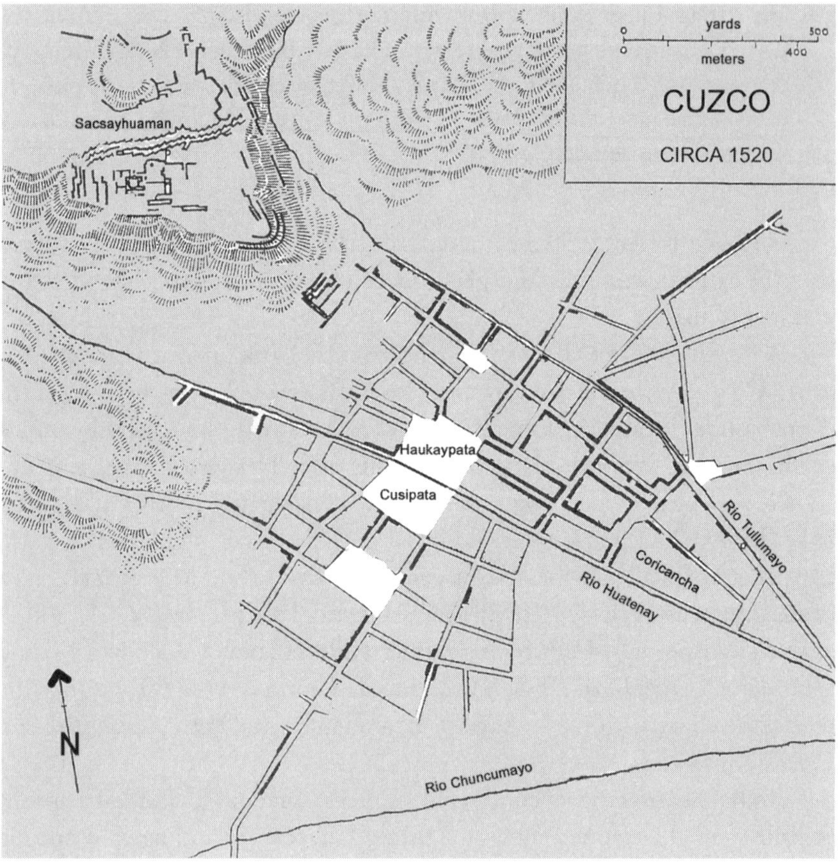

Figure 8.3. Map of the Capital Cuzco

of iconicity exist at multiple scales and across numerous features, none of the new or other Cuzcos is a precise physical copy of each other or the capital itself. The importance of both similarity and difference in scale and features between a new Cuzco and the capital requires analysis.

While a detailed discussion of replication and difference among the Cuzcos is beyond the scope of this chapter (see Coben 2003 for such discussion), certain features or groups of features recur in particular sequences and patterns at the capital and some of the other identified Cuzcos, including zigzag walls, double plazas, *kallankas*, roads, site layout, topography, merging bodies of water (Figs. 8.3, 8.4), and many of the Inka structural settlement principles described above. Zigzag walls are found in

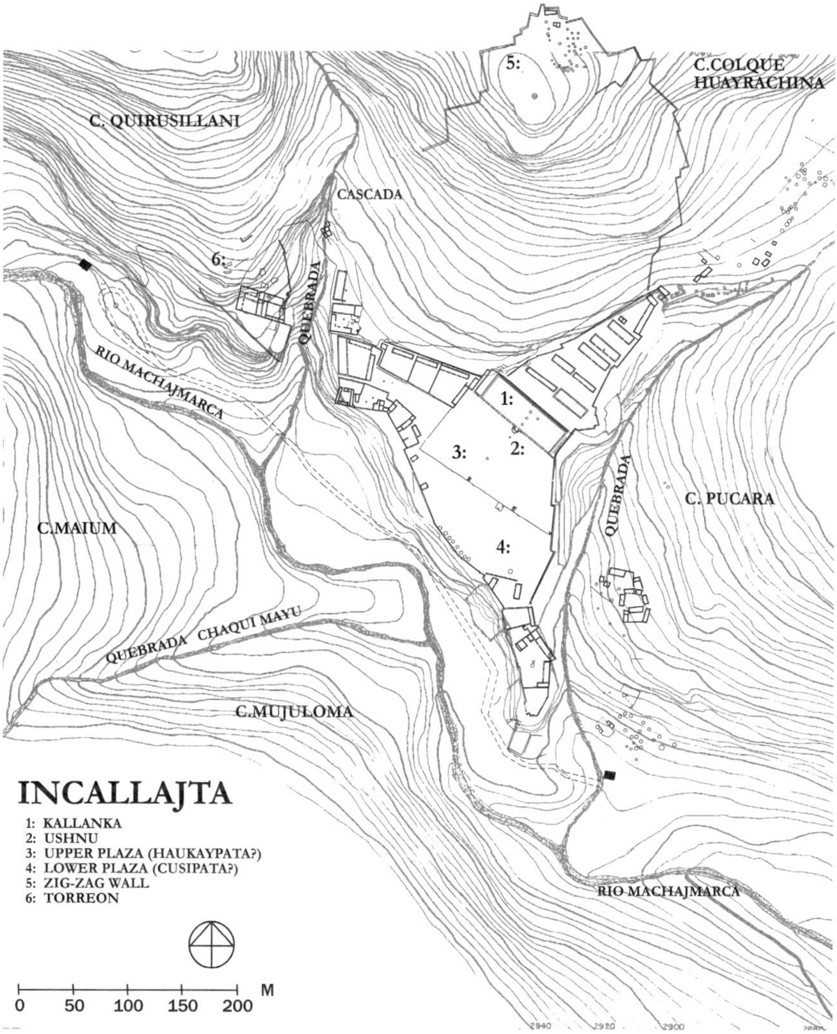

Figure 8.4. Map of Incallajta, a New Cuzco. Courtesy of Proyecto Inkallakta

Cuzco at Sacsayhuaman and at Incallajta on hills located to the north of their respective central precinct. Both hills are associated with *colcas* (storehouses), and rivers or streams flowing in a north–south direction flank such hills. *Colcas* are also found on hills to the north of Huánuco Pampa (Morris and Thompson 1985). Large central double or divided plazas are found in the centers of Cuzco, Incallajta, and Inkawasi (Hyslop 1985). *Kallankas*, large, multidoored, single-room buildings, are found on plazas

Figure 8.5. The *Ushnu* of the Upper Plaza of Incallajta. Photo by L. Coben

at Huánuco Pampa (Morris and Thompson 1985), Incallajta, Tomebamba (Idrovo 2000), and on the main plaza in Cuzco at the time of the Inka Huayna Capac (Garcilaso de la Vega 1987). Two streams or rivers, one flowing in a north–south direction and the other northwest–southeast, with the largest confluence occurring at the southeast corner of the site, are characteristic of Cuzco, Tomebamba, Huánuco Pampa, and Incallajta. The Temple of the Sun is located at this point in Cuzco, and similarly designed large, multidoored, single-room structures are found at this location at both Tomebamba and Incallajta. Utilizing a Peircean replication-based approach, I identified Incallajta as another Cuzco, arguing that both sites could be described as (1) approached by a major road, (2) with increasingly restricted access to the site's core, (3) a zigzag structure to the north of the site atop a hill flanked by streams or rivers overlooking (4) a large double plaza, with one plaza higher and larger than the other, (5) a stone/platform *ushnu* (See Fig. 8.5) complex in the higher plaza, which is bordered by a *kallanka*, (6) two streams or rivers with the largest confluence occurring at the southeast corner of the site, where the site appears to come to a point and where a large and significant structure is situated, (7) surrounded by an arrangement of hills, and (8) on a distant hill, a tower structure or structures (Coben 2003) (see Figs. 8.3, 8.4).

Inka settlement planning principles, including some of those described above, are often manifested at sites not designated as new or other Cuzcos. Polo de Ondegardo (1990:47–50) documented *ceque* systems across the empire in a large number of towns and describes their ubiquity as "universal." His description suggests that the complexity of these systems varied with the size and importance of the individual communities (Bauer 1998:17). Moiety and quadripartitioning have been observed at numerous sites, and numerous buildings and other features associated with Cuzco have been found at other locations (Hyslop 1990). Some level of replication of Cuzco appears to be manifested at most larger Inka sites. Cobo (1990:190, 1979:194) distinguishes larger towns, characterized by planning of streets and central squares, from other smaller settlements, described as housing one hundred inhabitants with houses that were "jumbled together with no order or coherent relation between them." Yet even smaller settlements may contain plazas or performance spaces (Coben and Stanish 2005; Arkush 2005).

Spectacle and Performance in the Inka Empire: The Play's the Thing

Ceremonial and ritual performance was ubiquitous throughout the Inka empire and the Andean region (Moore 1996; Sillar 2002). The ruler Pachacuti established a regular monthly calendar of major festivals and sacrifices, each of which contained spectacular dramatic elements and presentations. Pachacuti was also said to have composed many of the prayers associated with these performances (Cobo 1990:119).

Two of the most important of these spectacles were one for the investiture of boys as warriors centered around the December equinox, Capac Raymi, and another important spectacle centered around the June equinox, dedicated to the maize harvest (Betanzos 1996; Cobo 1990; Bauer 1996). During the latter festival, Inti Raymi,

> Those who had become *orejon* warriors . . . put on tunics woven of gold, silver and iridescent feathers. Dressed like that with this plumage, gold disks and bracelets, they would come out to the fiesta. There they would

> end their fasts and sacrifices, which they had made from the time they were made *orejon* warriors until then. . . . they would start to enjoy themselves and celebrate . . . since it was necessary to give thanks to the Sun for the crops. This fiesta . . . started in May and lasted until the end of June. . . . He [Pachacuti] ordered that this fiesta be celebrated in the square . . . in the city of Cuzco which is the exit from this city called Limapampa. For this fiesta the lords of Cuzco were to come out dressed in red tunics that reached down to their feet. He ordered great sacrifices to the idols for this fiesta. They were to burn much livestock, food, and garments. . . . And at these *guacas* [*huacas*] they would make many offerings of jewels of gold and silver. (Betanzos 1996:66)

Cobo (1990:142) describes this festival as commencing on the nearby hill of Manturculla and finishing in the main plaza of Cuzco. A dance called *cayo* was performed four times a day. The participants include the Inka, the *mamaconas*, cloistered women dedicated to the service of the Inka gods, and "his lord and knights." According to Cobo (1990:142), "This festival was performed only by the Incas of royal blood, and not even their wives participated in it; instead the wives stayed away in a patio. The *mamaconas* . . . would give drink to the Incas, and all of the vessels from which they ate or drank were made of gold."

Cobo also provides a detailed description of Capac Raymi, the investiture ceremony, and the preparation for it.

> When the first of the month came, the principal Incas got together in the Temple of the Sun, and there they organized the festival and everything that needed to be done for it. They ordered all of the provincials to leave the city, and none of them returned until the end of the festival. Both those who were leaving and those coming to the court [Cuzco] were instructed to stay at a certain place designated for this purpose at the beginning of each road, and at each of these places the people gathered who were from the *suyu* to which that road went. (Cobo 1990:127)

Preparations for the ceremony began well in advance of the spectacle proper. A number of richly dressed "noble maidens," ages twelve to fourteen and likely *accla*, went to a nearby hill called Chacaguanacauri to spin the thread for the fringe of the *guaras* (loincloths or britches). The boys went to the same hill to collect straw. The *guaca* (sacred idol) of Guanacauri accompanied the maidens while they were on the hill. The remaining items required for the ceremony, including the animals and clothing to be sacrificed, *chicha* (corn beer), clothing, and emblems for the boys, was provided by their parents and relatives, who also wore special clothing.

All of the boys who participated in this ceremony were twelve to fifteen years old and descendants or relatives of one of the Inka rulers, including the "crown prince" who was to succeed to the throne, and his brothers. This ceremony included the piercing of the boys' ears for earplugs and putting on of their *guaras*. The ceremony, which took place over several days, began with the presentation of the boys at the Temple of the Sun by Inka nobles. Idols of the Inka gods and the mummies of Inka ancestors were placed on low benches to drink with the ceremony's participants. Cobo notes that these gods and mummies participated in most of the ceremonies of the regular calendar. The Inka and the priest of the Sun then joined the ritual, which proceeded with animal sacrifices. Parts of the ceremony also took place on the sacred hill of Guanacari and in the main plaza of Cuzco, Hawkaypata. A dance called *guari*, which included singing, was performed several times, first by the boys alone and later by all present. Later, in the presence of the Inka, the priest of the Sun gave the boys certain clothing. The ceremony also included running to *huacas* on other hills, beatings of the boys by their older male relatives, and reminders of the victories of the Inkas. The rite concluded with a gift of weapons, and after being brought to the agricultural fields, the piercing of the boys' ears. The only stated role for the maidens during this entire ceremony was the carrying and serving of *chicha* and encouraging the boys during their runs up and down the hills.

At the conclusion of the ceremony, the people who had been excluded from Cuzco were permitted to reenter the city. Everyone gathered in Hawkaypata to perform the *cayo* dance. Each person was given a cake, served on a consecrated silver or gold plate, ostensibly "given to them by the Sun so that they would be content and not say that the Sun had neglected them by paying attention only to those who had participated in the festival" (Cobo 1990:129). The participants danced and drank for several days. Four drums, belonging to the Sun, were played during the dances to set the beat. Four "important Indians," each wearing a special costume dominated by puma skins worn such that "the head and neck of the lion came down over the head of the person wearing it and the animal's skin came down over the back" (Cobo 1990:129), played these drums. The description implies that the drummers appeared as anthropomorphized pumas. The Inkas sacrificed animals in the main plaza and then at all of the *huacas* of the Cuzco region.

The primary Capac Raymi ceremony was staged in Cuzco, "and there the festival included more spectators and greater ostentation because the number of boys who were knighted was large" (Cobo 1990:128). Capac Raymi was also staged concurrently in those provinces whose governors were of royal blood. Such governors knighted their sons and other young nobles, most likely in the provincial capitals and the other Cuzcos.

Descriptions of the entire ritual calendar of Cuzco are found in many of the chronicles (e.g., Betanzos 1996: bk. 1, chap. 15; Cobo 1990: chaps. 25–30) and will not be repeated here. (See D'Altroy 2002:152–153 for a discussion of the calendars and the discrepancies among them.) These descriptions reveal that in almost all of the ceremonies the moiety division of Cuzco between *hurin* and *hanan* and the empire division into four *suyus* are important organizing principles of the festivals. The participants wear distinctive and different costumes and perform different songs and dances at each festival. Every rite occurs in a designated location or locations, and movement between performance areas is common and often part of the spectacle itself. Idols and mummies were generally present and "participated" in the ceremonies, "consuming" *chicha* with other participants. The Inka ruler led or was present at these rites (Bauer 1996). People from the provinces were frequently required to leave or barred from entering Cuzco. The two rivers that border and define the central zone of Cuzco, the Huatenay and Tullomayo, play an important role in many of these ceremonies—ashes or goods are thrown into them or *chicha* is poured into them. The intersection of these two rivers is a particularly significant location. The participants sacrifice animals in each of these major festivals. Many of the ceremonies are associated with the agricultural cycle (Bauer 1996). Women were at times active participants, such as in the dance with the rope during the month of Camay.

Performance was not limited to these fixed events on the ritual calendar. Numerous other ceremonies occurred only in times of great need or stress, such as after an earthquake or during a drought or on an occasion of significance, such as the Inka personally going to war (Cobo 1990:112). One important ceremony was the Itu (Cobo 1990: chap. 31). Prior to its commencement, men abstained from women, salt, *aji* (chili), and *chicha.* All persons from the provinces were ejected from the city, as were women who had dogs and other animals. Guards were placed to ensure that no people or animals entered Cuzco. The first day of the ceremony required silence from all participants. After animal sacrifices, specially costumed young men moved in a procession around the main plaza, playing drums rhythmically and grimacing, followed by a noble spreading coca on the ground. An evening of prayer ensued, followed by two days of rejoicing, singing, and dancing. If the Inka were going to war or in times of great need, children might be sacrificed, and the drumming would be performed by "the most important nobles and knights of Cuzco," followed by their wives carrying the men's weapons in their hands (Cobo 1990:153).

The Itu was

> a *specifically Inca festival*, and they were the only ones to perform it for a long time, but later, as a means of showing favor, permission was granted for the festival to be held in their lands by other lords who were ruled by the Incas. Such permission was granted mainly when the Inca married one of his daughters or nieces to some provincial lord . . . [A] s a very special favor, the Inca granted the lord permission to celebrate this Itu festival in his land. (Cobo 1990: bk. 1, chap. 31:152; emphasis added)

Concurrently with the Itu, outside of Cuzco and these authorized locales, "another festival Ayma was performed in all of the provinces" (Cobo 1990: bk.1, chap. 31:153). Ayma included many of the same ceremonies as Itu, though the costumes were different.

Performance in Cuzco extended beyond the imperial spectacles described above. Cuzco-based kin groups were assigned to make offerings to *huacas* on specific *ceques* pursuant to another ritual calendar (Cobo 1990), establishing a schedule of performances at predetermined times and locations (Bauer 1998). These performances included the burning of objects, animal sacrifice, and at times child sacrifice. While the exact timetable of these offerings is uncertain, the number of *ceques* (41 in total) and the 328 *huacas* associated with this system suggest that this system of kin-based performance was a frequent if not daily part of Inka life in Cuzco. *Ceque* systems were said to be present in many Inka towns, and I propose that so were the rituals that characterized them (Polo de Ondegardo 1990:47).

Ceque-located and -related performance was likely pervasive throughout the Inka empire.

All of these performances were highly structured and regimented. While each ceremony and its related offerings, prayers, declarations, and sacrifices were different,

> The form to be followed in the sacrifices was so well established, with the rites and ceremonies designated for each one, that no one was permitted to exercise his own free will in changing, adding, or eliminating anything from what was ordained, *particularly with respect to the general and public ceremonies.* (Cobo 1990:110; emphasis added)

General and public ceremonies refer to the most important Inka ritual performances—these were the most regimented. The primary actors in each ceremony were similarly designated. This regimentation extended to the provinces.

> The priests of one *guaca [huaca]* did not interfere with the priests of another *guaca [huaca]*. . . At every town and *guaca [huaca]* attendants were assigned for each sacrifice, and it was stipulated when each sacrifice was to be made, the form and manner in which it was to be carried out, as well as the different types of things for it. . . . They also made a distinction in the words that were used at the time of making the offering. (Cobo 1990:110)

Cobo (1990) provides an elaborate description of Inka songs, dances, and instruments, many of which were associated with a particular ritual, occupation, or social class. Yet amid the structure and regimentation, the Inka reveled greatly during their ceremonies and festivals. Their "prayers were accompanied by banquets and drinking bouts, where they enjoyed themselves with dances, games and songs which they had especially for each *guaca [huaca]* and festival" (Cobo 1990:121).

Inka performance was not limited to Cuzco and the provincial capitals. Large plazas and other areas for public ceremony are found at Inka royal palaces (Niles 1999:171–173; Burger and Salazar-Burger 1993). At the ruler Huayna Capac's royal estate, Quispiguanca, the main plaza constituted two-thirds of the site's area (Niles 1999:171). Inka pilgrims frequently followed routes through sacred geographies, performing rites and rituals

(Sillar 2002; Arkush 2005; Bauer and Stanish 2001; Stanish and Bauer 2004). While a few of these, such as that at the sacred Islands of the Sun and Moon, were state-sponsored and subject to highly restricted terms of access and regimented rites, others were local in origin and practice and open to broad classes of people (Bauer and Stanish 2001:21–22; Arkush 2005). And in some strategic valleys, the Inka superimposed a series of performance spaces and ritual structures, such as platforms, plazas, and large stones, in the center of previously existing non-Inca settlements, including residential ones on a road and fortified ones above it (Coben and Stanish 2005).

Performance within the empire was not limited to the Inka and their ceremonies, although the Inka likely influenced such other performance to varying degrees. No spectacles were scheduled on the Cuzco ritual calendar for certain months of the year (Betanzos 1996; Cobo 1990). During the eleventh month, when no festivals were scheduled for Cuzco, the Inka granted the people of certain towns or ethnic groups the right to conduct ceremonies in their towns (Betanzos 1996:68). The Inka exercised dominion over certain ethnic groups or polities by moving their *huacas* and sacred objects to Cuzco and requiring the elite of such groups and polities to come to Cuzco to worship and celebrate such objects (Cobo 1990). Certain rites, such as marriage, were performed differently in every place, pursuant to local norms (Cobo 1990:206). According to Cobo (1990:244), "Every province throughout the Inka Empire had its own special dances which were never exchanged," as did the "Indians of Cuzco."

The Review: Theaters of Power and Community on Tour

Paul Wheatley (1971), in his classic comparative study, *The Pivot of the Four Quarters: A Preliminary Enquiry into the Origins and Character of the Ancient Chinese City*, describes Shang dynasty cities as material expressions of cosmological order and religious symbolism. These cities served as *axis mundi*, the sacred center of a conceptualized space and world that embody religion, ideology, and worldview. Such centers were frequently associated with the origin of a particular civilization and were designed pursuant to certain urban planning principles that incorporated and represented Shang cosmology and placed these cities at its core. Urban centers were thus an earthly depiction of an otherworldly ideal or archetype; in a Peircean framework, they were iconic instantiations (sinsigns/tokens) of the idealized cosmological type (legisign) that existed at the time of their construction—Peircean replicas of the *axis mundi* and its surrounding space.

Kings and rulers maintain a close association with such cities and their layouts in order to embody the power and sacrality that emanate from them. Upon the founding of a Chinese city, the king was to "assume responsibility for the work of God on High and himself serve . . . at the center of the land . . . and from there govern as the central pivot" (Wheatley 1971:430).

Cuzco, the Inka capital and cosmological center, was the empire's most important and precise physical manifestation of a model conceptualized city. Designed by Pachacuti, modified and augmented by later rulers, the city was the center of the Inka universe, and it represented and embodied their religion, ideology, and worldview. Cuzco was the physical and earthly depiction of an otherworldly Inka archetype—a representation of the cosmological ideal. Such an ideal is a Cuzco type or legisign, of which the actual city is a Peircean replica, the most important and iconic instantiation of this type/legisign.

The idealized type Cuzco and its primary replica at the capital incorporated more than the architectural features, topography, and layout of the idealized city and cosmos. Cuzco was the sacral theater of the Inka cosmos, the setting for an elaborate calendar of ritual ceremonies, and the stage on which many of the most important performances occurred. These performances replicate the idealized social actions and rituals undertaken in the idealized Cuzco's designated spaces, and the various calendars that govern such performances. Replication also includes theatrical properties of any production, such as dance, utterance, movement, lighting, set, and sound transmission. Many of such properties are integrally related to physical orientation, solar and lunar movement, and prevailing wind conditions.

The physical Cuzco and its idealized cosmological equivalent were not fixed or static but changed over time. New buildings were constructed, new spaces and zones created, and new shrines named or dedicated, while others were rebuilt or ceased to be ceremonial locations. Accompanying such physical modifications were changes in cosmology, ideology, religion, and ritual performance. The Inka "elite of Cusco reinstated and redefined their right to rule through their control of rituals and their dominant position in the state cosmology . . . in most, if not all, state-sponsored celebrations of the imperial city" (Bauer 1996:333). Urton (1990) describes how the Inka origin myth was modified and manipulated for ideological purposes. Cobo (1990:5) observed that

> from the beginning of their empire the Incas were not always steadfast in their religion, nor did they maintain the same opinions and worship the same gods . . . They were prompted to make such changes because they realized that this way they improved their control over the kingdom and kept it more subservient.

While a change in ideology or belief need not be accompanied by a corresponding change in material culture (see the "We the people" example above, or the continued use of such structures as the House of Parliament, the White House, or St. Peter's Basilica), architectural and spatial modifications necessarily alter the performances within and about them, and in a cosmological center likely parallel developments in religious belief and ritual practice.

While various Cuzco-like features were present in towns, cities, and provincial capitals, the Inkas designated only a few places in the empire replicas of the idealized cosmological legisign: the other or new Cuzcos. These instantiations of Cuzco are not identical copies of each other but icons of a type. Certain structures, spaces, layout, and landscape features may be absent, rearranged, or present at different scales. Nor should replication be considered on a single feature by single feature basis. Rather, both the co-occurrence and ordering of these features are equally if not more critical to an analysis of Peircean replication. A Peircean replica suggests identity of meaning when experienced by a person. Just as a type-sentence in whose instantiation a word is out of order or missing might carry a vastly different meaning or be incomprehensible, so might the mere recurrence of features without regard to their location, relationship to one another, and order of encounter; that is, as with words, the features must be considered both as co-occurring tokens and as a chain of signs in which sequence is critical.

Thus a site's layout, topography, ingress, egress, and surrounding landscape must all be analyzed in any examination of replication. The nature and degree of iconicity may vary over time within a given replica, as well as over time and space from other Cuzco to other Cuzco. I will analyze these changes and innovations, and their tension and dialectic with replication, to provide insight into Inka imperial expansion. Such dialectic exists not only in architectural form, but also in landscape, site design, ritual, and social action.

Such evidence suggests that the other Cuzcos replicated the capital's role as a sacred theater, the venue for the calendar of state-sponsored performances. At Huánuco Pampa, which was a provincial capital as well as an other Cuzco, elements of ceremonial architecture and layout predominate over administrative ones (Morris and Thompson 1985). A large platform (*ushnu*) with fine Cuzco-style masonry rests in the center of the site's enormous main plaza. Plazas were the focal points of Inca spectacles (Moore 1996). Additional evidence of feasting and ceremonial activity is found to the east in a subsidiary complex consisting of two additional plazas and a compound of elaborate architecture and waterworks also containing such masonry. Ceramic vessels found in this area are characterized by a predominance of jars of larger size than average for the site, especially wide-mouthed ones. These materials have been interpreted as evidence for large-scale food and *chicha* preparation and serving (Morris and Thompson 1985:90). The city was clearly designed for large gatherings as part of a system of governance in which ritual and spectacle played the leading role (Morris and Thompson 1985).

Tomebamba was the sacral theater of the northern part of the empire. Idrovo (2000:81–100) states that Tomebamba replicates Cuzco not only in an administrative sense, but also in physical and religious appearance. He focuses on the placement of sacred spaces and describes a site that "produces a miniature sacred geography, transmitting well the religious symbols of the capital" (Idrovo 2000:83; translation by author). This sacred geography includes a large central plaza bordered on the north by a large *kallanka* (a large, single-room building with multiple doorways), identified by Uhle (1923) as a temple dedicated to the creator god Viracocha, and to the southeast by a large structure, identified by Idrovo as a Sun Temple. Finely made stones from Cuzco of the type used in imperial structures were likely transported to Tomebamba and utilized in its construction (Ogburn 2004).

The recently completed mapping of the site of Incallajta by the author and Maria de los Angeles Muñoz reveals numerous large plazas, including a large pair of abutting central plazas that dominates the site. The largest *kallanka* (approximately 78 by 25 meters) in the Inka empire borders the larger and higher of these two plazas on the north side. Each central plaza contains an elevated platform, likely an *ushnu*, at its highest point. A person standing on either platform can be seen from anywhere within the plaza. A dramatic entrance can be made directly from the *kallanka's* centermost door onto a rock in the center of the upper plaza's *ushnu* (Fig. 8.5). The rock, the platform on which it rests, and a basin found a few meters in front of them suggest the description of an *ushnu* complex that was central to many spectacles in the Haukaypata plaza of Cuzco described above. The site of Incallajta replicates the sacred core of Cuzco, and its location and landscape features evoke the memory and ritual power of those of the Inka capital (Coben 2001, 2003).

The Inkas' intensive replication of their theaters and performances enhances the latter's power by calling attention to their highly structured nature. Parmentier (1994:129–130) observes that

> rituals are not just structured; they are "hyperstructured" in that these cultural forms literally call out: behold the structure! . . . ritual can be interpreted as hyperstructured social action, in which segmentation, hierarchy, and stereotypy are not just contingent aspects of performance but are the means of calling attention to the structuredness of action.

Hyperstructured performances are highly indexical and self-referential; in other words, they call attention to themselves and the structures that they represent and embody. They are "so conventionalized that they highlight or call attention to the rules, that is the pattern [or] model . . . which the ritual action instantiates" (Parmentier 1994:133). These performances invoke and powerfully ground themselves in a society's cosmology, worldview, and ideology, the sources of such rules and structures, and of existing societal order.

The power of a ritual is not maximized by a highly patterned setting alone, or from the mere decontextualized performance of a ceremony (Parmentier 1994:133), but rather when a regimented performance takes place within a replicated theater according to a fixed ceremonial calendar, thereby maximizing the hyperstructured nature of the performatic action and the invocation of the cosmology from which it emanates. Such performance

> is a token which is an instance of a general regularity, that is, a Peircean replica that brings *into* context the legitimized authority, divine precedent or mythological charter behind ritual action. . . . Ritual performance signals not just cultural conventions but conventionality itself. (Parmentier 1994:133)

These hyperstructured performances call attention to and emphasize their culturally derived cosmological, religious, and ideological underpinnings, highlighting and institutionalizing the existing order. They are "the contextual anchoring of hyperconventional . . . forms which have regimenting power due to their association with original or transcendent cultural types" (Parmentier 1994:134).

The original and other Cuzcos and their *ceque* systems, layouts, and features serve as ideal theaters for hyperstructured performances. While all ritual performance is to some degree hyperstructured, it reaches its apogee at the Cuzcos. From the beginning of a performance's preparation through the event itself, the idealized cosmological type Cuzco and all of the power, history, religion, and ideology associated with it are constantly evoked. The other Cuzcos provide the contextual and physical anchoring for the hyperconventional and scripted ceremonial performances of the ritual calendar, many of which are associated with Inka origins, the highest gods of their pantheons, and the rulers themselves. Outside of the capital, no sites so strongly exemplify and project the structure of Inka society. And in their role as settings of and integral elements in Inka ritual, they, together with the performances, replicate, contextualize, and bring to life most forcefully the live performance event that, when combined with structure, maximizes the power of Inka religion and ideology.

While the Inka built numerous provincial capitals and other cities, only a few were designated as other or new Cuzcos. They are generally associated with war and conflict. Quito, Tomebamba, and Incallajta are located near border regions characterized by numerous fortified sites, both Inka and those of other groups (Hyslop 1990; Pärssinen and Siiriäinen 1998; Querejazu 1998). The high wall surrounding much of Incallajta and portions of Tomebamba may have served a defensive function (Nordenskiold

1957; Idrovo 2000). Hatuncolla was built on the site of the Colla capital. The Colla rebelled against the Inka unsuccessfully on numerous occasions and were treated harshly in return (Stanish 2000; D'Altroy 2002:71; Cobo 1979:143, 153). The ruler Topa Inka constructed Inkawasi during his successful conquest of the Huarco valley, perhaps to house his army. Apparently the Inka abandoned Inkawasi after such valley was conquered and incorporated into the empire (Hyslop 1985; Cieza de Leon 1959; Garcilaso de la Vega 1987), and was no longer an area of intense warfare. Huánuco Pampa has no known association with a particular war, rebellion, or conquest.

Much of the capital's ritual calendar, which I suggest would have been performed in the other Cuzcos, is closely associated with warfare. The Inka invested new warriors during Capac Raymi, and at Inti Raymi these new warriors broke their fast and celebrated the harvest. During the annual ritual planting of corn, the Inka sang *haylli*, a song linked with both war and agriculture, and "this ritual was codified in the language of warfare" (Bauer 1996:328, 331). The Inka closely associated agriculture, the theme of many of the ceremonies of their ritual calendar, with warfare (Bauer 1996:328, van de Guchte 1990:335–338; Zuidema 1977:230). Special ceremonies, such as the Itu festival described above, were performed in Cuzco when the Inka went to war personally.

The ruler Huayna Capac designed and rebuilt Tomebamba in present-day Ecuador (Idrovo 2000:83; Cabello Balboa 1951) and likely reconstructed Incallajta while visiting the Pocona region in present-day central Bolivia (Querejazu 1998; Sarmiento de Gamboa 1947). Cabello Balboa (1951), Sarmiento de Gamboa (1947), and other chroniclers specifically state that these two sites were erected on settlements originally constructed by Huayna Capac's father, Topa Inka. The inclusion of this "fact" in the oral histories told by Inka descendants (or perhaps in a few cases, those who had actually witnessed the events in question) to Spanish scribes at least fifty years later, at first blush seems unusual and is not characteristic of these tales. I suggest such inclusion represents an effort by Huayna Capac to parallel and invoke the legendary triumph at and reconstruction of Cuzco by Pachacuti that marked the beginning of the expansive Inka empire.

Pachacuti remains behind to defend Cuzco after his father, the ruler Viracocha Inka, abandons the city, and offers to submit to the ruler of the neighboring Chancas, a local ethnic group threatening the capital and the

Inkas. Against all odds and with mythical assistance, Pachacuti triumphs over the Chancas. His father abdicates in his favor. Pachacuti then redesigns and rebuilds the city of Cuzco, his father's abandoned capital, including the canalization of the Huatenay and Tullomayo Rivers, the creation of the plazas Haukaypata and Cusipata, and the construction of the Coricancha Sun Temple. According to these stories, he also creates a warrior class and the ceremonial and ritual calendar of Cuzco described above. (See Betanzos 1996:21–75 for a more detailed telling of this story and the establishment of the calendar.) After his own successful military campaigns, Huayna Capac reconstructed other Cuzcos atop sites built by his father, thereby equating himself with his legendary grandfather and the founding of the Inka empire while diminishing the legacy of his father by associating him with Viracocha Inka.[6] His designation of Tomebamba as the second capital of the Inka empire further supports this hypothesis.[7]

As discussed above, the ritual order of Cuzco was dynamic and flexible, adapted by various leaders and others for their own strategic purposes (Bauer 1998:161; Niles 1999:52; Rowe 1980, 1985; van de Guchte 1999). Both the *ceque* system and the ceremonial calendar are closely related to Inca mythology and history (Bauer 1996; van de Guchte 1999). Through the manipulation of architecture, such system, and such calendar, Huayna Capac likely utilized other Cuzcos not simply as a response to war and rebellion, but as a powerful tactic to change Inka ritual and mythic history in order to elevate his own power and that of certain of his followers, particularly those in regions distant from the capital, at the expense of Cuzco-based elites.

Whether related to war or internal strife, the strategy of constructing other Cuzcos is directed primarily at the Inka themselves. Neither hyperstructured state-sponsored performance nor the Peircean replicated theaters in which they took place would have been meaningful to a newly conquered subject or a current foe. And non-Inkas were banned from the capital during many of the Cuzco-based ceremonies, a practice presumably followed in large measure at the other Cuzcos. The primary audience for and target of ritual in other Cuzcos were the Inkas. This was performance of the Inka, by the Inka, and for the Inka. These repeated performances served to legitimize, reinforce, redefine, and reformulate Inka hegemony and ideology (Bauer and Stanish 2001; Bauer 1996). They also served to reinforce an Inka's identification with and status and identity within the empire (Coben and Stanish 2005). Reassurance of Inka dominance, superiority, and destiny to rule would have been a particularly important and necessary practice during difficult military campaigns, when doubts about Inka victory in the field could undermine the people's confidence in their rulers. Huayna Capac's campaigns in both Ecuador and Bolivia were hard fought, with the Inka being defeated on certain occasions (Betanzos 1996; Sarmiento de Gamboa 1947). Inka troops in Ecuador at one point mutinied against their ruler and began to return to Peru, only to be lured back by various gifts, sacrifices, and ceremonies. Under these circumstances, the construction of and performance in other Cuzcos would have played an important role in reaffirming Huayna Capac's leadership and the loyalty of his subjects.

While my focus in this chapter has been on hyperstructured, internally directed performance, I suggest that the other Cuzcos may also have played an important strategic role with respect to the newly or sought-to-be incorporated ethnic groups within or across the borders of the empire. The *huacas* and rulers of newly conquered peoples were frequently transported to Cuzco. Local elites and persons were required to worship such *huacas* in the Inka capital (Cobo 1990). Originally they were housed in the Temple of the Sun (Betanzos 1996; Cobo 1990), though as they grew more numerous the Inka constructed separate temples for them elsewhere in the city. *Huaca* and ruler capture and transport was one strategy by which the Inka controlled conquered people and their resources. This strategy also served to demonstrate the superiority of, and inculcate the newly incorporated into, Inka religion. And the conspicuous consumption of animals, cloth, food, and *chicha* inherent in Inka ceremonial performance at these locations would have attracted elites and followers to the Inka to the detriment of other rulers who were unable to match such consumption due to Inka tribute requirements and the restrictions on performing in the Inka capital, and whose performances would have been less powerful due to the absence of and distance from their original, contextualizing local setting. Like the better known and closely related tactic of competitive feasting, superior "competitive performance" would have drawn followers to the Inka banner by winning the hearts, minds, and bellies of those coming to Cuzco to worship their own *huacas*. The construction of other Cuzcos in conflict regions would have facilitated this process greatly, as the geographic proximity of both rulers and *huacas* would have allowed for their manipulation and use in ongoing conflicts. In the case of Tomebamba, Quito, and Incallajta, such proximity would also have provided control over these rulers and *huacas* to Huayna Capac and his followers rather than competing Inka elite kin groups in Cuzco. While evidence of *huaca* capture at other Cuzcos is scant, the presence of several large structures with courtyards and multiple plazas at Incallajta is suggestive. In any event, the construction of massive religious centers would also have served as a statement of Inka presence, political authority, and permanence within a region.

Bring Down the Curtain: All The World's a Cosmological Stage

This chapter highlights the prominent and important role of replicated state-sponsored performances and their settings in the Inka empire, and how such performances reinforced, extended, modified, and transformed it. Performance was ubiquitous in the Inka empire. The Inka constructed numerous cities, settlements, provincial capitals, and pilgrimage routes in which state-sponsored or encouraged performance occurred. All of these theaters incorporated certain physical, structural, design, and religious elements associated with the Inka capital of Cuzco, the empire's cosmological, religious, and political center.

Cuzco was the site of a complex series of Inka ceremonies carried out according to a fixed ritual calendar, as well as other rarer and varied rites and festivals. The Inka constructed a small number of Peircean replicas of this city in troubled and war-related areas of their empire, in order to reproduce powerfully their most sacred theater and the performances within it. After the capital itself, these new and other Cuzcos would have been among the most important locales in the empire, incorporating much of the power of idealized type Cuzco and its ritual calendar while serving as the theaters for similar spectacles and ceremonies. The hyperstructure and replication of the theater itself would likely have militated the effect of the absence of the Inka ruler himself or, alternatively, provided him an appropriate venue from which to lead when he was present. Many of these other Cuzcos are associated with the ruler Huayna Capac, who utilized them not just to reinforce Inka hegemony but to remold it, finally creating a second capital and sacral theater at Tomebamba. Performance of the Inka, by the Inka, and for the Inka was a leading element of Inka imperial strategy, and it played a critical role in the negotiation and resolution of both internal and external strife and conflict.

Notes

I would like to thank Takeshi Inomata for asking me to join him in the creation of this volume, and for being a wonderful partner in all stages of the creative process. Thanks also to Clark Erickson, Robert Preucel, Charles Stanish, and Asif Agha for their incisive comments on earlier drafts of this "act," and to Peter Gallagher and Julie Bowen for providing a performer's perspective on it. Loretta Radice and Paul Boulifard were invaluable in the preparation of the images. My deepest gratitude to my many Bolivian colleagues who made my project at Incallajta possible, including though not limited to Javier Escalante, director of the Unidad Nacional de Arqueologia de Bolivia (UNAR). Thanks also go to José Tejeiro V., former director of UNAR; David M. Pereira Herrera, director of El Museo Arqueológico de la Universidad Mayor de San Simón; the investigators of that museum: Maria de los Angeles Muñoz, codirector of a portion of this project, Ramón Sanzetenea Rocha, Ricardo Céspedes Paz, and Walter Sanchez Canedo; the archaeologist Mali Salas; archaeology students Marcelo Ticona, Ruth Fontenla, and Denisse Rodas; and Ing. Carlos R Valenzuela, Igor Jaramillo, and Pablo Montalvo of the Centro de Levantamientos Aeroespaciales y Aplicaciones. My thanks also to the Peruvian archaeologist Eberth Serrudo and the Mexican archaeologist Juan Carlos Equihua for their work at the site. And my work would not have been possible without the enthusiastic participation of the people of the municipality of Pocona, particularly former mayor Eddy Morató, current mayor Jesús Gonzales Sánchez, former mayor Armando Valdivia Méndez, and municipal council member Vitaliano Córdova, and the subcentral of Incallajta, led by Damián Ricaldez and all of the projects' daily workers. Last, my thanks to Autodesk, and particularly Vice President Phil Bernstein, for an invaluable contribution of software and technical support, and to the Archaeology of the Americas Fund, which funded my research.

1. Taylor (2003:6) defines "performatic" as "the adjectival form of the nondiscursive realm of performance," as distinguished from "performative" and "performativity," which has become "less an adjective of performance than of discourse," especially as used by authors such as Austin (1962) and Butler (1993).

2. Much literature exists as to the historical accuracy of these chronicles, both from the perspective of the biases of their mostly Spanish authors and the likely Inka rewriting of their own history. A discussion of such accuracy lies beyond the

scope of this chapter. To the extent that this chapter discusses actions attributed to a particular Inka ruler, the arguments presented here are not materially affected should such actions ultimately be credited to another ruler.

3. The term "city" here refers to both Cuzco and the new and other Cuzcos. The term is used broadly with the understanding that a terminological debate as to what constitutes a "city" is ongoing in the anthropological literature.

4. Some accounts suggest that the city was laid out in the form of a puma. The puma shape may be apocryphal or a later Spanish invention.

5. Hatuncolla is located in Peru near the western shore of Lake Titicaca.

6. There are a variety of historical reasons why Huayna Capac or his *panaca* (royal house) may have wanted to diminish Topa Inka and thereby his *panaca*. These reasons are likely reflected in Huayna Capac's desire to name a second capital at Tomebamba and more generally shift power to regions away from Cuzco, and underlay some of the differences which led to the civil war that erupted when Huayna Capac died. A detailed discussion of such reasons lies beyond the scope of this chapter.

7. More study is required to determine the differences and similarities between Cuzco and Tomebamba, particularly with respect to ritual performance. I suggest such analysis will shed light on the factionalism between north and south that led to the Inka civil war.

References Cited

Arkush, Elizabeth

2005 Inca Ceremonial Sites in the Southwest Titicaca Basin. *In* Advances in the Archaeology of the Titicaca Basin. Charles Stanish, Amanda Cohen, and Mark Aldenderfer, eds. Pp. 209–242. Los Angeles: Cotsen Institute of Archaeology Press.

Austin, J. L.

1962 How to Do Things with Words. Oxford: Oxford University Press.

Bauer, Brian S.

1996 Legitimization of the State in Inca Myth and Ritual. American Anthropologist 98(2):327–337.

1998 The Sacred Landscape of the Inca. The Cusco Ceque System. Austin: University of Texas Press.

Bauer, Brian, and Charles Stanish

2001 Ritual and Pilgrimage in the Ancient Andes: The Islands of the Sun and the Moon. Austin: University of Texas Press.

Betanzos, Juan de
1996[1551] Narrative of the Incas. Austin: University of Texas Press.

Burger, Richard, and Lucy Salazar-Burger
1993 Machu Picchu Rediscovered: The Royal Estate in the Cloud Forest. Discovery 24(2):20–25.

Butler, Judith
1993 Bodies That Matter: On the Discursive Limits of "Sex." New York: Routledge.

Cabello Balboa, Miguel
1951[1586] Miscelánea Antárctica. Lima: Instituto Etnológico de la Universidad Mayor de San Marcos.

Cieza de Leon, Pedro de
1959[1552] The Incas of Pedro Cieza de Leon. Norman: University of Oklahoma Press.

Coben, Lawrence S.
2001 Signs of the Times: Inca Architecture, Cuzco and Peircean Replication. Paper given at the annual meeting of the Society for American Archaeology, New Orleans.
2003 Incallajta: El Otro Cuzco en las Charcas. Paper given at the 31st Annual Midwest Conference on Andean and Amazonian Archaeology and Ethnohistory, Chicago.

Coben, Lawrence S., and Charles Stanish
2005 Archaeological Reconnaissance in the Carabaya Region, Peru. *In* Advances in the Archaeology of the Titicaca Basin. Charles Stanish, Amanda Cohen, and Mark Aldenderfer, eds. Pp. 243–246. Los Angeles: Cotsen Institute of Archaeology Press.

Cobo, Bernabe
1990[1653] Inca Religion and Customs. Austin: University of Texas Press.
1979[1653] History of the Inca Empire. Austin: University of Texas Press.

D'Altroy, Terence N.
2002 The Incas. Malden, Mass.: Blackwell Publishing.

Ellefsen, Bernardo
1973 El patron urbano incaico segun el profesor Zuidema y su relacion con Incallacta. Bulletin de l' Institut Français d'études Andines 2(4):29–34.

Garcilaso de la Vega, El Inca
1987[1609] Royal Commentaries of the Incas and General History of Peru. Austin: University of Texas Press.

Guaman Poma de Ayala, Felipe
1980[1603] El primer nueva corónica y buen gobierno. Critical edition by John V. Murra and Rolena Adorno; translation and textual analysis of the Quechua by Jorge L. Urioste. Mexico City: Siglo XXI.

Hodder, Ian
1991 Interpretive Archaeology and Its Role. American Antiquity 56:7–18.

Hyslop, John
1985 Inkawasi: The New Cuzco. BAR International Series 234. Oxford: British Archaeological Reports.
1990 Inka Settlement Planning. Austin: University of Texas Press.

Ibarra Grasso, Dick Edgar
1982 Ciencia Astronomicay y sociologia incaica. Cochabamba: Editorial Los Amigos del Libro.

Idrovo Uriguen, Jaime.
2000 Tomebamba, arqueologia e historia de una ciudad imperial. Quito: Banco Central de Ecuador.

Julien, Catherine
1983 Hatunqolla: A View of Inca Rule from the Lake Titicaca Region. Berkeley: University of California Press.

Moore, Jerry
1996 The Archaeology of Plazas and the Proxemics of Ritual. American Anthropologist 98(4):789–802.

Morris, Craig
1990 Arquitectura y estructura del espacio en Huanuco Pampa. Cuadernos del Instituto Nacional de Antropologia 12:27–45.

Morris, Craig, and Donald E. Thompson
1985 Huánuco Pampa: An Inca City and Its Hinterland. London: Thames & Hudson.

Niles, Susan
1987 Callachaca, Style, and Status in an Inca Community. Iowa City: University of Iowa Press.

1999 The Shape of Inca History: Narrative and Architecture in an Andean Empire. Iowa City: University of Iowa Press.

Nordenskiold, Erland
1957[1915] Incallajta, ciudad fortificada fundada por el inca tupac yupanqui. Khana. Revista Municipal de Arte y Letras 25–26: 6–22.

Ogburn, Dennis
2004 Power in Stone: The Long-Distance Movement of Building Blocks in the Inca Empire. Ethnohistory 51:101–135.

Parmentier, Richard
1994 Signs in Society: Studies in Semiotic Anthropology. Bloomington: Indiana University Press.
1997 The Pragmatic Semiotics of Culture. Semiotica 11(6):1–115.

Pärssinen, Martti, and Ari Siiriäinen
1998 Cuzcotoro and the Inka Fortification System in Chuquisaca, Bolivia. Baessler-Archiv, new series, vol. 46:135–164.

Peirce, Charles Sanders
1931–1935 Collected Papers of Charles Sanders Peirce. Charles Hartshorne and Paul Weiss, eds. Cambridge: Harvard University Press.

Pizarro, Pedro
1978[1571] Relacion del descubrimeiento y conquista del Peru. Lima: Pontificia Universidad Catolica del Peru.

Polo de Ondegardo, Juan
1990[1571] Relacion de los fundamentos acerca del notable dano que resulta de no guardar a los indios sus fueros. Madrid: Historia 16.

Preucel, Robert W., and Alexander A. Bauer
2001 Archaeological Pragmatics. Norwegian Archaeological Review 34:85–96.

Querejazu Lewis, Roy
1998 Incallajta y la conquista incaica del collasuyu. Cochabamba: Editorial Los Amigos del Libro.

Rowe, John H.
1945 Absolute Chronology in the Andean Area. American Antiquity 10:265–284.

1946 Inca Culture at the Time of the Spanish Conquest. *In* The Andean Civilizations. Julian H. Steward, ed. Pp. 183–330. Handbook of South American Indians, vol. 2, bulletin 143. Washington, D.C.: Smithsonian.
1980 An Account of the Shrines of Ancient Cuzco. Nawpa Pacha 5:59–76.
1985 La Constitucion Inca del Cuzco. Historica 9(2):193–245.

Sarmiento de Gamboa, Pedro
1947[1572] Historia de los Incas. Buenos Aires: Emece Editores.

Sherbondy, Jeannette
1982 The Canal Systems of Hanan Cuzco. Ph.D. dissertation, Department of Anthropology, University of Illinois at Urbana-Champaign.

Sillar, Bill
2002 Caminado a través del tiempo: Geografías sagradas en cacha/raqchi, Departamento del Cuzco (Perú). Revista Andina 35:221–246.

Silverstein, Michael
1976 Shifters, Linguistic Categories, and Cultural Description. *In* Meaning in Anthropology. K. Basso and H. Selby, eds. Albuquerque: University of New Mexico Press.

Singer, Milton
1978 For a Semiotic Anthropology. *In* Sight, Sound, and Sense. T. A. Sebeok, ed. Bloomington: Indiana University Press.

Stanish, Charles
2000 Negotiating Rank in an Imperial State: Lake Titicaca Basin Elite under Inca and Spanish Control. *In* Hierarchies in Action: Cui Bono? M. Diehl, ed. Pp. 317–339. Southern Illinois University Center for Archaeological Investigations, Occasional Paper no. 27. Carbondale, Ill.

Stanish, Charles, and Brian S. Bauer, eds.
2004 Archaeological Research on the Islands of the Sun and Moon, Lake Titicaca, Bolivia: Final Results from the Proyecto Tiksi Kjarka. Los Angeles: Cotsen Institute of Archaeology Press.

Taylor, Diana
2003 The Archive and the Repertoire: Performing Cultural Memory in the Americas. Durham, N.C.: Duke University Press.

Uhle, Max
1923 Las Ruinas de Tomebamba. Quito: Sáenz Rebolledo.

Urban, Greg

2001 Metaculture: How Culture Moves through the World. Minneapolis: University of Minnesota Press.

Urton, Gary

1990 The History of a Myth: Pacariqtambo and the Origin of the Incas. Austin: University of Texas Press.

Van de Guchte, Martin

1999 The Inca Cognition of Landscape: Archaeology, Ethnohistory, and the Aesthetic of Alterity. *In* Archaeologies of Landscape: Contemporary Perspectives. W. Ashmore and A. Knapp, eds. Oxford: Blackwell.

Wheatley, Paul

1971 The Pivot of the Four Quarters. Chicago: Aldine.

Zuidema, R. Tom

1980 El Ushnu. Revista de la Universidad Comlutense 28(117): 317–361.

1977 The Inka Calendar. *In* Native American Astronomy. Anthony F. Aveni, ed. Pp. 219–259. Austin: University of Texas Press.

1964 The Ceque System of Cuzco. Leiden: Brill.

SCENE 9

PUBLIC CEREMONIAL PERFORMANCE IN ANCIENT EGYPT: EXCLUSION AND INTEGRATION

John Baines

While historians and social scientists accept the centrality of ritual and performance, including performance as public display, in constituting, representing, and sustaining authority in and between societies, archaeologists can have difficulty in identifying correlates for this social centrality in the material record. Ritual actions in small-scale societies may leave little trace if their enactment requires no more than the existence of a suitable space, without constructed features. Nonetheless, in studies of Neolithic and Bronze Age Europe, for example, the identification and interpretation of ritual spaces is a significant focus of research, even where the material evidence is sparse and takes such forms as enclosures and cursus monuments (Bradley 2002:87–89). Results like these should encourage the search for comparable elements in regions where little that is relevant has been identified.

For complex societies and civilizations, spaces for ritual performance and ritually organized features of the built environment are often readily identifiable and major features of the record. Their importance is widely appreciated, even though their large scale and patterns of their use and reuse may make it difficult to investigate them archaeologically. Such difficulties are compounded by the modern history of the sites, which were cleared as tourist attractions without being excavated archaeologically, so that progress on the ground would depend on identifying unexcavated sites.

If the role of such spaces in ancient societies is to be modeled, there arise issues of access and of the "public" addressed by performances that were sited there. Because ruling groups in early civilizations were small and initiation and other restrictions surrounded many of their core activities, one must ask how much those states were concerned with public spectacle, performance, and competitions, of a kind that would be comparable, for example, with what is typical of Greek and Roman civilization. Were central elite concerns enacted in such a way as to address only small numbers of people—as against such groups as deities and the dead—or did performances held in larger arenas of the built or managed environment address wider sections of the community? If such performances occurred, what character did they have?

Major ancient Egyptian sites pose these questions in acute form. Because the scale of monuments such as pyramids and major temple complexes is vast and dominates whole landscapes, in some sense they addressed audiences additional to the deities together with the rulers and elites who commissioned them, or even the considerable sectors of society involved in constructing the biggest of them. Yet despite the monuments' size, the spaces within pyramid complexes in particular were small, while most or all of them were accessible only to a limited group of qualified personnel. This contrast between scale and restricted access conveys a powerful message of exclusion or seclusion—of visual spectacle in the built environment while what is done inside salient features of that environment is withheld from participation and from view. In the modern world such a contrast has come to seem increasingly problematic, but its occurrence is not unique to Egypt. The architectural evidence for exclusion is unequivocal: sacred spaces were enclosed and symbolically protected from the outside world; major public performances were presumably not held within them. Any "secular" public performances that took place are essentially unknown (I mention public proclamations of deeds below). Other possible locations, such as palaces and the cityscapes surrounding them, are largely inaccessible to archaeology (on processional approaches to temples, see Cabrol 2001). Do some features of sacred spaces nonetheless point to public performances that could be called theatrical, in the broad sense of public enactment of significant rituals, of events, or for example of narratives? (I introduce an alternative understanding of theater below.) Is there evidence for such performances in other sources?

These wide-ranging questions can only be addressed selectively. Few have been pursued in detail for Egypt, and I approach them through case studies. An essential issue is how far elites created spaces and performances that acted as focuses for communities, or how far they followed the more inward-looking strategy of appropriating space and performance to themselves and addressing the rest of society principally through exclusion. Norman Yoffee and I studied some of these questions on a theoretical level, with Egypt and Mesopotamia as our comparative examples (Baines and Yoffee 1998; see Richards and Van Buren 2000 for a range of civilizations). We sought to model the maintenance of elites through a common high culture that, although in principle communicative, subverts communication between elites and others. In a more positive perspective, our arguments have parallels in social and political scientists' studies of the self-legitimation of ruling groups in the modern world (Barker 2001). In this chapter, extending the arguments of studies in preparation on elite exploitation of the environment (see also Baines 2004), I revisit our model in relation to communication between elites and others and to the enactment of power.

It is difficult to imagine any but the smallest-scale and least differentiated society that would exist without some sort of spectacle. In order to situate discussion in relation to other possibilities and societal types, one should consider what kinds of institutions and evidence are relevant to the questions I have outlined. I review potential sources, including a couple of more or less universal categories of spectacle, and move to other arenas and thematizations of display and concealment, returning at the end to comparative issues.

Sources

Accessible Egyptian urban sites are few, while terrain and patterns of discovery have been unconducive to studying uses of monuments and traces of ephemeral practices (Fig. 9.1, Table 9.1). The principal exception is the short-lived capital of el-Amarna (c. 1350–1330), which was constructed on a large, impressive tract of low desert and seems to have been unusual for its spacious layout and potential for the spectacular conduct of the ruler's daily life (Kemp 1976; Kemp 1989:261–294; O'Connor 1987–1988; O'Connor n.d.), as well as for less frequent large-scale events (Meskell 2002:168).

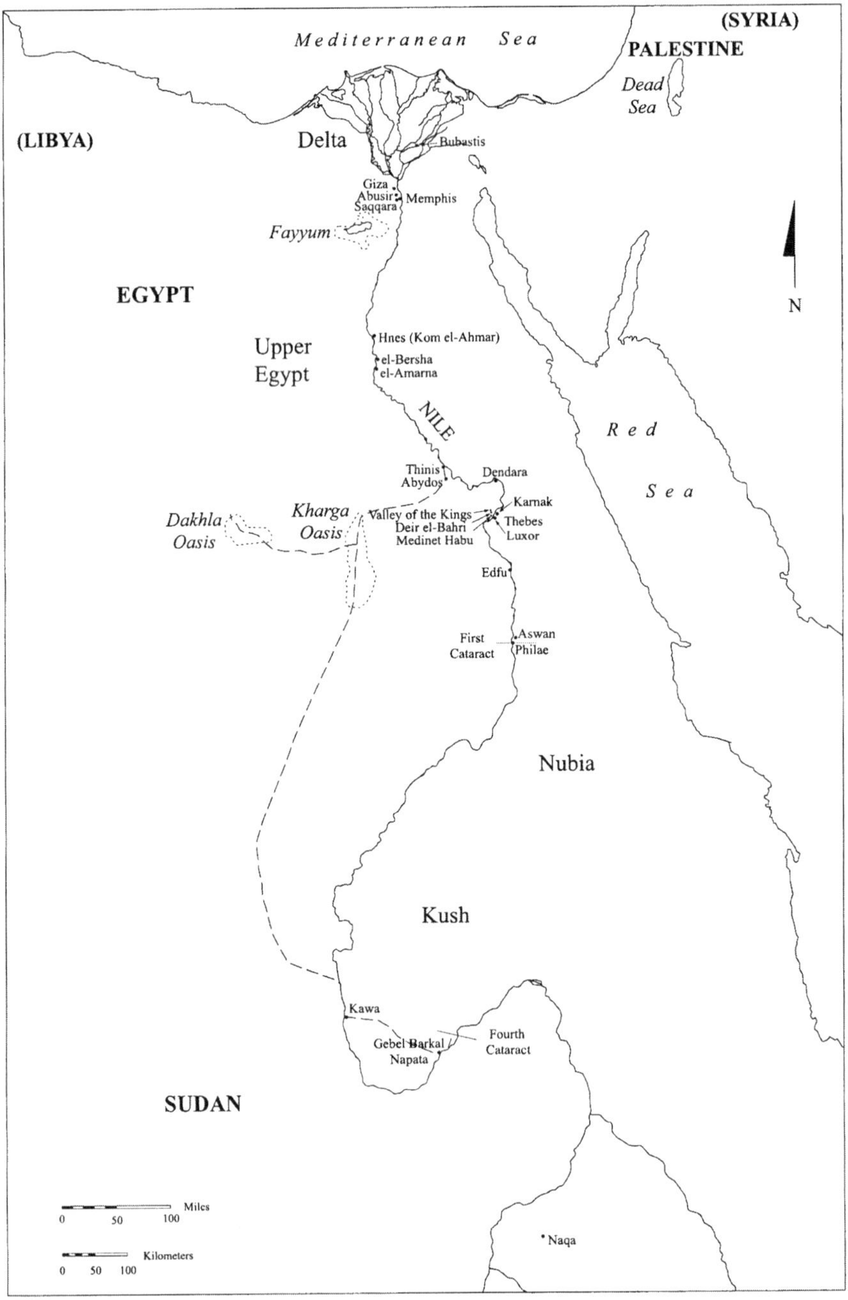

Figure 9.1. Map of Egypt and Northern Sudan, with Sites Mentioned in the Text

Table 9.1. Chronology of Egypt

Early Dynastic period (dynasties 1–3)	2950–2575
Old Kingdom (dynasties 4–8)	2575–2150
First Intermediate period (dynasties 9–11)	2150–1975
Middle Kingdom (dynasties 11–14)	1975–1640
Second Intermediate period (dynasties 15–17)	1640–1525
New Kingdom (dynasties 18–20)	1525–1075
Third Intermediate period (dynasties 21–25)	1075–656
Late period (dynasties 26–31)	664–332
Ptolemaic period	332–30
Roman period	30 B.C.E.–395 C.E.

Note: Dates before 664 are rounded and approximate.

The site is difficult to interpret in relation to general Egyptian patterns of discourse and ideology because it was the arena for promulgating King Akhenaten's consciously revolutionary religion. While the revolution did not affect all aspects of ceremonial life, one of its concomitants was that different events were represented pictorially from those attested for other periods, making comparison with other sites difficult. Nonetheless, the evidence for ceremonial events and practices there, indications of comparable institutions elsewhere, and the impossibility that any revolution could touch all of social life encourage one to investigate these issues in relation to other material. In this chapter I do not study el-Amarna or, for example, Abydos, which produces evidence for "theatrical" rituals performed outside the temple, especially in the Middle Kingdom (O'Connor forthcoming).

In default of detailed archaeological data, I use evidence from iconography, texts, and architectural spaces. A notable gap in evidence relates to the River Nile as an arena for display, which is known from texts and images, whereas archaeological material relating to the river is sparse. The pictorial material was not intended for broad consumption, but some of it depicts events that would have meaning only if enacted on a large scale, whether or not many saw them, which is a central question here. Some rituals and festivals were celebrated simultaneously by many in parallel enactments, for example, around kin groups, that must have affected whole communities.

While the architectural evidence is in principle relatively "objective," even though it is difficult to establish who could enter spaces and what they were used for, images and texts pose more problems. They were produced for small, even theoretical numbers of viewers and readers. The majority of known examples were set up in places to which few had access, and in any case they were difficult or impossible to view; literacy was scarce. While it is probably not useful to ask what their impact was, they can be analyzed as they stand, and one can suggest how ideas they incorporate related to practice. I start with examples from the third millennium and move to a major monument of the second as well as later outliers. Analogous material could be cited from other periods and contexts.

Monuments, Their Purposes, and Their Celebration

Construction

From the time of the great pyramids in the third millennium onward, mortuary monuments were decorated with elaborate pictorial reliefs, some of which ostensibly commemorated events. Others instantiated the notion that the world of the gods and the humanly organized cosmos of Egypt came together to impart gifts of victory, order, generalized benefits, and material provision to the king's mortuary complex. The flow of provision and signification from outside was most strikingly depicted in long processions of figures bearing offerings and representing areas of the country, estates, or abstract qualities (notably Jéquier 1940: pls. 19–28; Jacquet-Gordon 1962). Deities could also be shown leading captives toward pyramid temple interiors (Borchardt et al. 1913: pls. 5–7; Jéquier 1940: pls. 12–14). None of this necessarily corresponded to anything that was enacted, while details show that some scenes should not be taken literally, but there may have been occasions when local representatives symbolically presented products to institutions at the capital. These processions are not temporally situated and should be seen as perpetually available to the king in this world and the next. Some of the reliefs depict possible spectacles, but that is not their prime purpose.

All this decoration made the pyramid complex central to its owner's cosmos. The monument was displayed as the result and product of the activities symbolized by the processions, which signified both single events and repeated activities. Single events can be complemented by more detailed material. A scene from the approach causeway of the Fifth Dynasty pyramid temple of Sahure (c. 2425) shows the pyramid's capstone, which is said to be of electrum—presumably it is gilt with electrum—being dragged, no doubt to the site of the pyramid itself (Hawass and Verner 1996). Other registers show prepared food, perhaps in booths, the bringing of pieces of furniture, slaughter of oxen, and groups of deferential courtiers. Further blocks discovered nearby include possibly connected scenes of dancing and wrestling. All of this suggests that the final stage of construction may have been celebrated for its own sake. As in many societies, ritual enveloped the earlier stage of laying out ground plans, which was depicted with divine actors and is attested from the Early Dynastic period onward (Engelbach 1934), as well as other stages in the creation of a monument. While access to such events is generally limited and hierarchical, the many years it took to build a pyramid complex, the size of labor force, and the vast amount of craft work that went into its decoration mean that events like these reverberated among a far larger group than those performing the rituals. The dragging of the capstone involved large numbers of people and was a ready vehicle for "dramatized" performance.

The potential for celebrations offered by construction practices can even be seen in old photographs. At the beginning of the twentieth century, the colossal columns of the hypostyle hall in the temple of Karnak were reconstructed following a collapse, partly using the ancient method of building rubble ramps up which the blocks were dragged. Blocks were garlanded with palm fronds and workers posed beside them (Azim and Réveillac 2004:2:56, 67–68, 77–79). This was done partly for photography, but the practice was probably traditional. In an early second millennium depiction of the transport of a colossal statue, groups of celebrants are shown running and waving palm fronds beside the men pulling the ropes (Newberry [1893]: pls. 12, 15; Baines and Malek 2000:126–127; Davies 1999). Along the registers are inscribed songs of joyful participation and praise of the statue's owner, the local potentate Djehutihotep. The songs are stated to be performed by the dragging crews, who are dressed in ceremonial clothing and represent various districts of the province in whose capital the statue was to be set up. Behind the statue, its owner and his family and retinue are shown in formal attire.

Such an image need not be taken literally, but events like these involved many people. The design of the relief showing the statue transport is formally close enough to that of the Sahure (see above) on a probably stereotyped ceremonial hunt (Borchardt et al. 1913: pl. 17) to make it plausible that Djehutihotep's designer adopted a template from a royal model. Apart from this artistic correspondence, it is likely that royalty and nonroyal elites staged both unique and cyclical events so as to maximize their impact in the community. While the reliefs are not visual records of the events—such a notion might be anachronistic—the creation of an idealized representation of what happened outside within the microcosm of a monument gives them some credence as a source. The treatment of such events varies from the relatively "realistic" to the entirely symbolic, so that examples need to be evaluated individually. The assumption that construction projects were generally well known is supported indirectly by the early Eighteenth Dynasty biography of Ineni, which states that he supervised the construction of what may have been the first tomb in the Valley of the Kings at Thebes, "none seeing, none hearing," which implies that this was not normally the case (Sethe 1906:57; Dziobek 1992:51, 53).

From altogether later, the construction of the temple of Edfu (c. 235–80 B.C.E.) is recorded in texts that emphasize celebration by the entire city (De Wit 1961; Kurth 1994:71). This focus on celebration and joy is characteristic of many Egyptian texts, especially from later periods (Baines 1997:218). The wider impact of the completed temple is not clear. While its vast complex came during a century and a half to dominate Edfu and its construction was celebrated locally, its longer-term local meaning is not straightforward. Only priestly personnel could enter. At most its outer court was accessible to a wider group. Its prime purpose was centripetal and cosmological, not local and devotional. Among the rituals shown or mentioned in the hundreds of reliefs and inscriptions covering its walls, only those which involved journeys outside the temple presented its divine inhabitants to the wider population. On those occasions the images of deities were kept inside shrines which were themselves shrouded from view by cloths draped over them. Concealment was part of display. Almost all deities were concealed in this way, so that this paradox was a constant feature of public cult.

In summary, the construction of a monument had a fairly broad impact, especially if it was a rapidly built structure like a pyramid, on which vast numbers of people were employed for a decade or two. A temple like Edfu, where construction by a smaller labor force lasted for generations, must have had a different but also powerful resonance among the population. In another sense such temples were strongly anchored in their communities by the networks of land holdings and social obligations that accrued over centuries, in a rhythm that was not closely related to the structures themselves and was anything but spectacular (Meeks 1972).

Funerals: What Is Absent from Mortuary Monuments?

The ultimate purpose of pyramid complexes and tombs was to serve as a resting place for the deceased and a location for mortuary cult. As Dieter Arnold (1977) has shown, they cannot have been used for the performance of funerals, because crucial transition points in them were too narrow to accommodate funerary equipment. Preparation of the body for burial could take most of a year (Dunham and Simpson 1974:8), while the processes and materials involved were probably polluting and were discarded ceremonially (Münch 2000). A First Dynasty tomb belonging to one of the two or three leading people in the country bears a likely reminder of the funeral in the form of hundreds of cattle horns set into the plastered bench of the facade (Emery [1954:8–9] estimated 300). The most plausible interpretation of this feature is that animals—whether or not these ones or this number of them—were slaughtered at the funeral and their horns were placed there as a token of that event. If so, the meat could have been distributed to vast numbers of people. A comparable scale of performance is suggested by the text of a funerary liturgy that enumerates events lasting a number of days and involving many people (Gardiner 1955; ms Middle Kingdom but composition probably older). In the Old Kingdom, grave goods were sparse, yet tomb decoration shows the preparation of large amounts of furniture, sometimes in association with statuary. The statuary was meant for deposition in the tomb, so it is logical to assume that the furniture too was funerary. Since it does not seem to have been included in burials, it may have had a role in the funeral, which would have been very elaborate if such artifacts were used once and ceremonially discarded (compare Münch 2000).

Traces identified on the surfaces of Old Kingdom tomb structures support the assumption that funerals were performed in the open; offering pottery suggests that numerous people were present or that there was much accompanying ritual activity (Alexanian 1998). Images of funerals from the New Kingdom, when numerous grave goods commonly formed part of elite burials, show elaborate processions, part of the meaning of which seems to have been to display what was to be buried. In some examples, the holders of leading state offices walk in hierarchical order behind the coffin, rather as in modern state funerals (cf. Meskell 2002:189–193; Lange and Hirmer 1968: pls. 28–29, 171; Martin 1987: nos. 21–24, 62–64, 66–67, 100–102; hierarchical order: Schulman 1965: pl. 30). Booths with refreshments are set up alongside. In some cases, the booths or their contents seem to have been destroyed after a procession passed, presumably symbolizing the closure of the deceased's life and associations. The booths also imply some wider presence, of attendants of the processing elites or of the general population. The setting-up of the processional way and the funerary cortege for elites would have been a significant spectacle for many people—as was no doubt also true of kings: unless access to royal funerals was severely restricted, they must have been elaborately orchestrated. A suggestive detail is the mortuary cortege shown in the tomb of Tutankhamun (Reeves 1990:72). Simply to take Tutankhamun's tomb equipment to the Valley of the Kings for burial would have been a significant undertaking; when some of the excavated material was brought to the river for transport to Cairo, the parade became a heavily photographed ceremony.

Comparable ceremonial funerals are attested for the major animal cults of the first millennium. The Apis Bull, which was kept in a temple complex in Memphis, was buried in a closed mausoleum in the Saqqara necropolis. The preparation of the vault, the transport of the massive hardstone sarcophagus, which may have been done well in advance, and the funeral and burial were major episodes in city life. Between the death of one bull and the next, the mausoleum seems to have been kept sealed except during the excavation of the next vault, so that major activity was focused around one or two periods in the bull's career, of which its death was the most important (Vercoutter 1975; Smith 1972:64–82: fictional presentation from primary sources for the bull's mother). From the same period a captioned relief on a mortuary stela the funeral for a member of the priestly elite in Upper Egypt as having named executants, lasting four days, and including visits to Thinis, Abydos (where the stela was found), and a third locality, in a journey of more than twenty kilometers (Jansen-Winkeln 2001:135 n. 17).

Funerals were presumably replicated in less elaborate forms right down the social scale, but it is not possible to trace nonelite performances. As an arena of display and participation, they probably both divided disparate social groups and drew them together. Among ruling elites in many complex societies, funerals have been and continue to be very major public events (for renaissance Europe, see Giesey 1960; Howarth 1997:153–190). Even in the Muslim world, where burial should be before the next sundown, funeral corteges are significant displays. The scale of Egyptian mortuary monuments alone makes it likely that this was the case in antiquity.

Commemoration of Deeds and Events: Arenas of Display

The pictorial decoration of mortuary complexes commemorated a specific life or an ideal life colored with a few individual elements. The person of the royal or nonroyal owner was celebrated in the first instance in images and secondarily in inscriptions that minimally identified him or her through titles and epithets, but did not necessarily make more specific statements. Since this volume focuses on public events, of which many would be repeated, this dearth of distinctive materials may not be a handicap, but for many periods it may be impossible to study how the unique was integrated with the repeated.

Such an integration, however, was at the heart of the performance of kingship and of rule, as is clear from annals from the beginning of the historical period, in which a biennial royal progress or tour of duty through the country figures prominently. This progress was named the "Following of Horus," where "Horus" was both the king, who performed an office that manifested an aspect of the principal god, and that god himself (Wilkinson 2000). The "Following of Horus" was also the name of a set of standards that accompanied the king when he appeared in public, signifying both protection and aspects of kingship (Kaiser 1959). This institution, which may have disappeared by the end of the Early Dynastic period, created a regular spectacle of rule that may in part have been superseded by the intense focus on the center of the country which is evident in the enormous Old Kingdom mortuary monuments.

Until the New Kingdom, most compositions in mortuary decoration were either small scale or rather abstract in character, as with the processions mentioned above. Among exceptions, some scenes depict the king in a natural environment, hunting hippopotamus, fish, and birds in the marshes or game in the low desert (Borchardt et al. 1913: pls. 15–16). These suggest that the king occasionally showed himself in the world at large. The most significant scenes in terms of public performance are two in the mortuary complex of Sahure. In one, a group of ships is shown presumably returning from an expedition abroad (Borchardt et al. 1913: pls. 12–14; fragmentary scene of ships setting out, pl. 11). Above each ship is inscribed part of a litany that states that the king is beloved of a range of deities (Fig. 9.2); this is presumably being declaimed by the crews, some of

Figure 9.2. Ship with Crew, from Ceremonial Relief of the Arrival of an Expedition from Abroad from the Mortuary Temple of Sahure (5th Dynasty) at Abusir (after Borchardt et al. 1913: pl. 13)

whose members are not Egyptian (Bietak 1988). High- and lower-ranking court personnel are shown in upper registers, in a pose of deference and at a larger scale than the images of the boats. The pose and differences in scale probably relate to a lost figure of the king that would have dominated the composition. The design implies that an expedition abroad is significant not so much in itself as because its celebration contributes to the king's position and enhances it in relation to the gods. Events like these—this one is probably generic, even if captions gave it a specific cast—exploited the river and were presumably orchestrated as spectacles, although their ultimate focus on the king and the gods pointed toward a sphere that was inaccessible for most people. The modern viewer's sense that this shows an event that could have occurred is reinforced by a different relief which shows the king's own, more splendidly furnished ship, together with members of his retinue (Borchardt et al. 1913: pl. 9), and by contrasting those examples with scenes of the king triumphing over his Libyan enemies, which contain numerous imaginary features (Borchardt et al. 1913: pls. 1, 7).

An annal inscription of the nineteenth century B.C.E. mentions the dispatch of a military expedition abroad and its successful return, presumably months later. There follow a short journey, a celebratory hunt, a distribution of rewards primarily to the expedition leaders, and the creation of statues for the gods (Altenmüller and Moussa 1991; Baines in preparation; the word for "dispatching" is written with a ship determinative). These events bring together motifs that form separate captioned pictorial compositions in Old Kingdom mortuary complexes. The sequence moves toward progressively smaller audiences, starting with a publicly observable expedition that reaches outward and on its return brings the world outside Egypt to the center. Such patterns are theatrical in the sense that theater is about gathering events from outside and representing them within a separate, restricted space. They are not, however, fictional in the literary sense of performed imaginary narratives or situations. Much of the aim of the celebrations was no doubt to reinforce the impact of the events abroad that were evoked; there is no evidence that these were recreated in staged renderings.

From the Eighteenth Dynasty come texts recounting military expeditions that have an overall structure comparable to the one just described. Kings of the period, however, participated in the campaigns, making their return to Egypt, from regions in Sudan and Syria, into a visible parade of victory. Thutmose I (c. 1493–1483) brought a slain captive back from Nubia hanging upside down from the prow of his ship (Sethe 1906:9; Lichtheim 1976:14). Amenhotep II (c. 1427–1401) stated that at the end of his early campaign to Syria-Palestine he similarly hung seven corpses of slain rulers from his ship. He then displayed six of them on the walls of Thebes and dispatched the seventh to be hung on the wall of Napata in the Fourth Cataract, at the southern end of Egyptian territory in Nubia (Helck 1955:1297; 1961:31–32).

Difficulties of navigation and topography render it improbable that any ship would have made exactly this journey, but the text's visual rhetoric fits into a tradition of display on the river. On the decks of royal ships were baldachins in which the king could show himself; a full-scale example is preserved from the Great Pyramid complex at Giza (Jenkins 1980: figs. 79, 93; pl. 7); models are also known (Werner 1986). The hull projections of New Kingdom royal ships often bore scenes of the king clubbing enemies with a mace or related motifs (Landström 1970:98–113). These were located close to the position where Amenhotep II hung the rebel corpse. Thus as the king traveled by river, he visibly asserted his rule, and in the process made the main cabin of his ship into a proper, sanctified location in which he could appropriately sit on his traveling throne, protected by representations of the defeat of enemies.

This iconography constitutes both spectacle and exclusion. The king's presence on the river is a spectacle, while the protective decoration reinforces exclusion; the ship itself is accessible only to specific personnel. The public spectacle might seem limited in impact to our eyes because ancient ships were not large, but such matters depend on expectations. Texts praise the dimensions of ships, many of which are also depicted as extravagantly decorated. Texts, depictions, and practicalities show that a normal royal progress would be a flotilla, not a single vessel. From the third millennium to the first, texts and reliefs celebrated exceptional exploits and speeds of navigation, ranging from overcoming the storms which can render the river treacherous (Schott 1977), to transporting monoliths such as obelisks or colossal statues along the Nile through much of the land (Lichtheim 1973:21–22; Naville n.d.: vol. 6, pls. 153–156; Helck 1958:1822–1823; 1961:272–273). The latter required large numbers of people, often traveling many hundreds of kilometers.

Boatmanship itself was an object of display, as in an inscription of Amenhotep II which states that he acted as stroke for two hundred oarsmen, and when they were exhausted after five kilometers of rowing, he took over and single-handedly rowed another twenty-five kilometers (Lichtheim 1976:41; the "miles" of the translation are units of 10.6 kilometers). It is irrelevant that this achievement is far less possible than Mao Zedong's hour-long swim in the Yangzi at the age of seventy-three in 1966. What is relevant is that the river was an arena of spectacle, and that the size of ships and their crews, as well as feats of navigation, were topics for presentation, narration, and celebration.

We know of some events and feats of navigation from the material evidence of the monoliths themselves, as well as from depictions and texts. The latter, which can be checked against surviving monuments that are mentioned in texts, appear not to exaggerate unduly. But once the monoliths had been set up, even the grandest of them were accessible to relatively few people, either because they were inside sacred spaces or just because they were in a place that only a minority, in the long, thin land of Egypt, would visit. Their transport served the centripetal, "theatrical" purpose mentioned above. The commemorative inscriptions and reliefs did this much less, because they were in locations where few would see them—they were far less public than the monoliths themselves—and because they were in specialized media, especially the hieroglyphic script, which few were competent to read.

Were there other arenas in which these exploits were made public? Royal inscriptions of general import were often set up in temples across the country, while under Amenhotep III (c. 1391–1353) sets of scarabs asserting royal dominion and announcing royal exploits were distributed in hundreds of copies that have been found from Nubia to Syria (Blankenberg-Van Delden 1969; Baines 2003). The process of creating inscriptions would have disseminated their content, but one cannot say how widely it became known. It is possible to imagine royal deeds being proclaimed around the country, as the accession of a king seems to have been (Sethe 1906:79–81, Eighteenth Dynasty accession of Thutmose I, known from three examples; Černý and Gardiner 1957: pl. 69:1, Twentieth Dynasty accession of Ramesses V). But it should not be assumed automatically that there was much concern to make events widely known. This also might not have been a difficulty. Among perhaps a couple of million people, few of whom lived very far from the travel artery of the river, it may have been possible to rely on social networks and, for example, on military draft, corvée, and such institutions to spread awareness as far as was desired.

Two related features of the material are relevant here. These are the almost complete absence of public narratives of anything other than victory and success—the suppression of failure is common enough in any society—and the joy and celebration that permeate the record. This enforced optimism, which can be seen to be such because different perspectives exist in belles lettres (Parkinson 2002) and some other sources, is part of the high-cultural assertion with which the central elite confronted the gods and their own destiny. Sustaining such a position must have involved ignoring available information and so could have worked against public proclamation.

Monuments as Representations of Rituals: Journeys to Festivals

The questions reviewed so far are well exemplified in the architecture and texts in the ceremonial capital of Thebes from Amenhotep III to the end of the Eighteenth Dynasty. Amenhotep III remodeled Thebes and constructed temples throughout the city, transforming its cosmological character (O'Connor 1998) and linking sacred areas on the East Bank with avenues of sphinxes (Cabrol 2001). Most evidence for these avenues dates to the fourth century B.C.E., when a text states that they were backed by walls (Abd el-Razik 1969:157). The eastern approach to the Karnak temple was remodeled, seemingly without sphinxes but including walling off the sacred way from neighboring courtyards. Thus even these thoroughfares running through the city were not freely accessible.

Amenhotep III also replaced the ceremonial bark (as ships of deities are termed) of Amon-Re, in which the principal god traveled between temples on the east and west banks of the river during the major festivals of "Opet" and of the "navigation of the West" (on barks, see Karlshausen 1997). This bark is described in the longest building inscription from the reign:

> The Dual King Nebma'atre, exemplar of Re,
> Son of Re, Amenhotep ruler of Thebes.
> Again I made a monument for the one who bore me,

> Amon-Re, Lord of the Thrones of the Two Lands,
> who established me on his throne:
> Making for him a great bark for river travel,
> (named) Amon-Re is Great of Prow,
> in fresh pine which His Person felled on the uplands of God's Land,
> being dragged from the mountains of Syria
> by the chiefs of all foreign lands,
> being made very broad and large, its like never having been made before,
> its interior purified with silver,
> and it was worked with gold throughout,
> its great shrine being of electrum.
> Its prow doubled its length
> and was endowed with vast crowns,
> their cobras encircling on its two sides,
> acting in protection all around.
> Flagpoles were set up before it (the shrine),
> worked with electrum,
> with two great obelisks between them.
> It was beautiful on all sides.
> The Souls of Pe performed a dance of jubilation for it,
> and the Souls of Nekhen adored it.
> The Meret goddesses of Upper and Lower Egypt propitiated its presence.
> Its prow illuminated the primeval waters,
> like the rising of the sun in the sky,
> in order to make its perfect navigation at his (the god's) festival of Opet,
> (and) at his navigation of the West
> of millions and millions of years. (Helck 1957:1652–1653; Lichtheim 1976:45)

This description makes the bark into a mobile temple with numerous divine associations. Representations of divine barks match this description, showing either consistency with its real appearance or a mutually reinforcing fiction; a particularly elaborate example dates to the same reign (Schwaller de Lubicz 1999: pls. 98–99; Landström 1970:119 fig. 368, 121 fig. 370). In imagery that is paralleled in other texts, the precious metals—either used or simulated in paint—make the bark gleam, emanating the solar character of the god it bore and spreading its luster through reflections in water. While this radiance could spread the bark's meaning among people who saw it on the river, the text does not mention them, instead returning repeatedly to the king's relationship with the god. There was a tension between divine presence and its concealment, as well as its dissemination on the river, from the moment deities came out of temples, because their shrouded images in their shrines were set on portable, ideally gilded barks that made movement into a symbolic, fictionalized river journey.

Thus the iconography of river barks both constituted spectacle and conveyed a message of exclusion. This tension between display and concealment also lay at the core of temple design, and it was reinforced by a unique development of the reign of Amenhotep III. The forward part of the temple of Luxor at the southern end of the city (Fig. 9.3), which was visited by Amon-Re of Karnak (at the city's northern end) at the festival of Opet, consisted of a relatively narrow facade to a colonnaded corridor of enormous dimensions (Epigraphic Survey 1994, 1998; Wolf 1931). This

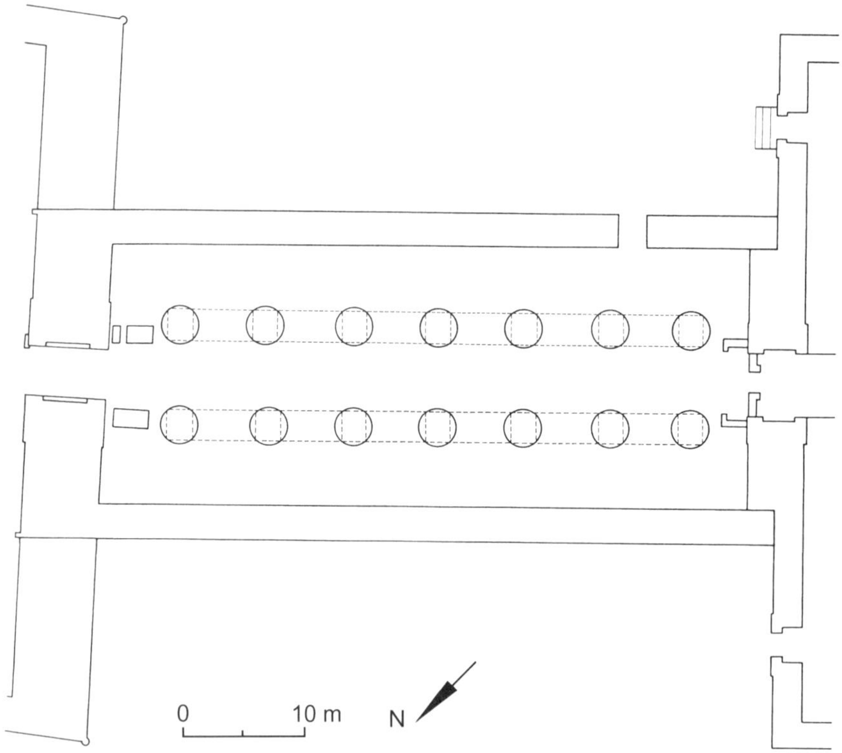

Figure 9.3. Plan of the Luxor Temple, with the Colonnade Hall of Amenhotep III; Fourteenth–Thirteenth Centuries B.C.E. The Broad Walls on the Left of the Plan Are a Later Addition to Amenhotep III's design.

long, not very wide space is not an obvious focus for ritual performance but seems to have constituted something like a "stage," on the interior walls of which the festival of Opet was depicted. One can imagine the portable barks of the gods being set up temporarily in the colonnade hall, but neither this nor the court behind it was a public space (here, I differ from Bell 1997; Teeter 1997). Rather, these areas served the theatrical purpose of incorporating the parts of the ritual that took place outside the temple within its confines, so that they too could be perpetually celebrated and rendered present to the god. This function may have been particularly valuable for the Luxor temple, which seems to have been a ritual outlier of the cult of Amon-Re more than a cult center in its own right (Bell 1985).

The decoration of the colonnade hall was executed around 1330–1280 under Tutankhamun, Haremhab, and Sety I. They may have followed designs of Amenhotep III, because it is difficult to imagine that such a vast construction would be completed without a plan for its decoration, but little survives from his reign (Epigraphic Survey 1998:xvii–xix). In the interior, only the lowest register of three or four is preserved to any great extent. It is likely that the upper registers had repetitive scenes of the king adoring deities and not the rare material of the lowest register, which was also the only one that could be viewed at all effectively—as also with such tall relief compositions as Trajan's Column in Rome—and then only by those qualified to enter the temple.

It is difficult to comprehend the magnitude of this unitary composition, which at two reliefs, each more than fifty meters long, is on a larger scale than almost any Western work of representational art. The theme of these vast scenes is the journey of the cult barks of the three main deities of Karnak, Amon-Re, Mut, and Khonsu, together with that of the king, from Karnak to Luxor for the festival of Opet, and their return to Karnak at the end of the festival (Fig. 9.4). The move is completed in stages, from the king's emergence from his palace and entry into the temple, through the appearance of the images of the gods in their portable shrines and transfer to their river barks, to their entry into the Luxor temple and receipt of worship there. The journey, which is less than three kilometers, is presented as a huge and active celebration. The barks are towed upstream by teams of haulers on the shore and are accompanied by soldiers, musicians, and dancers, in addition to priestly personnel. Booths with refreshments, comparable with

Figure 9.4. Section of the Relief of the Festival of Opet in the Colonnade Hall of Amenhotep III at Luxor; Reigns of Tutankhamun/Haremhab. The Upper Register Shows the Bark of the Goddess Mut, Preceded by a Service Ship with a Large Personnel. In the Lower Register Are Men Hauling a Bark from the Shore on the Left and Other Attendants on the Right. Photograph Courtesy of the University of Leipzig

those shown for funeral processions, imply that many people are present and enhance the celebratory atmosphere. However, all the figures in the composition seem to be participants, for whom the refreshments may be intended. Spectators are not depicted. Crowds of people may have observed and cheered on the progress of the barks, but they are not shown in the reliefs. A biographical text states that late in the reign of Thutmose III (c. 1430 B.C.E.) its protagonist Amenemhab formed part of the crew sailing and mooring the bark of Amon-Re at the festival of Opet, and that "all the Two Lands (i.e., Egypt) were in rejoicing," so that by implication there was mass participation (Sethe 1907:895–897). "All the Two Lands" could, however, mean all those who mattered—elites and others directly involved. Despite the visibility of the event and this seemingly explicit statement, one cannot say how widespread participation was. If people of the highest rank, such as Amenemhab, played apparently practical, but no doubt also prestige-laden, roles in the festival ritual, this suggests that the event was not primarily addressed to the people as a whole.

None of the groups of people depicted in the reliefs belongs to categories that are shown in central areas of temple decoration, so that the composition is explicitly "exterior," even though it is located inside a columned hall. Much of the material is specialized and learned, notably a mildly erotic song about the encounter of the king with the goddess Hathor (Epigraphic Survey 1994:12–14, pl. 26), which is cryptically formulated in language and orthography that seemingly derived from ancient models.

Thus, despite the vast scale and hundreds of figures, nothing in this composition relates to a mass audience, and some material is recondite. This contrast between scale, ostentation, and specialized content fits with the location. The hall makes the grandest architectural statement and must have been visible from the river and from the city, but its specific content, which was inscribed only on the inside, was not revealed by its form. The ground plan created by this extra element was most unusual. The long hall led to a wider double-colonnaded court that merged in turn, without any closure, into a broad hypostyle (columned) hall, behind which were the temple's cult areas. The very rare absence of any screening to the hypostyle hall may be related to the presence of the colonnade, the back portal and door of which interrupted any view of the temple interior from outside the temple entrance. Probably the court too was in some sense an "interior" space, even though it was open to the sky.

All these features mean that the outer areas at Luxor form a space where the festival of Opet, including its more public and spectacular parts, was incorporated into the very structure of the temple where its core was celebrated, while the court was probably a special part of the interior where some stages of the ritual could take place. The temple structure and decoration "sacralized" the entire festival, not just its intimate rites. This was the most significant annual ritual in Thebes. Haremhab, under whom the colonnade reliefs were completed, legitimized his accession to the throne, to which he was not entitled by descent, by enacting his acceptance by Amon-Re, through the mediation of his local god Horus of Hnes, at the festival of Opet. He recorded the episode in an extensive inscription on a pair statue of himself and his queen (unprovenanced but probably from Thebes: Gardiner 1953—the "coronation" in the article title is inexact). The temple of Horus of Hnes was about four hundred kilometers to the north, and the journey from there to Thebes no doubt formed a spectacle that brought not just Horus but also the land in general toward a ritual performance that had enormous symbolic import (Baines 2004:42–44). The festival thus had political as well as ritual significance. The text does not state where Amon-Re accepted Haremhab, but it "dramatizes" and almost fictionalizes the event by stating that Amon-Re happened to be away from Karnak at the festival when Horus of Hnes arrived. The acceptance may have been within the Luxor temple because images of gods were only revealed to view inside temples. Later rulers used roughly the same trajectory as Haremhab for similar purposes. These include the High Priest Osorkon of the ninth century B.C.E. (Caminos 1958:162–163) and Psammetichus I (664–610), who installed his daughter Nitokris as the adoptive successor to the then leading dynastic figure in Thebes, the Divine Adoratrice of Amun (Caminos 1964).

Haremhab exploited the festival as well as the colonnade hall. There is no specific evidence for why its new design was created under Amenhotep III. Despite the latter's grandiose remodeling of Thebes as a whole and his building inscription's emphasis on display on the river, the hall appropriates the crucial ritual to the temple interior, creating something both visible and more exclusive to the gods and less accessible than the public parts of the festival. Materially, aesthetically, and theatrically, the architecture internalized ritual performance and display.

More than two centuries later, around 1075, Herihor, a high priest of Amon-Re and ruler of the Theban area who adopted kingly titles, created the only other known extensive representation of the festival of Opet (Epigraphic Survey 1979: pls. 19–23, 26). This is in the forecourt of the temple of Khonsu at Karnak, a slightly more accessible and considerably smaller space than the colonnade hall. In addition to scenes of the barks sailing to Luxor, the register includes figures of the children of Herihor (Epigraphic Survey 1979: pl. 26). The essential relevance of these reliefs is that Herihor exploited the ritual for political purposes in a manner comparable to Haremhab. In Herihor's case the reliefs themselves included the political theme, whereas Haremhab made his claim in a separate inscription and his reliefs have a more timeless appearance, while probably deriving from designs of Amenhotep III.

The large numbers of participants in all these reliefs raise a more general question. Egyptian temples seem not to have been accessible to any broad public, yet they enclose spaces whose vastness people now find difficult to comprehend if they were never filled with crowds. To state the question thus is to suggest that in one respect it is wrongly posed because its perspective is that of the densely populated modern world. Moreover, large ordered and enclosed spaces are almost universally a mark of status. Where those spaces are dedicated to deities, the grander they are, the more strongly they assert the deities' majesty and power. The relatively small numbers of personnel in the courts and halls contribute to this message. It is hard to gain a sense of the ancient appearance of temples because they contained vast numbers of statues and must have been far more cluttered than they are now. Votive offerings, and occasionally surplus statues, were buried or otherwise disposed of within the sacred precinct, presumably in order to disencumber the ritual spaces. A cache of statuary found in the main court of the Luxor temple is an example of the furnishings that are almost entirely lost (El-Saghir 1991; see Azim and Réveillac 2004:1:275–335, 2:201–302: Karnak).

There has been a tendency to interpret the pictorial evidence for participation in temples rather too literally. In contrast with the Opet festival compositions, most reliefs inside temples represent only the king and deities. In marginal and special areas priests are depicted, notably carrying portable barks. They are shown both because it takes many people to carry a bark and because barks take deities outside temples. In another sense, the priests are tokens of their wider presence within temples. The cult was performed by priests. At most, the king was the principal executant when he was present for a major ritual. The depiction of the king offering to the gods is in keeping with decorum but does not represent any straightforward reality, as is evident from texts describing the actions of priests, which do not disguise the fact that they, not the king, performed the rituals (Roccati 1982:235–236).

An element that is absent from temple decoration is subordinate staff. Temples like Karnak and Luxor had enormous staffs, but their existence can be established only from documentary sources (which cannot be studied here), as well as from general considerations of the numbers that might be needed to service rituals, maintain structures, and so forth. Greco-Roman period temples add homilies on proper conduct addressed to personnel entering by the side doors around which these texts are inscribed (e.g. Gutbub 1973:144–184). As in many societies, those of lower status who were required for practical reasons were not absent; they were simply not depicted or mentioned. In order to enact the Opet festival, many people were needed, more outside than within the temples because of the scale of the river craft, among other factors. The courts and halls may not have felt crowded—I see no way usefully to estimate the numbers of participants—and the spaces may have awed and dwarfed those privileged to take part, but one should not use the size of the buildings to argue for mass participation (contra Bell 1997, with fig. 74; on functions of palace and temple in such contexts, see O'Connor 1995). As indicated, the openness of the Luxor court to the interior is cogent evidence for the closed character of the whole.

The later mortuary temple of Ramesses III (c. 1187–1156) at Medinet Habu integrates action in the world, ritual, and sacrality in another way (Murnane 1980). To one side of its outer court is a modest ceremonial palace linked to a small esplanade for the king's appearance. As if to emphasize the performance of the king's self-display, the low screen of the esplanade bears reliefs of soldiers wrestling archetypal foreigners to the ground before the king, with accompanying, slightly humorous captions (Epigraphic Survey 1932: pls. 111–112). On either side of the king's "window of appearances" are scenes of him about to smash the heads of enemies. The wrestling and ritual slaughter are agonistic, emblematic counterparts to the military campaigns which cover large areas of the temple's exterior in an intricate and unusual pattern with multiple orientations (Van Essche-Merchez 1994). The military theme is present in an almost theoretical way on the wall opposite the window of appearances, where the scenes revolve around the region of Amurru in Syria, which may no longer have existed and is unlikely to have been within range of Egyptian campaigns (Epigraphic Survey 1932: pls. 94, 96, 98–99). The final scene shows the king presenting the fruits of victory to the gods. Opposite the esplanade, attached to the range of pillars in front of the wall reliefs, are architectural colossi of the king in conventional clothing, as against the undifferentiated and divinized form of colossi in the inner court. Thus the outer court is relatively "secular" and suited to interaction between king and people. Its reliefs thematize both performance and its transformation into what is dedicated to the gods. It is not possible to say who had access to this area.

The inner court has a colonnade and a rise in floor level, as well as an extra range of columns forming a portico that marks a significant transition, making it into two symbolic spaces rather than one. In the outer, lower part, the bottom register on the south side unusually bears representations of Ramesses III's first Libyan war (Epigraphic Survey 1930: pls. 19, 23–28); these are presumably determined by the complex distribution of the decoration mentioned above. On the north side, the bottom register shows the king arriving at the temple, being inducted into it by gods, and making offerings (Epigraphic Survey 1940: pls. 229–234). The top register throughout the court bears reliefs of festivals (Epigraphic Survey 1940: pls. 196–208, 218–226). These are not closely comparable with those of the festival of Opet, but they too show a wider range of figures than the inner, cult areas of the temple that begin with the portico (Epigraphic Survey 1957).

There is thus a progression through the temple toward areas where public display is less relevant. This progression must start with the "High Gates" that acted as ceremonial entrances to the entire complex, outside the areas just considered. On these (only the eastern one is preserved above ground level), the exterior walls have generalized images of the king defeating his enemies, while the interior rooms have intimate scenes of the king with royal women, in an iconography that is not known from temple interiors, although its implications could be compared with the erotic song mentioned earlier for the Luxor colonnade (Epigraphic Survey 1970; O'Connor in press). The first court, which lacks such intimate scenes, might be a location for "performing" the king's ceremonial appearance. The axis of the king's appearance is at a right angle to the main divine axis, marking it as distinct in character. The inner court, like the Luxor colonnade, brings rituals that are performed in the outside world into the temple space and sacralizes them. The cult areas are not metonymic in the same way because their reliefs have a direct meaning in context.

Luxor and Medinet Habu show different styles of appropriation of spectacle and performance in the outer parts of temples. Medinet Habu is a unitary conception with a logic in its architecture and decoration that runs from the outer, symbolically fortified gate to the temple's inner sanctuary. Since the Medinet Habu complex was surrounded by a high, mud-brick enclosure, as well as an inscribed low, crenellated stone wall (Hölscher 1951:2–3, figs. 1, 13, pl. 6), it is again clear that this organization was not for all to see but for those who were entitled to enter, as well as for the gods, the temple's true inhabitants. The architecture itself is theater. As a "set," it addresses its performance not only to the actors, including the gods who inhabit it and comprehend its meaning, but also to those who are not entitled to enter.

A Note on Participation in Festivals

The festival of Opet and its depiction in Luxor and Karnak temples is the extreme case of a large-scale event that has a centripetal function and was presented as broadly participatory. There were festivals with large-scale participation (Assmann 1991). The "Perfect Festival of the Wadi," in which the people of Thebes—which was mainly on the east bank of the Nile—visited their dead in the necropolis on the west while the image of Amon-Re was taken to the temple of Deir el-Bahri, which was furthest removed from the Nile Valley, created much parallel ritual action (Graefe 1986). Many smaller local festivals were occasions when gods were brought out from their temples and interacted with people, notably by having oracle questions presented to them. Like the Festival of the Wadi, these provided multiple arenas (Valbelle 1985: 318–331; McDowell 1990:107–141; Meskell 2002:168–177). In the fifth century B.C.E. Herodotus (2.60) stated that around 700,000 people attended a festival at Bubastis in the Delta, and in the Greco-Roman period the goddess Hathor of Dendara visited Horus of Edfu, more than 150 kilometers away, in a major festival that is said to have drawn a large audience (Cauville 1984:7–8, 69–70). Barks that allude to the journey of Hathor are depicted at the wall bases in the entrance to Edfu's outer court (Fig. 9.5). Building inscriptions state that at the inauguration of part of the construction both sexes of the population of both cities mingled and there was great drunkenness (Kurth 1994:71). A propitiatory festival hymn at Philae states that "men and women" adore the goddess Hathor, in addition to many other categories of being (Daumas 1968:10–11). These statements express at least a folklore and an ideal of participation.

The issue is not whether there were festivals that encouraged large-scale attendance, but how major festivals were "staged" and how temple construction, design, and decoration incorporated their significance. It is not possible here to investigate the broader organization and deployment of festivals.

Succession as Spectacle

Structures of the mid first millennium adopt a new approach toward themes similar to those of the Luxor colonnade. The Twenty-Fifth Dynasty Kushite kings of Sudan and Egypt, notably Taharqa (c. 690–664), constructed monumental colonnaded approaches to temple complexes. In the ideal case these seem to have been created along any approach axis. Four survive at Karnak (Lauffray 1970), and forward colonnaded extensions or comparable freestanding structures in various forms are known at many first millennium and later temples (Arnold 1999:282–285), both in Egypt and in the Napatan–Meroitic central Sudan (e.g., Naqa'; Wildung and Schoske 1999:58–59 figs. 53, 55). They could also be separate structures (for Kushite examples, see Macadam 1955:53–57), developing a type that went back at least to the Middle Kingdom.

The Kushite colonnades show similarities with first millennium hypostyle halls, which typically have screen walls that block the interior from view while letting light into their upper parts and integrating the columns architecturally. Proportions in the two contexts are different. The colonnade before the second pylon at Karnak has five pairs of columns, originally twenty-one meters high, that are as massive as those in the interior of the hypostyle hall behind the pylon. Linking the columns are screen walls that

Figure 9.5. Relief of Arriving at Edfu for the Festival of the Meeting of Hathor of Dendara and Horus; Temple of Edfu, Inside Entrance to Courtyard; First Century B.C.E.; Photograph Courtesy of Richard Parkinson

seem to have been only a little above human height. These walls prevented spectators from seeing whatever rituals took place inside but would not have made the colonnade an "interior" space. These forward extensions probably had more than one function. They may have acted as way stations, where the portable bark of the god would have been set on a pedestal for a stage of ritual that mediated between the temple interior and the world outside (Lauffray 1970: fig. 2). Another possibility connects with the use Haremhab and Herihor made of the festival of Opet. The salient theme of Kushite royal inscriptions is the election of the new king (Eide et al. 1994: nos. 9, 21, 29, 34, 37). In several cases this depended on an oracle. On occasion it related to a procession to and from a palace; the army was also involved, both because it was leaderless without a king and, no doubt, because the new king had to be acceptable to it. Ursula Verhoeven (1998) has discussed these aspects of succession most valuably, but I would not accept her view that the stela depicting and describing the election of Aspelta (c. 590 B.C.E.) was intended as a broadly accessible display of the meaning of the events. Rather, in Kush as in Egypt all these activities were managed among elites and in sacred spaces.

The forward projection of the temple would have been a suitable venue for an oracle that was visible only to immediate personnel while being perceptible to the slightly larger audience entitled to enter the temple complex. Deities commonly issued oracles when they went out from temples in their barks, so that this location would fit such a possibility. This is not to claim that oracles were the sole function of the colonnades, but these offered an excellent location for rituals that mediated between the temple and the world outside, among which oracles were prominent. Since the king was the leading symbolic executant of temple ritual, he would appropriately have entered this special space in order to receive the result of an oracle. The coincidence in date between the Kushite rulers, with their organization of succession through oracles, and the introduction of this prominent new architectural form in Sudan and Egypt is striking.

Like their New Kingdom predecessors, the Kushites used the Nile as an arena for display. The victory stela narrating the campaign by which the conqueror Piankhy (Piye) imposed himself on the north of Egypt around 730 B.C.E. is a prime example (Lichtheim 1980:66–84; Grimal 1981). Battles were to be fought according to a proper order more than tactical imperatives, and sieges are presented in highly dramatic terms. In addition to oracles, rulers exploited travel through their realm as a strategy to organize selection and succession (Eide et al. 1994: nos. 9, 21, 29, 34, 37). Royal succession was anchored in the core region around Napata near the Fourth Cataract, but while the two countries were united, the major area of rule was Egypt. Kings therefore summoned possible successors, as well as their own mothers, from Napata to Egypt. These journeys paused at temples both in Sudan (Macadam 1949: no. 4) and in Egypt. When Piankhy (Piye) announced that he would join his army in Egypt, he spoke first of attending the festival of Opet in Thebes, which was already part of his realm, and thus attached his military intentions to an old ceremonial tradition (Lichtheim 1980:71).

Discussion and Conclusion

Exclusion

Egyptian material poses acutely the question of who is addressed by display and performance. I have argued that, while some displays encompassed the entire managed environment and distinctively exploited the arena of the Nile as the country's essential means of travel and transport, and hence of social encounters, much symbolic incorporation of spectacle was exclusionary. In a sense, exclusion of humanity in general was inclusion of those who mattered more: sacred spaces that were dedicated to the gods while signifying celebration in the world outside enabled society's most important members, who were not human but divine, to benefit more fully from human performance. The actors may have seen this exclusion as self-evident, especially since requirements of purity and limited access to temples were ancient and seemingly universal. As indicated, the dearth of pictorial material relating to spectators in festivals may have more to do with who were the recipients of the display than with audience. Other contexts such as processional ways, together with associated evidence, suggest that complementary patterns of gatherings of people occurred and effected communication from social superiors to inferiors. These areas would need separate study (compare Cabrol 2001).

The aspect of performance that I have left aside is fully fictional dramatization. This can take the thoroughgoing form of role-play and "staging." Such practices are well attested for Egyptian rituals, but there is no clear evidence for their being addressed to a "secular" public and they are not fictional in the literary sense (O'Rourke 2001). Less elaborate forms, such as the performance of narrative tales, can confidently be posited, not least because written genres ultimately look to oral forms, even though they depart radically from them (Parkinson 2002: 55–60, 78–85). Verhoeven (1996) has suggested that one version of the tale of Horus and Seth was staged locally in celebrations of the accession of Ramesses V (c. 1150–1145). This relatively humorous and uncomplicated telling of a well-known myth (Lichtheim 1976:214–223) is unlikely to have been performed only on that occasion. The core tales and instructions of Egypt's classical literature may have been performed before audiences—a far more likely mode of dissemination than distribution on papyrus for private reading—but they are complex, high-cultural products, some of which make play with "simple" narrative. These works are part of central elite culture, not anything that would have been a vehicle for broad spectacle, and their audiences were presumably elites. Here one might compare the Indian dramas of Kālidāsa, whose topics and treatments might seem at first sight to have a broad appeal—and have had some success in the West in the past two centuries—but which are composed in a mixture of two languages, of which Sanskrit was no longer a vernacular at the time they were written in the early centuries C.E. They can only have had full effect as performances addressed to an inner elite (Johnson 2001).

As with so many other questions relating to the material, pictorial, and textual legacy of early civilizations, spectacle and performance cannot be seen simply as socially integrative displays that legitimized Egyptian inequality or, for example, as offering diversion or distraction on the lines of the "bread and circuses" evoked by the Roman ruling elite. People were mobilized for great projects, which constituted goals that involved much of society. The processes of construction and inauguration of those projects created performances and spectacles that necessarily involved vast numbers of people, or smaller numbers over long periods. In as monument-focused a civilization as Egypt, these processes were almost constant in several historical periods. Despite assertions that communities were included, the motivations which those who led projects were able to impart to participants and to audiences remain elusive. While "theatrical" performance may have been one medium for such imparting, the most potent and distinctive Egyptian legacy of spectacle is where it was appropriated and dedicated for the gods and the elite in temples and mortuary monuments.

Integration

Thus, whereas it is possible to analyze the exclusion of potential participants and spectators in relation to Egyptian spectacle, the integration of different social groups of actors is less easily addressed—not because such integration was lacking but because sources are sparse and the examples I have used have a different focus. Here, comparison with other contributions to this volume is particularly valuable. The Egyptian material I discuss hardly relates to local-scale performances, such as the Puebloan (Triadan), or to the subjectivity of groups or individuals, both of which are ideally vital to understanding spectacle and are addressed notably by Moore.

Among societies studied in this volume, Egypt was large in scale, long-lasting, and centralized. The cosmological anchoring of institutions like major festivals is common to most complex societies, but the deities may have been more central in ancient models of Egyptian society than in some others. It is meaningful to see integration of spectacle within the spaces of deities as more symbolically important than broad involvement of people, while legitimizing aspects may have been less significant in a relatively stable Egypt than in fragmented and competitive Maya city-states (Houston, Inomata) or the short-lived Inka empire (Coben). Little Egyptian material evokes the creation of an integrated state, as against its maintenance, reaffirming an established order rather than affirming a new one. The case that is perhaps closest to Egypt is Urartu, where Smith elegantly develops the salient aesthetics of performance.

These parallels and differences throw into relief both commonalities and distinctive elements among the cases analyzed in this volume, but they also demonstrate how much differences of focus relate to the particular sources used. Despite the vast range of societies gathered in the chapters—perhaps a representative subset of societies that are addressed through archaeology—differences are evident in source material as much as in the character of spectacle: it is possible to paint a richer and more diverse picture of human interaction in societies where ethnohistoric evidence is available than for ones without postarchaeological successors. Lessons from ethnohistoric cases cannot be simply imposed on diverse societies and periods, but the insights they offer bring out to the archaeologist and ancient historian both the social centrality of spectacle and the difficulty of approaching its meaning. In this context, the most distinctive element in the Egyptian material is celebration of the creation of monuments and spaces, as reflexively depicted in scenes of the completion of pyramids and transport of colossal statues discussed above. This is where mass participation was most necessary and probably most involving across different social groups (festivals are less unambiguous in this respect). Monument as spectacle is a visibly fundamental idea that resonates in Egypt as in many places. The appropriation of the monument's meaning to the very center, both for its creation and for the spectacles held within it and depicted in places where deities more than people had access, is perhaps characteristic of large-scale, territorial societies.

Note

This chapter was written while I held the Norman Freehling Visiting Professorship in the Institute for the Humanities of the University of Michigan, which I thank for providing a wonderful research environment. Much is lightly referenced. I give citations of primary publications, while for theoretical background I rely in part on chapters in this volume. I am grateful to Takeshi Inomata and Lawrence Coben for their invitation to contribute even though I was not present at the original session, to Richard Parkinson for reading a very rough draft, to Stephen Houston for stimulating initial thoughts, to Neal Spencer for references, to Matthew Stolper for enabling me to do checking, and to Christina Karlshausen for sight of her unpublished dissertation. Alexey Vinogradov kindly showed me several studies on Kushite succession and kingship before publication; I have not been able to cite these specifically here.

References Cited

Abd el-Razik, Mahmud

1969 Study on Nectanebo Ist in Luxor Temple and Karnak. Mitteilungen des Deutschen Archäologischen Instituts, Abteilung Kairo 23:156–159.

Alexanian, Nicole

1998 Ritualrelikte an Mastabagräbern des Alten Reiches. *In* Stationen: Beiträge zur Kulturgeschichte Ägyptens, Rainer Stadelmann gewidmet. H. Guksch and D. Polz, eds. Pp. 3–22. Mainz: Philipp von Zabern.

Altenmüller, Hartwig, and Ahmed M. Moussa

1991 Die Inschrift Amenemhets II. aus dem Ptah-Tempel von Memphis: Ein Vorbericht. Studien zur Altägyptischen Kultur 18:1–48.

Arnold, Dieter

1977 Rituale und Pyramidentempel. Mitteilungen des Deutschen Archäologischen Instituts, Abteilung Kairo 33:1–14.

1999 Temples of the Last Pharaohs. New York: Oxford University Press.

Assmann, Jan

1991 Das ägyptische Prozessionsfest. *In* Das Fest und das Heilige: religiöse Kontrapunkte zur Alltagswelt. J. Assmann and T. Sundermeier, eds. Pp. 105–122. Gütersloh: Gerd Mohn.

Azim, Michel, and Gérard Réveillac

2004 Karnak dans l'objectif de Georges Legrain: Catalogue raisonné des archives photographiques du premier directeur des travaux de Karnak de 1895 à 1917. 2 vols. Paris: CNRS.

Baines, John

1997 Temples as Symbols, Guarantors, and Participants in Egyptian Civilization. *In* The Temple in Ancient Egypt: New Discoveries and Recent Research. S. Quirke, ed. Pp. 216–241. London: British Museum Press.

2003 On the Genre and Purpose of the "Large Commemorative Scarabs" of Amenhotep III. *In* Hommages à Fayza Haikal. N. Grimal, A. Kamel, and C. M. Sheikholeslami, eds. Pp. 29–43. Cairo: Institut Français d'Archéologie Orientale.

2004 Die Bedeutung des Reisens im alten Ägypten. 13. Siegfried-Morenz-Gedächtnis-Vorlesung. Leipzig: Ägyptisches Museum der Universität.

N.d. Hunting and Annals under Amenemhat II.

Baines, John, and Jaromir Malek

2000 Cultural Atlas of Ancient Egypt. Rev. edition. New York: Facts on File.

Baines, John, and Norman Yoffee

1998 Order, Legitimacy, and Wealth in Ancient Egypt and Mesopotamia. *In* Archaic States. G. Feinman and J. Marcus, eds. Pp. 199–260. Santa Fe: School of American Research Press.

Barker, Rodney S.

2001 Legitimating Identities: The Self-Presentation of Rulers and Subjects. Cambridge: Cambridge University Press.

Bell, Lanny

1985 Luxor Temple and the Cult of the Royal Ka. Journal of Near Eastern Studies 44:251–294.

1997 The New Kingdom "Divine" Temple: The Example of Luxor. *In* Temples of Ancient Egypt. B. E. Shafer, ed. Pp. 127–184. Ithaca, N.Y.: Cornell University Press.

Bietak, Manfred

1988 Zur Marine des Alten Reichs. *In* Pyramid Studies and Other Essays Presented to I. E. S. Edwards. J. Baines, T. G. H. James, A. Leahy, and A. F. Shore, eds. Pp. 35–40. London: Egypt Exploration Society.

Blankenberg-Van Delden, C.

1969 The Large Commemorative Scarabs of Amenhotep III. Leiden: E. J. Brill.

Borchardt, Ludwig, et al.

1913 Das Grabdenkmal des Königs Śa3ḥ u-Re‘ II, Die Wandbilder. Leipzig: J. C. Hinrichs.

Bradley, Richard

2002 The Past in Prehistoric Societies. London: Routledge.

Cabrol, Agnès

2001 Les voies processionnelles de Thèbes. Leuven: Peeters.

Caminos, Ricardo A.

1958 The Chronicle of Prince Osorkon. Rome: Pontificium Institutum Biblicum.

1964 The Nitocris Adoption Stela. Journal of Egyptian Archaeology 50: 71–101.

Cauville, Sylvie

1984 Edfou. Cairo: Institut Français d'Archéologie Orientale.

Černý, Jaroslav, and Alan H. Gardiner

1957 Hieratic Ostraca I. Oxford: Oxford University Press for Griffith Institute.

Daumas, François

1968 Les propylées du temple d'Hathor à Philae et le culte de la déesse. Zeitschrift für Ägyptische Sprache und Altertumskunde 95:1–17.

Davies, W. V.

1999 Djehutyhotep's Colossus Inscription and Major Brown's Photograph. *In* Studies in Egyptian Antiquities: A Tribute to T. G. H. James. W. V. Davies, ed. Pp. 29–35. London: British Museum.

De Wit, Constant
1961 Inscriptions dédicatoires du temple d'Edfou. Chronique d'Egypte 36:56–97, 277–320.

Dunham, Dows, and William Kelly Simpson
1974 The Mastaba of Queen Mersyankh III G 7530–7540. Boston: Department of Egyptian and Ancient Near Eastern Art, Museum of Fine Arts.

Dziobek, Eberhard
1992 Das Grab des Ineni, Theben Nr. 81. Mainz: Philipp von Zabern.

Eide, Tormod, Tomas Hägg, and Richard Holton Pierce
1994 Fontes Historiae Nubiorum: Textual Sources for the History of the Middle Nile Region between the Eighth Century BC and the Sixth Century AD. Vol. 1. Bergen: University of Bergen, Department of Classics.

El-Saghir, Mohammed
1991 Das Statuenversteck im Luxortempel. Mainz: Philipp von Zabern.

Emery, Walter B.
1954 Great Tombs of the First Dynasty. Vol. 2. London: Egypt Exploration Society.

Engelbach, R.
1934 A Foundation Scene of the Second Dynasty. Journal of Egyptian Archaeology 20:183–184.

Epigraphic Survey
1930 Medinet Habu I: Earlier Historical Records of Ramses III. Chicago: University of Chicago Press.
1932 Medinet Habu II: Later Historical Records of Ramses III. Chicago: University of Chicago Press.
1940 Medinet Habu IV: Festival Scenes of Ramses III. Chicago: University of Chicago Press.
1957 Medinet Habu V: The Temple Proper Part I. Chicago: University of Chicago Press.
1970 Medinet Habu VIII: The Eastern High Gate. Chicago: University of Chicago Press.
1979 Scenes of King Herihor in the Court, with Translations of Texts. The Temple of Khonsu 1. Chicago: Oriental Institute, University of Chicago.
1994 The Festival Procession of Opet in the Colonnade Hall. Reliefs and Inscriptions at Luxor Temple 1. Chicago: Oriental Institute, University of Chicago.

1998 The Facade, Portals, Upper Register Scenes, Columns, Marginalia, and Statuary in the Colonnade Hall. Reliefs and Inscriptions at Luxor Temple 2. Chicago: Oriental Institute, University of Chicago.

Gardiner, Alan H.
1953 The Coronation of King Haremhab. Journal of Egyptian Archaeology 39:13–31.
1955 A Unique Funerary Liturgy. Journal of Egyptian Archaeology 41: 9–17.

Giesey, Ralph E.
1960 The Royal Funeral Ceremony in Renaissance France. Geneva: Droz.

Graefe, Erhart
1986 Talfest. *In* Lexikon der Ägyptologie. W. Helck and W. Westendorf, eds. Vol. 6, cols. 187–189. Wiesbaden: Otto Harrassowitz.

Grimal, N.-C.
1981 La stèle triomphale de Pi(ʻankh)y au Musée du Caire, JE 48862 et 47086–47089. Cairo: Institut Français d'Archéologie Orientale.

Gutbub, Adolphe
1973 Textes fondamentaux de la théologie de Kom Ombo. 2 vols. Cairo: Institut Français d'Archéologie Orientale.

Hawass, Zahi, and Miroslav Verner
1996 Newly Discovered Blocks from the Causeway of Sahure. Mitteilungen des Deutschen Archäologischen Instituts, Abteilung Kairo 52:177–186.

Helck, Wolfgang
1955 Urkunden der 18. Dynastie, Heft 17. Urkunden des Ägyptischen Altertums IV. Berlin: Akademie-Verlag.
1957 Urkunden der 18. Dynastie, Heft 20. Urkunden des Ägyptischen Altertums IV. Berlin: Akademie-Verlag.
1958 Urkunden der 18. Dynastie, Heft 21. Urkunden des Ägyptischen Altertums IV. Berlin: Akademie-Verlag.
1961 Urkunden der 18. Dynastie: Übersetzung zu den Heften 17–22. Berlin: Akademie-Verlag.

Hölscher, Uvo
1951 The Excavation of Medinet Habu IV: The Mortuary Temple of Ramses III, Part II. Chicago: University of Chicago Press.

Howarth, David
1997 Images of Rule: Art and Politics in the English Renaissance, 1485–1649. Basingstoke, U.K.: Macmillan.

Jacquet-Gordon, Helen
1962 Les noms des domaines funéraires sous l'Ancien Empire égyptien. Cairo: Institut Français d'Archéologie Orientale.

Jansen-Winkeln, Karl
2001 Eine Familie im Totenkult. Zeitschrift für Ägyptische Sprache und Altertumskunde 128:133–141.

Jenkins, Nancy
1980 The Boat beneath the Pyramid: King Cheops' Royal Ship. London: Thames & Hudson.

Jéquier, Gustave
1940 Le monument funéraire de Pépi II, III: Les approches du temple. Cairo: Institut Français d'Archéologie Orientale.

Johnson, W. J.
2001 Kālidāsa, The Recognition of Śakuntalā: A Play in Seven Acts; Śakuntalā in the Mahābhārata (Mahābhārata 1.62–69). Oxford: Oxford University Press.

Kaiser, Werner
1959 Einige Bemerkungen zur ägyptischen Frühzeit I: Zu den *Šmśw-Ḥr*. Zeitschrift für Ägyptische Sprache und Altertumskunde 84:119–132.

Karlshausen, Christina
1997 L'iconographie de la barque processionnelle divine en Egypte au Nouvel Empire. Ph.D. dissertation, Université Catholique de Louvain.

Kemp, Barry J.
1976 The Window of Appearance at el-Amarna and the Basic Structure of This City. Journal of Egyptian Archaeology 62:81–99.
1989 Ancient Egypt: Anatomy of a Civilization. London: Routledge.

Kurth, Dieter
1994 Treffpunkt der Götter: Inschriften aus dem Tempel des Horus von Edfu. Zurich: Artemis.

Landström, Björn
1970 Ships of the Pharaohs: 4000 Years of Egyptian Shipbuilding. London: Allen & Unwin.

Lange, Kurt, and Max Hirmer

1968 Egypt: Architecture, Sculpture, Painting. 4th edition. London: Phaidon.

Lauffray, Jean

1970 La colonnade-propylée occidentale de Karnak dite "Kiosque de Taharqa" et ses abords: Rapport provisoire des fouilles de 1969 et commentaire architectural. Kêmi 20:111–164.

Lichtheim, Miriam

1973 Ancient Egyptian Literature: A Book of Readings I, The Old and Middle Kingdoms. Berkeley: University of California Press.

1976 Ancient Egyptian Literature: A Book of Readings II, The New Kingdom. Berkeley: University of California Press.

1980 Ancient Egyptian Literature: A Book of Readings III, The Late Period. Berkeley: University of California Press.

Macadam, M. F. Laming

1949 The Temples of Kawa I: The Inscriptions. 2 vols. London: Oxford University Press/Griffith Institute, Oxford.

1955 The Temples of Kawa II: History and Archaeology of the Site. 2 vols. London: Oxford University Press for Griffith Institute, Oxford.

Martin, Geoffrey Thorndike

1987 Corpus of Reliefs of the New Kingdom from the Memphite Necropolis and Lower Egypt. Vol. 1. London: KPI.

McDowell, Andrea G.

1990 Jurisdiction in the Workmen's Community at Deir el Medina. Leiden: Nederlands Instituut voor het Nabije Oosten.

Meeks, Dimitri

1972 Le grand texte des donations au Temple d'Edfou. Cairo: Institut Français d'Archéologie Orientale.

Meskell, Lynn

2002 Private Life in New Kingdom Egypt. Princeton: Princeton University Press.

Münch, Hans-Hubertus

2000 Categorizing Archaeological Finds: The Funerary Material of Queen Hetepheres I at Giza. Antiquity 74:898–908.

Murnane, William J.
1980 United with Eternity: A Concise Guide to the Monuments of Medinet Habu. Chicago: Oriental Institute, University of Chicago/American University in Cairo Press.

Naville, Edouard
N.d. The Temple of Deir el Bahari. 6 vols. London: Egypt Exploration Fund.

Newberry, Percy E.
N.d. [1893] El Bersheh. Vol. 1. London: Egypt Exploration Fund.

O'Connor, David
1987–1988 Demarcating the Boundaries: An Interpretation of a Scene in the Tomb of Mahu, el-Amarna. Bulletin of the Egyptological Seminar 9: 41–52.
1995 Beloved of Maat, the Horizon of Re: The Royal Palace in New Kingdom Egypt. *In* Ancient Egyptian Kingship. D. O'Connor and D. P. Silverman, eds. Pp. 263–300. Leiden: Brill.
1998 The City and the World: Worldview and Built Forms in the Reign of Amenhotep III. *In* Amenhotep III: Perspectives on His Reign. E. H. Cline and D. O'Connor, eds. Pp. 125–172. Ann Arbor: University of Michigan Press.
In press The Eastern High Gate: Sexualized Architecture at Medinet Habu? *In* Structure and Significance: Thoughts on Ancient Egyptian Architecture. P. Jánosi, ed. Pp. 421–436.
Forthcoming Abydos: The Evolution of a Sacred Landscape. London: Thames & Hudson.
N.d. City and Cosmos in Ancient Egypt. London: Equinox.

O'Rourke, Paul F.
2001 Drama. *In* The Oxford Encyclopedia of Ancient Egypt. D. B. Redford, ed. Pp. 1:407–410. New York: Oxford University Press.

Parkinson, R. B.
2002 Poetry and Culture in Middle Kingdom Egypt: A Dark Side to Perfection. London: Continuum.

Reeves, Nicholas
1990 The Complete Tutankhamun: The King, the Tomb, the Royal Treasure. London: Thames & Hudson.

Richards, Janet E., and Mary Van Buren, eds.
2000 Order, Legitimacy, and Wealth in Ancient States. Cambridge: Cambridge University Press.

Roccati, Alessandro
1982 La littérature historique sous l'Ancien Empire égyptien. Paris: Editions du Cerf.

Schott, Erika
1977 Die Biographie des Ka-em-tenenet. *In* Fragen an die altägyptische Literatur: Studien zum Gedenken an Eberhard Otto. J. Assmann, E. Feucht, and R. Grieshammer, eds. Pp. 443–461c. Wiesbaden: Dr Ludwig Reichert.

Schulman, Alan R.
1965 The Berlin "Trauerrelief" (no. 12411) and Some Officials of Tut'ankhamun and Ay. Journal of the American Research Center in Egypt 4:55–68.

Schwaller de Lubicz, R. A.
1999 The Temples of Karnak. Rochester, Vt.: Inner Traditions.

Sethe, Kurt
1906 Urkunden der 18. Dynastie. Urkunden des Ägyptischen Altertums IV:1. Leipzig: J. C. Hinrichs.
1907 Urkunden der 18. Dynastie. Urkunden des Ägyptischen Altertums IV:3. Leipzig: J. C. Hinrichs.

Smith, H. S.
1972 A Visit to Ancient Egypt: Life at Memphis and Saqqara (c. 500–30 BC). Warminster: Aris & Phillips.

Teeter, Emily
1997 The Presentation of Maat: Ritual and Legitimacy in Ancient Egypt. Chicago: Oriental Institute, University of Chicago.

Valbelle, Dominique
1985 "Les ouvriers de la tombe": Deir el-Médineh à l'époque ramesside. Cairo: Institut Français d'Archéologie Orientale.

Van Essche-Merchez, Eric
1994 Pour une lecture "stratigraphique" des parois du temple de Ramsès III à Médinet Habou. Revue d'Egyptologie 45:87–116.

Vercoutter, Jean
1975 Apis, Apis-Bestattung. *In* Lexikon der Ägyptologie. W. Helck and W. Westendorf, eds. Vol. 1: cols. 338–350. Wiesbaden: Otto Harrassowitz.

Verhoeven, Ursula

1996 Ein historischer "Sitz im Leben" für die Erzählung von Horus und Seth des Papyrus Chester Beatty I. *In* Wege öffnen: Festschrift für Rolf Gundlach zum 65. Geburtstag. M. Schade-Busch, ed. Pp. 347–363. Wiesbaden: Harrassowitz.

1998 Amun zwischen 25 Männern und zwei Frauen: Bemerkungen zur Inthronisationsstele des Aspelta. *In* Egyptian Religion, the Last Thousand Years: Studies Dedicated to the Memory of Jan Quaegebeur. W. Clarysse, A. Schoors, and H. Willems, eds. Pp. 2:1487–1501. Leuven: Peeters.

Werner, Edward K.

1986 Montu and the "Falcon Ships" of the Eighteenth Dynasty. Journal of the American Research Center in Egypt 23:107–123.

Wildung, Dietrich, and Sylvia Schoske

1999 Die Stadt in der Steppe: Grabungen des Ägyptischen Museums Berlin in Naga, Sudan. Berlin: Stiftung Preussischer Kulturbesitz.

Wilkinson, Toby A. H.

2000 Royal Annals of Ancient Egypt: The Palermo Stone and Its Associated Fragments. London: KPI.

Wolf, Walther

1931 Das Schöne Fest von Opet: Die Festzugsdarstellung im grossen Säulengange des Tempels von Luksor. Leipzig: J. C. Hinrichs.

SCENE 10

VISIBLE AND VOCAL: SOVEREIGNS OF THE EARLY MERINA (MADAGASCAR) STATE

Susan Kus and Victor Raharijaona

Like the Sun Rising above the Mists

There is a moment recounted in the recorded official oral traditions of the ruling nobles of Imerina in the central highlands of Madagascar (see Fig. 10.1) that will initially engage our attention.[1] At the end of the eighteenth century, according to these traditions, Ramboasalama, the "Vigorous, healthy dog," was informed that his maternal uncle, Andrianjafy, who had been a cruel and unjust ruler over the northeast corner of Imerina, was to be surrendered to him. Speaking for the people who had apprehended Andrianjafy, their leader *advised* Ramboasalama, who was standing on "the sanctified stone" (*ambatomasina*), to have his uncle taken to [a place to] the east to be put to death. Ramboasalama replied that Andrianjafy was deserted (by his attendants) and powerless. The people, through their leader, spoke again saying that Andrianjafy had caused much suffering for their wives and children. The leader of the people once again advised Andrianjafy's death. Andrianjafy was taken to *Antsahafady*, "At the tabooed field," where he was killed (Callet 1981:430). It is because of this act that this place came to be called "At the tabooed field," and subsequently it became taboo for the ruling sovereign and for his possessions to pass through this area (Callet 1981:430).[2]

First "At the holy field" (*Antsahamasina*), then mounted on the central of three stones which subsequently came to be called "At the stone(s) with the red head" (*Ambatomenaloha*), and then at "At the place of consecration"

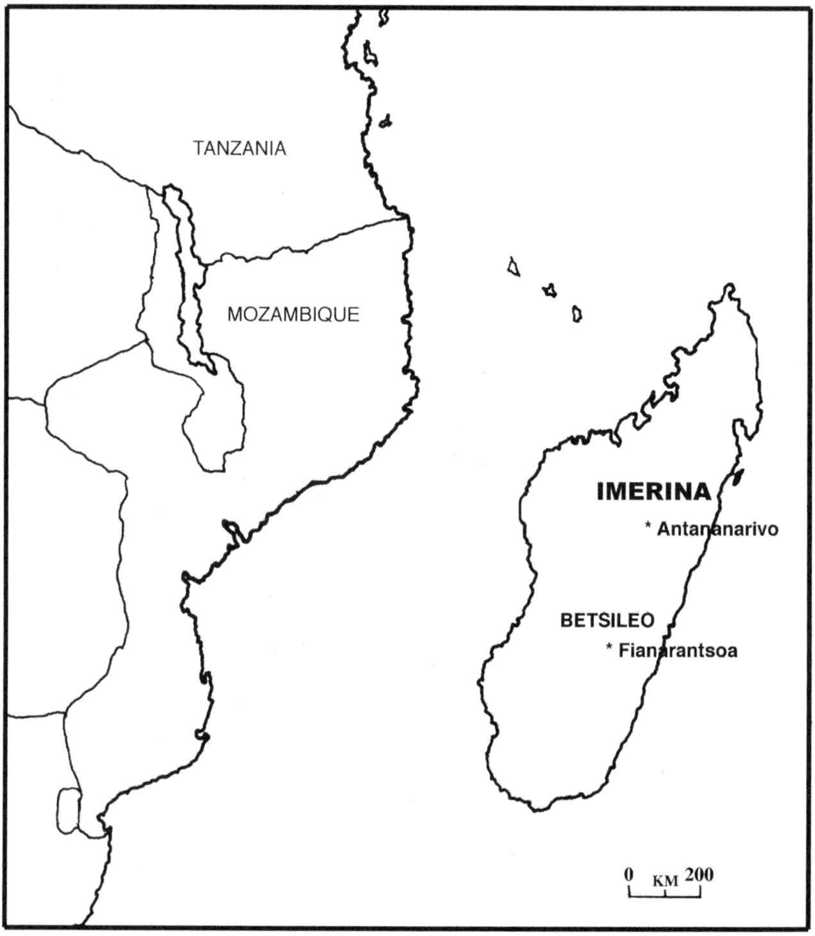

Figure 10.1. Map of Madagascar and Imerina

(*Ankasina*),[3] the "Vigorous, healthy dog" (*Ramboasalama*), who took the name Andrianampoinimerina, the "Noble desired in the navel of Imerina," declared before the assembled populace that he was in possession of the polity. He was met by the populace at "At the place where one stands upright" (*Ambohiniarenana*) and they sang:

> Our noble, Eh! Eh! Eh! Is a good lord. Eh! Eh! Eh!
> Our noble, Eh! Eh! Eh! Is our sun. Eh! Eh! Eh!
> Our noble, Eh! Eh! Eh! Is our god. Eh! Eh! Eh!
> Our noble, Eh! Eh! Eh! Is a good lord. Eh! Eh! Eh! (Callet 1981:390; authors' translation)

The "Noble desired in the navel of Imerina" spoke to the assembled multitude with well-chosen words and images to testify to his satisfaction. *Sitraka sy telina ary mamy ny atao nareo* (Callet 1981:431) were among the words he used. If we were to translate the official French translation (Callet 1974:88) of this phrase into English, it would read, "That which you have done for me is sweet; I approve and I am satisfied." Yet the term *telina*, which can be translated as "meeting with approval," has a more concrete definition: "the action of swallowing." This act of swallowing complements the word *mamy*, which designates both the tangible sensation of sweetness and the more intangible image of cherishing. Indeed, the Malagasy often remark that "life is dear/sweet" (*mamy ny aina*), and life was to be sweet for the assembled crowd with the peace brought by "the noble that they desired in their navel." Additional words were exchanged between the sovereign and the people, and Andrianampoinimerina said that he had come to rule by consent of the people, and now it was for them to have confidence in him (Callet 1981:431).

Proceeding then to the "Sacred place of [rice] threshing" (*Ampamoloanamasina*), this sovereign, who would later claim that his "only equal was rice,"[4] moved seven times around the area and then standing in the northeast corner he declared himself head of the polity. Rejoicing, singing, dancing, and drumming, the people were given many fatted cattle to share among themselves and were promised more in the days of celebration to come. The "Noble desired in the navel of Imerina" then told them in his *kabary* (public address) the day on which to reassemble and on which he would "appear" (*hiseho*) to them, that is, the day on which he would formally take office (Callet 1981:432).

On the appointed day the people dressed themselves in new robes, or *lamba*, with braided fringes and adorned themselves in the silver of anklets, bracelets, and necklaces, and wore earrings of coral and silver and beads. Those of high status wrapped themselves in silk cloths with tiny beads of tin worked into the fine weave. The men wore red headbands or tall decorated hats with long tails and they too wore earrings and bracelets of silver. The "Vigorous, healthy dog," that "noble desired in the navel of Imerina," wore anklets of red coral beads and bands of red coral and white beads above his knees, a loincloth of finest silk and a scarlet robe and red coral headdress (Callet 1981:432). When he took office, that is, when he "appeared" (*niseho*) in his resplendent garb, the image, traditionally attached to Merina rulers, of "the god seen with the eyes" (*andriamanitrahitamaso*) was made stunningly salient. Before the crowds of people whom, attired in their white *lamba*, "one compared to the morning mists that filled the depths of the valleys" (Julien 1908:157; authors' translation) he "appeared" (*niseho*) before them as the sun appears (*miseho*) at daybreak.

The population greeted the sovereign. The twelve chiefs of the population offered the "Noble desired in the navel of Imerina" several gifts, including (1) an *omby volavita,* or a cattle marked with white spots on the forehead, back, rump and legs, (2) an *omby malaza,* or cattle of remarkable beauty and size, and (3) a *volatsivaky*, or uncut silver coin (Maria-Theresa thaler) whose round shape and intact form symbolized not only the fullness of the moon but duration, perpetuity, and completeness (Callet 1981:432). The chiefs of the population declared with well-chosen words in the name of the people that "even if the sky should fall and the earth lift itself up" they would remain faithful to the sovereign. The sovereign acknowledged that it was because of the people that he had come to reign and he vowed that their history would never be lost (would continue to be told). Vows of loyalty and promises of support were exchanged between the "Noble desired in the navel of Imerina" and the populace. He made known to them his intentions: "I will make the sea the limits of my rice field" (*atao ko ny ranomasina no valamparia ko*) (Callet 1981:433).

Turning to two of his attendants, Tsimahàka and Andriantiana, the "Noble desired in the heart of Imerina" appropriated their names for himself. Declaring to the populace that it was he who treated all his subjects equally, he "who does not make a distinction between friends and other," he took for himself the name Tsimahàka. Declaring to the populace that it was he the sovereign beloved by the Merina, and declaring that it was he "the beloved noble," he took for himself the name Andriantiana (Callet 1981:433).

There were two villages nearby, Tafohasina and Soavinimerina. The "Noble desired in the navel of Imerina," declaring himself the one "covered in grace" took the name Tafohasina. Declaring himself "blessed by the Merina," he appropriated the name of Soavinimerina (Callet 1981:433).

These various acts were accomplished upon the *fisehoana*, or "appearance" (inauguration) of the "Noble desired in the heart of Imerina." The people in their contentment danced, sang, beat on drums, blew on conch shells, and feasted on fattened cattle (Callet 1981:433) offered to them by the "Big-eyed bull" (another of this sovereign's sobriquets). After taking control of the northeast corner of Imerina, the "Noble desired in the navel of Imerina" went on to reunite the four corners (fiefdoms) of Imerina and prepare the way for his son to take control of two-thirds of the fourth largest island in the world. The dates traditionally given for the political rule of Andrianampoinimerina are 1787–1810.

In the Thickness of Description

There is much delight and wonder for the anthropologist in the sensuous tales of times, places, and cultures other than one's own. To linger in the thickness of captivating visual, oral, aural, and palpable descriptions, to engage in "sensuous scholarship" (Stoller 1997), is one of the delights of the trade. Perhaps it should also be one of the obligations of the trade, to share more widely this edification anchored in tangible delights of diversity. Small and large objects, phrases, and gestures, chosen and executed with attention, should merit our attention as forms of poetry before we subject them to critical analysis.

For anthropologists of certain theoretical persuasions there is a daunting exegetical challenge in the thickets of such alternative ways of being in the world. Let us take up that challenge for a moment now. "The god seen with the eyes" (*andriamanitrahitamaso*) is a designation of the sovereigns of Imerina. The name harkens back to the time when a daughter of the creator was sent to earth to create an alliance between the powers of the earth and the sky by marrying a noble (*andriana*) of the earth. The visibility of a god finds resonance in the name given to the polity of Imerina. This name is said to come from the word *manerinerina*, which means "to dominate, to be in view, eminent, visible from afar" (Abinal and Malzac 1955:129; authors' translation). This eminence transitions into singularity. Only sovereigns are allowed to wear coral on their heads and solid scarlet or deep purple robes; only sovereigns are allowed to carry red parasols and be buried in singular tombs (rather than the collective tombs of those under their dominion). To the sovereign belong the singular bulls of renowned size and strength (*omby malaza*). To the sovereign belong the *omby volavita*, the cattle that bear the marks of sanctity. The sovereign is likened to such bulls, such images of strength and brutal beauty without rival. It is a ruler without rival that guarantees the peace of the polity and the "sweetness" of life (prosperity with security) for women and children, many fatted cattle on which to feast, and reason to don celebratory attire, to sing, and to dance. (See also Kus 1989.)

The sovereign is singular like the sun, and like the sun he cannot be measured; like the sky he cannot be delimited (Houlder 1960:117). The sun has dominion over "(all those) under the sun" (*ambaniandro*) and "(all those) under the sky" (*ambanilanitra*), the names that came to be used for citizens of the Merina state. Like the sun (and the full moon), the sovereign and his reign are complete in form and enduring ("from beginning to end"), and the sovereign and polity is complete like a round silver coin that has not been "broken/cut" (*volatsivaky*) for use in ordinary (if not vulgar) market exchanges of the day. So when a sovereign officially takes office, the term *miseho* is used, which is the verb "to appear, to become visible, to be in view." This verb is used also for the rising of the sun (and the appearance of the moon), for the sovereign is made visible and efficacious, as is the sun that rises.

Those who came to be called "those under the sun" and "those under the sky"[5] pledged their "unwavering" support even "if the earth should rise and the sky lower itself." This is an image that comes from one myth of early origins where the earth and sky began a battle. The mountains and hills rose up for attack and the lightning that attained the earth created the striking boulders that pierce deep into the hilltops. The conflict was ended when the creator being stepped in to restore peace; however, the prominences and (outcrops of) large boulders remained in their poised positions, giving Imerina its dramatic relief of today. As the sovereign moved across the landscape, his moves involved not only seven auspicious turns and the nobility and the sacredness of the northeast direction, but also his feet that stood above the ground on sacred stones. Stone is the most celestial of terrestrial elements. (See also Kus and Raharijaona 1998.) Boulders protrude from the earth attaining to the sky, remnants of that time when earth was poised to attack the sky. Other boulders penetrate the earth; they are remnants of the lightning sent by the sky to attain earth.

As the sovereign continued to move across the landscape, he avoided places of defilement (*antsahafady*). His moves resonated with the names of fields that were sacred (*antsahamasina*), stones of the color red of nobility (*ambatomenaloha*), and consecrated locations (*ankasina* and *ampamoloanamasina*). Other locations rendered their names of grace (*tafohasina*) and benediction (*soavinimerina*) to the sovereign.

Individuals also surrendered their beloved (*andriantiana*) and even-handed names (*tsimahàka*) to a sovereign who had and would change his name several times over the course of his career. The "Vigorous, healthy dog" (*Ramboasalamatsimarofy*) was so named at his birth. To avoid the jealousies of those who might wish a newborn or a young child harm, a child is often given a name to deflect envy. As a warrior he took the name Ombalahibemaso, which can be interpreted as the "big-eyed bull," the "Bull with the powerful gaze," or the "Bull with many eyes." Some interpret the "many eyes" as the extension of political control through the eyes of the many counselors to the sovereign. As is the case with the powerful performative language, evocative multiple references are edifying rather than obfuscating as they are creatively worked into public discourse *and* private thought.

There is much, much more to the poetics of the inaugural tales of the "Bull with the powerful gaze," but if you tend to the milk that is boiling over, what becomes of your in-laws at the door and your loincloth that has fallen down? This is a Malagasy conundrum that can be used to express the dilemma of being pulled in multiple directions. Milk is a precious commodity, one's body is to be appropriately presented in public, and it is a serious social obligation to show proper attention and respect to one's in-laws. In the case of this article, does one continue to present the poetry of Merina culture or engage in its exegesis, or does one attend to the theoretical implications of the Merina case for larger discussion of performance in early states?

"The Shifting Sensorium"

"Cultures vary greatly in their exploitation of the various senses and the way in which they relate their conceptual apparatus to the various senses" (Ong 1991:26). The "Noble desired in the navel of Imerina," as well as other Merina sovereigns, were above all else *visible and vocal.* Their visibility and vocalness played a critical role in Merina statecraft, particularly in the conceptual structuring of the domain of state ideology and in the state's claims to legitimacy.

In recent "vocalizations" of anthropological theory, we are offered an assortment of "names" underpinned by edifying discourse that allow us to conceptually articulate how the mind-body rift of earlier theoretical discourse fails to capture the nature of how alternative ways of being and understanding the world are constructed and found convincing. "Embodiment" as anthropological paradigm (Csordas1990) that articulates with "the mindful body" (Lock and Scheper-Hughes 1987), "body thoughts" (Strathern 1996), and "radical empiricism" (as used by Jackson 1989) are a few among such namings.

Pulling from these underpinnings, there are two points that will be explored in the discussion that follows. First, if we are to take seriously the embodied and experiential nature of thought and metaphor, particularly in traditional societies and premodern states, then we must further appreciate the aptness, if not the compelling nature, of certain symbols and symbolic domains within particular cultural contexts. Symbols become good to think with because they become multireferentially evocative as they are episodically layered in the experiencing body, applied by the performing mindful body, and appreciated as clever, beautiful, and/or profound by the embodied mind (see also Kus and Raharijaona 2001a, b, 2000, 1998). Second, while we certainly need to be aware that "the division of the world's cultures into two categories, literate and nonliterate, masks a far more interesting and complex reality of multiple, conflicting sensory and cognitive models which we really ought to be exploring" (Howe 1991:19), we would nevertheless urge people to appreciate the powerfulness, the efficaciousness of speech and naming in primarily oral societies (see also Kus and Raharijaona 2002). Powerful and poetic language not only affects, it effects.

"Seen from Afar": The Suggestiveness and Saliency of Symbols

Imerina is a country of resplendent and dramatic beauty. The poet Rabemananjara called it Imerine-la-Magnifique (1964:63). From its heights one can scan a countryside where seasons and relief reveal themselves as rainbows. The red slopes of its hills climb to blue heights that blend into the blue-gray clouds of a storm-laden sky. The valleys range across the spectrum of green—the iridescent yellow-green of rice nurseries, the vibrant green of the growing plant, the warm green-gold of the stalk ready for harvest, and the dark blue-green of forest growth. The ribbons of rivers wind their glistening way across the landscape, mirroring the passage of clouds that cross their paths from above.

Grand expanses of this "magnificent" countryside of Imerina can be encompassed from its central heights, heights that came to be occupied by heads of polities when the territory of Imerina became a political map. To be physically present in the landscape of Imerina is to appreciate the stunning saliency of the symbol of height not only as the sacred hills of Imerina captivate one's gaze when looking across the landscape, but also as one's gaze dominates the countryside from atop a central promontory. "Taking possession with the gaze of the eyes is incontestably a recurrent trait of Malagasy culture" (Domenichini-Ramiaramanana 1983:364; authors' translation). A ruling noble is "a god seen with the eyes" (*andriamanitrahitamaso*) whose position of visible occupation of Imerina's heights places him or her at the boundary of the celestial and the terrestrial and whose gaze brings all under its purview and domination.

In Imerina, the confounding of vision and height with authority is not the result of an intellectual fortuitousness or symbolic arbitrariness; it is anchored in a sensual persuasiveness and experiential compulsion for those who do not separate mind and body in practice and conviction. On and out from this compelling sensual motif, powerful themes of political ideology can be spun. "Between earth and sky there are only a few large boulders" (Vig 1977:49) as there are only a few powerful and singular individuals capable of ruling. Imerina, "visible from afar" and "eminent" (as its root word declares), was projected into a political agenda of expansion and domination of that which comes under the gaze of the sovereign. This was declared (according to tradition) by an earlier ruler, Ralambo, who, standing on one of the sacred hills of Imerina, conferred this name on his domain, saying, "I will call this Imerina under the sun . . . And here is the reason why I call it Imerina: I possess all the hills, and nothing under the sun is beyond my dominion" (Callet 1981:147).

Andrianampoinimerina, standing as well on one of the sacred hills of Imerina, laid claim to political authority and presaged his unification of Imerina's four corners in a public episode before "taking power" over Imerina. At the capital of his uncle, Andrianjafy, in the company of his counselors and representatives of the people, standing at the place of Ambatomiantendro, "At the boulder that attains to the summit" (see Fig. 10.2), he declared his intention to unite the twelve sacred mountains of the realm (Callet 1981:577). When he eventually did unite the polity, he placed his capital at Antananarivo, "At the town of 1,000." One

Figure 10.2. The View from Ambatomiantendro

thousand is the largest symbolic number for the Malagasy and represents that which is supreme, perpetual, enduring, and invincible (Molet 1979:85). This "town of 1,000" literally sits at the center or in the navel of Imerina, surrounded by a vast expanse of rice fields and marshes. These fields and marshes physically isolate and visually draw attention to the capital city. "It is a location befitting a sovereign with a knowledge of military defense, a concern for economic provisioning, and an artist's feel for a powerful metaphor" (Kus and Raharijaona 2000:107). One British missionary to the island expressed his wonder at the sight of this capital city: "Before rain and immediately after it the town can be seen with peculiar distinctness from a very great distance. It calls to mind Isaiah's description of Jerusalem: 'A mountain established in the top of the mountains'" (Griffith 1919:6).

Those in Imerina under the dominating gaze of a "god seen with the eyes," singular and overwhelming as the sun, occupying the heights of Imerina, and in particular, the central height of "At the town of 1,000," came to bear the collective name of "those under the sun." This name was insistently and persistently applied in public discourse to a population of numerous endogamous descent groups divided by territory, rank, and individual group histories, some of whose histories laid claim to sovereignty over various parcels of Imerina. The collective identity of this population "under the sun" was further reinforced in the sovereign's public discourse with well-chosen words to emphasize the population's unity: this population was like the feathers of the guinea fowl, all of one color, creating a whole as one creates a braid from tufts of hair, and before the sovereign they were equal as was the uniform and continuous rim of a cooking pot.[6] This "discursive" strategy accompanied the creation of state policy applied to all segments of the population (with the exception of a small number of privileged individuals). When the polity expanded out beyond Imerina into other territories and incorporated other "ethnicities," the poetically convenient collective term "those under the sky" was applied to the collectivity.

(Seen) Up Close and Personal

A European, Hugon, saw this "god seen with the eyes" in 1808 and described him as rich, very ugly, with straight hair, and reminding him of a Malay (Brown 2000:110). Raombana, the Malagasy secretary to a later queen of Madagascar in the mid-nineteenth century who had been given a Protestant and British education abroad, described the "Big-eyed bull" as "rather tall, and . . . bony and sinewy . . . and brave even to madness" (1980:249). Advisers to the "Noble desired in the navel of Imerina" from the east coast of the island, who were accustomed to dealing with ruling elite across the island and who recorded their impression in a document written in Arabic script, described him as "having a strong destiny, as being strong in body and mind, as being a gifted speaker, light-skinned, pleasing to look at and strong willed" (Kasanga 1982:20; authors' translation).

In the official royal oral histories of the kings, however, there is little by way of individualized physical description of the "Noble desired in the navel of Imerina," though he was noted as wearing his hair in a tuft at the top of his head when a child and as wearing purple, being crowned in coral or accompanied by a red parasol when ruling Imerina. Some local tales, however, speak of the "Vigorous, healthy dog" as showing distinctiveness in comportment at an early age, distinguishing himself from other contenders for the "throne" by sleeping with his head raised above theirs or leaning against central pillars of houses. However, such distinctiveness is actually what is traditionally expected of those who would be acceptable candidates for inheriting authority.

Vision can be "effected" by provocative-evocative language. If one is expecting to see a powerful big-eyed bull, a noble covered by grace and beloved by the Merina, or desired in the navel of Imerina, if one is expecting a god seen with eyes, this is who one might, in fact, see ornamented in silver and coral and draped in deep scarlet robes in orchestrated public display.

To name oneself is, as Erica Jong suggests, the first act of the revolutionary (and poet) (1977). It is acceptable and common in the highlands of Madagascar to change one's name over the course of one's life. One historian of highland cultures, DuBois, complained of difficulty in studying the oral historical traditions of the Betsileo (see Fig. 10.1) because of problems with genealogies of ruling elite whose members, following their individual caprices, changed their names "for the least reason or the smallest adventure" (1938:169). The "Vigorous, healthy dog" took for himself the name of Ombalahibemaso, the "Bull with the powerful gaze"[7] when he became the aggressive warrior intent on reuniting the four corners of divided Imerina. One finds in this name the reference to an encompassing gaze that is a metaphor for political aspiration, if not control. One finds also the image of the bull that has been continuously associated with the ruling elite of Imerina. The evocativeness of the image of the bull should not be underestimated, since the Merina were (and in part still are) a culture of cattle raisers "who did not cease to speak the language of cattle—as one speaks with the language of flowers—developing to an extreme their capacity for such expression" (Domenichini-Ramiaramanana 1983:352 n. 47; authors' translation). Such a tradition continues in the work of a number of twentieth-century Merina poets. Consider the first verse of "Zebu" by Rabearivelo (1960:59) (considered by many to be the foremost Merina poet), which incorporates many of the key symbols of the ideology of the Merina state that are invested in cattle in reverse fashion (testifying to an effective grafting of early state ideology onto popular imagination):

> Vaulted like the towns of Imerina
> [strikingly] evident on the hills
> or carved as are the boulders
> humped like the pinions of houses
> cast in shadow by the moon
> This is the powerful bull
> Of sovereign purple color like its blood

As the unification of Imerina proceeded, the "Bull with the powerful gaze" was given (or took, depending on the version of the oral tradition one refers to) the name of Andrianampoinimerina, the "Noble desired (or hoped for) in the navel of Imerina." Such a name was meant to suggest not only a desired acceptance on the part of the local population for the rule of this noble but also a sense of predestination and ultimate fulfillment of a political destiny.

It is most important for those of us from societies where "talk is cheap" and prose(aic) utterances are norm, to appreciate the power of language in a society where sensitivity to language is cultivated not only in the mouth of the orator, but in the ear of the listener as well. An assortment of Malagasy proverbs (Houlder 1960:10–11), for instance, testifies to the fact that assuming a name is not a "fait accompli." If people continue to use your nickname at home, a new name will not take hold. You may call yourself a "great field" but it will be evident to all if you are but a small clod of dried earth. However, if you are to grow groundnuts, what purpose does it serve to clear only a small portion of a field? So, if you assume a new name, do so with aplomb and assuredness.[8]

"So That Is Poetry Really Loving the Name of Anything and That Is Not Prose": Gertrude Stein (1935)

The appropriation of names given to individuals and places, the reinterpretation of names, and the conferring of names in public discourse was an important and powerful strategy on the part of the "Noble desired in the navel of Imerina" in making visible and vocal the nature of the new political order and making claim for its legitimacy. (See also Kus and Raharijaona 2002.)

In his appearance as he took power, it will be remembered that the "Noble desired in the navel of Imerina" moved across a named landscape of noble red boulders, sacred fields, and sacred thrashing areas, places covered by grace and blessed by the populace. It will also be remembered that he appropriated names from people and places that testified to his sanctity and belovedness, as well as his goodness. To these names became attached the history and tales of this sovereign, so that to later speak such names evoked reference to the "Noble desired in the navel of Imerina." The later unfolding of events in the royal oral traditions offers many additional examples of this powerful performative strategy of naming individuals, groups, and physical locations to which the oral history of the Merina state becomes inextricably grafted.

With time the "Noble desired in the navel of Imerina" became more explicit in developing an ideology that encompassed both the unification of Imerina and its eventual expansion into regions beyond its core. One theme of this ideology was that the political unification that would bring prosperity and peace to the polity could only be guaranteed by allegiance to the singular sovereign of Imerina. The theme of singularity became more explicit with time. (See also Kus 1997; Kus and Raharijaona 2000.) This theme was redundantly asserted in an amazing assortment of symbolic strategies, including those that involved the landscape of Imerina. Ambatomiantendro (see Fig. 10.2), "At the boulder that attains to the summit," provided a stunning visual and aural/oral symbol and metaphor for what was an announcement of treason against an uncle and a ruler, and an audacious act of usurpation.

It will be remembered that the term *miseho* is applied both to the rising of the sun (and the moon) as well as to the action of taking office as sovereign. This term can also be used to speak of "revealing the meaning or significance" of a word, a statement, or an action; this type of revelation is an implicit privilege and talent of the sovereign. This "epiphanic" quality of the sovereign's speech is wonderfully illustrated in the multiple interpretations given to the name of Ambatomiantendro, which bring additional poetic nuance to its meaning through "plays on words." The name can be interpreted to mean "at the boulder that attains the summit," as mentioned above, or it can be translated as "the boulder that surpasses (all) peaks." The name, translated according to one account as "at the boulder from where I can (visually) encompass all" (Callet 1981:577–578), brings us again into the domain of visual domination as equated to political domination. According to yet another account it is translated as "at the boulder where all the peaks meet" (Callet 1981:577–578, 603).[9] In this skilled "reinterpretation," if not the revelation of the "true" significance of the name Ambatomiantendro, it is evident that much political claim and ideology is compacted, including the image of a unified and expansive polity.

You Do Not Teach a Small Cow to Swim; You Do Not Teach a Noble to Speak [These Are Natural Gifts][10]

The appreciation of the ability in speech to startle[11] or to please,[12] to unfold or to nuance an image[13] or a conundrum[14] is recognized by many cultures and their members as the ability of a sage. The conferring of beautiful and surprising names is one ability accorded to the "Noble desired in the navel of Imerina." Plays on words, clever comparisons, colorful imagery, and citations of apt proverbs are other forms of verbal skill he demonstrated in such tales. Such skills when used to sustain arguments in powerful performances before assembled crowds can be persuasive.

To be persuasive is no mean challenge when the populace is skilled to hear and reflect upon oration. To make this discerning populace explicitly complicit in one's schemes through (orchestrated) dialogue is certainly a stroke of (political) genius (according to oral tradition it was the people and not the "Bull with the powerful gaze" that insisted on the death of Andrianjafy, the uncle that the the "Bull with the powerful gaze" replaced as sovereign). The tradition of *kabary*, or public discourse and dialogue, goes back before the time of the "Noble desired in the navel of Imerina." It is with the "Bull with the powerful gaze," however, that this tradition is put into force to exploit a shifting balance of power away from the diverse interests of convoluted factions of petty nobles to a base of more consolidated commoner support.

The *kabary* of the "Noble desired in the navel of Imerina" are numerous in the oral traditions. They most often begin and/or end with direct addresses to the assembled populace to offer advice and to give consent to the proposed projects. In these *kabary* the sovereign is said to *miera amin'ny vahoaka*, to consult the people. All proceeds as if by dialogic consensus: "Is that not true, 'Those under the sky' [my people]?" "Yes it is so!"[15] (Rahajarizafy 1961:26). Yet it remained the case that "the elder is charged with speech making and the younger with carrying the baggage."[16] Many of these official discourses were not only committed to collective memory but were also fixed with aide-mémoires in the form of standing stones (*orim-bato*). Even today in the countryside, these standing stones help elders who can still recite the historical events and *kabary* that transpired at the marked location. These royal histories include the conferring of privilege and/or honorable history on the groups that inhabit the territory on which the standing stones are found, and so the ideology of the state has been confounded/interwoven with local histories involved in past and contemporary social/class maneuverings. However, with time brute force came to speak louder than words under the successors of the "Noble desired in the navel of Imerina" and the *kabary* (d)evolved into the presentation of orders from royalty to be duly observed or implemented. Yet throughout the nineteenth century these successors (two kings and four queens) assembled crowds of "those under the sky," at times numbering 100,000 (Raison-Jourde 1991:50), to participate in *kabary* where the litanies of call and response were still recited, and the words of the sovereign were repeated from individual to individual across the crowd, and then upon returning home obligatorily repeated to the members of one's community who were not in attendance.

The powerfulness of speech and of acts of naming in public discourse, in public performance, lies in the fact that they can create a cultural landscape (and in some cases, displace other cultural landscapes), both literally and figuratively, where evocative names and compelling concrete images and metaphors are mnemonically and conceptually aligned with objects and places in the physical landscape as well as with the local histories of social groups occupying those spaces. They are thus also given center stage for further repetition, nuanced reworking, and fuller interweaving of images, concepts, and vocabulary in continued "official" public discourse and made available for, if not forced on, more publicly limited, and even private, discussion. To repeat the names of such sites as "Imerina that advances" (Imerimandroso) and "Imerina that cannot be pushed [aside, destabilized]" (Imerintsiatosika) publicly and privately is to reify polity and politics.

Words can enter into a common fund of popular image and discourse. *Atao ko ny ranomasina no valamparia ko*, "I will make the sea the limits of my rice field," are words found not only in the official royal traditions but in several recorded traditions other than those taken down by Callet (Delivré 1974:203–212). This phrase was used in *kabary* by the "Noble desired in the navel of Imerina" to formulize the unifying and expansionist intentions he had for the polity, and used to "galvanize the energy [and imagination] of his subjects" (Delivré 1974:210) to participate in this venture. These same words were used to pass on this charge to his successor, Radama, before the clouds covered the singular sun, the "Bull with the powerful gaze" (Callet 1981:1047). Delivré's studied analysis of the royal traditions collected by Callet attests to the correct assignation of this particular phrase to the "Noble desired in the navel of Imerina" (1974:203–214). The term *ranomasina* used for "sea" can be translated as "sacred water." *Masina/hasina*, the term for "sacred," is used in public discourse to acknowledge the sanctity of the sovereign. Thus this choice of words to designate "the sea" that surrounds the island echoes the claim to sovereignty and sacredness of the "Noble desired in the navel of Imerina." The phrase "the sea is the limit of my rice field" occurs a number of times in the royal traditions recorded by Callet (1981), but there is only one instance where it occurs formulated as *Ny riaka ny valampariko*, where the word *riaka* replaces *ranomasina* (Delivré 1974:211). This particular phrasing is most likely an addition to the royal traditions in a later sovereign's reign. The term *riaka* can by translated as the "torrential waters or moving waters [of the sea]." This is certainly a colorful image, but its choice is also an oral poetic choice where the resonant syllables of *riaka* and *rik[i]o* create a powerful play on word/image and a lyrical rhythm of phrasing. It is this phrasing using *riaka* rather than *ranomasina* that has endured in popular discourse. One appreciation of this popular reworking of the "Noble desired in the navel of Imerina's" words, in a culture where exact recall of complex phrasing is not problematic, is to understand the aesthetics of proverbs. Malagasy proverbs (*ohabolona*), which are an ancient, rich, and common fund of Malagasy knowledge and often serve as the central building blocks of *kabary*, are characterized by "brevity, symmetry, parallelism, and metaphor" (Fox 1990:37). This reworking of the sovereign's words fits better the "proverbial" aesthetic sensibilities of the Malagasy. Most recently, this phrase of political propaganda, *Ny riaka/ranomasina ny valamparihiko* (The sea is the limit of *my* rice field), has been coopted by a force of the modern "political" economy, a mobile phone company, to incite the popular imagination in its advertising campaign. One of its "displays" (see Fig. 10.3) shows a small indigenous child from the coastal region holding up a conch shell to her ear as a "vacationing" woman, presumably from the highlands, looks on smiling. The image is accompanied by the phrase, *Izao tontolo izao, no valamparihantsika*, or "All of this [the world] is the limit of *our* rice field," to suggest that the wireless signal encompasses (and "unifies") the entire island of Madagascar (and all Malagasy).[17]

Words can also be used to contest. When dialogic skills, however, are still finely honed on both sides, when words still carry significant performative power, the words of contest must be carefully crafted if spoken publicly.

Figure 10.3. "The World Is the Limit of Our Rice Field"

There is the occasional example in the surviving oral traditions where contestations take place publicly. From the mouth of Rabodolahy, the son of the "Noble desired in the navel of Imerina," who was originally to inherit the polity, came words spoken publicly to his father in angry, yet poetic, formulation when he was passed over and Radama became heir apparent. "Be sanctified, sire. When you have given us nothing, when you sent us, we did not refuse to leave [to fight for you]; we have killed crocodiles; there he stands [reference to Radama], the one who bedecks himself with their teeth; we weave the cloth and there he is, the one who dresses himself in it; it is we who clear and prepare a public space; it is he who dances there" (Callet 1981:1027). Rabodolahy was banished subsequently upon the advice of the sovereign's counselors. (Later he was executed for attempting to kill Radama and lead an insurrection against his father.) In another instance according to other recorded traditions, the "Bull with the powerful gaze," in preparation for battle against the Betsileo, the Merinas' neighbors to the south (see Fig. 10.1), as part of a public performance, organized a contest of verbal eloquence between Rabefiraisana, a representative of the troops of Imerina's northern territory, and Rafiara, a representative of the troops from a territory in the south. Such public oratory contests were traditionally used to bolster the courage and ardor of troops assembled for battle. Rabefiraisana presented powerful images of the northern troops as the spades of iron that brought prosperity to the sovereign at the sacrifice of their own crops, making of their heads shields and leaping across defensive ditches as offerings to the sovereign and the polity. Rafiara's response included images such as, if the northerners were the lightning waiting to strike, they from the south were the rocks offered for it to dance on; if the northerners were a whirlwind ready to blow, they from the south were a grand immovable boulder (Domenichini-Ramiaramanana 1983:356–357). The "Bull with the powerful gaze" judged Rafiara, representative from the south, to be the winner according to one tradition. In a compelling and nuanced close reading of multiple versions of these speech poems, Domenichini-Ramiaramanana (1983:370–379) argues that one version of Rafiara's speech exists in oral traditions where the images are woven so as to present a veiled contestation of the legitimacy of the "Bull with the powerful gaze." Further, according to tradition, the "Bull with the powerful gaze" was duly outraged by Rafiara's audacity, but he held himself back (astutely assessing the politics of the situation). The basis of the contestation of the "Bull with the powerful gaze's" authority was that his authority was a political one backed by a popular *commoner* force from the north, whereas the south was the source of sacred and *noble* authority of divine origin. Among the powerful additional images of Rafiara's speech in this alternative version are several including the comparison of the the "Bull with the powerful gaze" that bellowed on the land to the hippopotamus that bellowed in the water, and the comparison of a feral bull born from an errant humpless cattle, to a wild bull born from a ferocious sire (Domenichini-Ramiaramanana 1983:361–378). Drawn from "the language of cattle," the power and beauty of these images are unavailable to most of us from such a cultural distance.

Despite the preceding discussion of the speech acts of sovereigns and other members of the Merina state, it should be obvious, nevertheless, to anthropologists and archaeologists of early states that the Merina state was not simply a creation of rhetoric. Material, economic, and social issues from the establishment of a new working capital to the repairing and building of defensive ditches and irrigation ditches (to allow a second and even third annual crop of rice), to colonizing of new territories, to market reforms (including standardization of weights and measures), to the whittling away of class privilege, to multiple campaigns of expansionist warfare, and to engagement in the international slave trade and the importation of guns, also played critical roles in the creation of the Merina state under the "Noble desired in the navel of Imerina." Nevertheless, at one point in the official royal oral traditions, a group that accepts to become part of the expanding Merina state says to the "Noble desired in the navel of Imerina," "The sound of a gun travels only so far; it is rather speech that travels the distance" (*Ny basy tsy re ny lavitra fa ny teny re ny lavitra*) (Callet 1981:989). The allusion in this statement is that the reputation of fair treatment for his subjects by the "Noble desired in the navel of Imerina" is well-known. One Malagasy proverb also states, *Ny tenin'andriana mahafiadana* ([it is] the words of the sovereign [that] create prosperity) (Houlder 1960:117). Powerful words fill more than 1,000 pages of the royal oral traditions of Imerina. Our preceding examination of speech acts contained in those oral traditions has allowed us to understand why the "Noble desired in the navel of Imerina," despite the material and political machinations that underpinned his rise to power, would claim publicly before all "those under the sun's dominion," "But for all the sovereign that I am, it is you, my people, who have made me so; my mouth only indicated [the way]; it is you that accomplished it, and I am pleased and satisfied for [the plans] which I have indicated to you, you have followed through to completion all without exception" (Callet 1981:745).[18]

Conclusion: Speech Is Like a Wrapped Package: The One Who Wraps and Ties It Is the One [Who Knows How] to Unwrap It

The highland Malagasy of the countryside speak of their history as "a heritage of the ears" (*lovan-tsofina*) and as a history "seen with the eyes" (*hita-maso*).[19] The latter image of "seen with the eyes" speaks not only of the witnessing by oneself or by one's ancestors of historic action, but also refers to the "seeing" of the places where historic events transpired (Kus 1997:210), places which often carry the physical marks of standing stones or bear the names from such events. This is a history that is still *vocal* in its oral recitation and *visible* in a landscape of named places and named groups and the many standing stones erected as commemoratives of such performative speech and powerful acts.

The preceding discussion of the public performances of the Merina sovereign and the "performative" (Austin 1962) language of royal public discourse argues that such performances and speech acts have the power to not only affect but also "effect" the state, and that early state "crafting" involves a nonnegligible, if not integral, component of symbolic construction. In particular, under the "Noble desired in the navel of Imerina," idioms of topography, self-presentation of the sovereign in dress, name, public appearance, placement in and movement across the landscape, and sensuously salient concrete imagery dexterously presented in elegant and traditional styles of discourse shaped, and in part *created*, the conceptual domain of the state's existence and its legitimacy. (1) The concept of political unification was made coterminus with the image of a singular sovereign without rival. (2) A singular "imagined community" (Anderson 1991) of "those under the sun/sky" was created to reinforce the popular base of support that brought the "Noble desired in the navel of Imerina" to power, and to displace a social network of multiple classes of divided allegiance with multiple petty lords holding competing claims to authority, privilege, and territory. (3) A concept of an expansionist state with "the torrential waters as its limit" was envisioned for the popular imagination and subsequently put into political practice. (4) The traditional practice of *kabary*, or public speech making by the sovereign, was crafted in word and performance style to present the work of the state as a complicity on the part of the "imagined community" and its sovereign.

It is not that archeologists have not recognized the role that symbols and metaphors, sumptuary materials, grand rituals, and spectacles have found in premodern state formations. We do have compendiums in our literature of ostentatious materials of (theatrical) display and performance, plastic art, ritual paraphernalia and attire, monumental architecture of royal residences, temples, and tombs, and so on, and in some cases, elements of speech acts that accompany performance. Yet, taken as a whole within a "science of the abstract," we are left with apples and oranges in the same pile. If, however, we come to understand that a sensorial ethos is implicated in any alternative way of being in the world, then we are challenged to come to understand the "how" of the *specific* materials used to create and sustain the political within the premodern state formations we choose to direct our attention to. We are encouraged to become "scientists of the concrete," encouraged to take our gut-level anthropological fascination for the practices of others and our archaeological idolatry of "other people's garbage" and to linger longer "on small things forgotten" (homage to Deetz 1977) and large things reexamined in an attempt to explore the "metaphorical entailments" between the technological and the philosophical, between the quotidian and the cosmological, in early states where ideologies are neither gratuitous nor fortuitous in the construction of those states.

Notes

The authors would like to thank Larry Coben and Takeshi Inomata for the stimulus to put pen to paper for the original working group and for the pressure that gave final form to this chapter. The authors are also grateful to the great uncle of Landy, Rakotomalala, for his patience in explaining Merina ways of being in the world, and to the grandfather of Landy, Rakototiana Raoelina, for having put together an invaluable library of resources on Malagasy history, literature, and custom.

1. The *Tantara ny andriana eto madagascar* (History of the [Ruling] Nobles in Madagascar) is a thousand-page document that was collected and published in the Malagasy language during the middle of the nineteenth century by François Callet, a French Jesuit missionary to Madagascar.
2. There are several additional tales that attach other acts of taboo to this location (including the execution of an earlier rule); thus its name is historically multireferential rather than singular.
3. *Ankasina* lends itself to several interpretations: "where one becomes sanctified," "the place of sanctification," and "the sanctified place."
4. The political ideology of Andrianampoinimerina presented him as a singular and unique sovereign who had no equal and would suffer no rival. His singularity as head of the polity was the guarantee of peace in place of the former periods of famines. Some famines were so severe that the memory of their horrors survived in their names: to "Assuage [the hunger of] children with promises" and to "Eat without the effort to peel off the skin" (see also Kus 1997). Peace brought with it prosperity, including an abundance of rice, the staple of the Merina diet. Equating himself to rice was a powerful metaphor to remind/convince the populace of the benefits of his rule.
5. "Those under the sun" referred to the Merina citizenry proper and "those under the sky" included populations that subsequently came under the domination of the Merina.

6. Today the appellation *ambaniandro* ("those under the sun") is used by the populations of the island to refer to the Merina. The Merina themselves do not ordinarily use that term as one of self-designation, but rather use the term "Merina" or a finer named group distinction, making it quite evident that the distinctions within "the braid" or the "rim of the pot" continued and continue to exist and to call into question the political identities crafted by the state.

7. As mentioned earlier, this name can take several other interpretations as the "Big-eyed bull" and the "Bull with many eyes."

8. *Ny anarana no tsy raikitra, ny antrano no manivaiva.* (A [new] name does not take if one's diminutive continues to be used at home.) *Anarany no nomeny trano be, ka sondro-drahona; anarany no nomeny vala be, ka sakamaina.* (He calls himself the "mansion" but is only a cabin; he calls himself the "great field" but is only a small clod of dried earth.) *Ny anarana tanim-boanjo, ka izay kely famaritra no ratsy.* (The name that one takes is like a field of groundnuts, to clear only a little patch is of little worth.) *Toy ny tsimbolavola ka anarany ihany.* (Like the name of the brown grasshopper [that would pretend to silver with its name that contains the word for silver, *vola*], it is only a name.)

9. In one interpretation there is a play on words involving the term *tendro, le sommet, le point culminant, la cime* (Abinal and Malzac 1955:695) and the term *tendry, désignation, indication* (Abinal and Malzac 1955:695) in its first-person singular form *tendro*. In other interpretations, Ambatomiantendro is recorded as Ambatomihaotendro. One interpretation involves an additional play on pronunciation making reference to the verb *mihoatra*, or "*excéder, dépasser, franchir, surpasser, être mieux ou meilleur, l'emporter sur*" (Abinal and Malzac 1955:256). In another interpretation there is also a play on pronunciation involving the term *mihaona*, "*se rencontrer, s'aboucher*" (Abinal and Malzac 1955: 216).

10. *Ny zanak'omby tsy ampianarin-domano, ny andriana tsy ampianarin-kabary.*

11. One highland-named speech genre is the *kipotsaka*, a type of joke or farce to gain people's attention. Another genre is the *dombolana*, or "the shock or blow of speech" (Michel-Andrianarahinjaka 1987:340).

12. One highland genre is the *isamanga*, or "beautiful/excellent song" (Michel-Andrianarahinjaka 1987:338).

13. One highland genre is the *hainteny*, or the "science/art of speech." Another is the *sangaly*, or "ingenious/skilled song" (Michel-Andrianarahinjaka 1987:338).

14. One genre of the *fampariahitsa*, or the scatter seeds of the *ahitsa* plant with the image being to plant a shade of doubt or regret on a given subject so that it will take root and mature in the heart/mind of the individual (Michel-Andrianarahinjaka 1987:338).

15. *Tsy izany va, ry ambanilanitra? Izay! Hoy ny firedon'ny vahoaka.*
16. *Mananjandry afaka olan-entana; mananjoky afaka olan-teny.*
17. The Malagachisant will notice in the foreground of the picture an individual wearing a T-shirt with the words: *Tiako i Madagasikara* (I love Madagascar). This is a piece of more prosaic contemporary political rhetoric (sometimes appearing as "♥ *Madagasikara*"), a slogan used in a recent presidential election.
18. *Kanefa na andriana aza aho, hianareo vahoaka no nanana'ko izany; ny vava ko foana no manoro, f'hianareo mahavita, dia mankasitraka aho mankatelina, izay atoro ko dia vita nareo avokoa.*
19. *Ny teny toy ny fonosana, ka izay mamono no mamaha* (Houlder 1960:43).

References Cited

Abinal, Antoine, and V. Malzac
1955[1888] Dictionnaire Malgache-Français. Paris: Editions Maritimes et Coloniales.

Anderson, Benedict
1991 Imagined Communities: Reflections on the Origin and Spread of Nationalism. London: Verso.

Austin, John
1962 How to Do Things with Words. Cambridge: Harvard University Press.

Brown, Mervyn
2000 A History of Madagascar. Princeton, N. J.: Marcus Weiner.

Callet, François
1974 Histoire des Rois. G.-S. Chapus and E. Ratsimba, trans. Antananarivo: Librairie de Madagascar.
1981[1908] Tantara ny andriana eto Madagascar: Documents historiques d'après les manuscrits malgaches. Antananarivo: Imprimerie Nationale.

Csordas, Thomas
1990 Embodiment as a Paradigm for Anthropology. Ethos 18:5–47.

Deetz, James
1977 In Small Things Forgotten: The Archaeology of Early American Life. Garden City, N. Y.: Doubleday.

Delivré, Alain
1974 L'Histoire des rois d'Imerina: Interprétation d'une tradition orale. Paris: Klincksieck.

Domenichini-Ramiaramanana, Bakoly
1983 Du ohabolona au hainteny: Langue, littérature et politique à Madagascar. Paris: Karthala

DuBois, H.-M.
1938 Monographie des Betsileo. Paris: Institut d'Ethnologie.

Fox, Leonard
1990 Hainteny: The Traditional Poetry of Madagascar. Cranbury, N. J.: Associated University Presses.

Griffith, Robert
1919 Madagascar: A Century of Adventure. London: London Missionary Society.

Houlder, J. A.
1960 Ohabolana ou proverbes malgaches. Antananarivo: Imprimerie Luthérienne.

Howe, David
1991 Introduction: To Summon All the Senses. *In* The Varieties of Sensory Experience: A Sourcebook in the Anthropology of the Senses. David Howe, ed. Pp. 3–21. Toronto: University of Toronto.

Jackson, Michael
1989 Paths toward a Clearing: Radical Empiricism and Ethnographic Inquiry. Bloomington: Indiana University Press.

Julien, Gustave
1908 Institutions politiques et sociales de Madagascar. Paris: Guilmoto.

Jong, Erica
1977 How to Save Your Own Life: A Novel. New York: Holt, Rinehart, Winston.

Kasanga, Fernand
1982 Tantaran'ny Antemoro Anakara teto Imerina tamin'ny andron' Andrianampoinimerina sy Ilaidama. Antananarivo: Société d'Imprimerie Antananarivo.

Kus, Susan
1989 Sensuous Human Activity and the State: Towards an Archaeology of Bread and Circuses. *In* Domination and Resistance. Daniel Miller, Michael Rowlands, and Christopher Tilley, eds. Pp. 140–154. London: Unwin Hyman.

1997 Archaeologists as Anthropologists: Much Ado about Something after All? Journal of Archaeological Method and Theory 4(3–4):199–213.

Kus, Susan, and Victor Raharijaona
1998 Between Earth and Sky There Are Only a Few Large Boulders: Sovereignty and Monumentality in Central Madagascar. Journal of Anthropological Archaeology 17:53–79.
2000 House to Palace, Village to State: Scaling Up Architecture and Ideology. American Anthropologist 102(1):98–113.
2001a Matters of Life and Death: Mortuary Rituals as Part of a Larger Whole among the Betsileo of Madagascar. *In* Social Memory, Identity, and Death: Intradisciplinary Perspectives on Mortuary Rituals. Meredith Chesson, ed. Pp. 56–68. Archeological Papers of the American Anthropological Association, 10.
2001b To Dare to Wear the Cloak of Another before Their Very Eyes: State Co-Optation and Local Re-Appropriation in Mortuary Rituals of Central Madagascar. *In* Social Memory, Identity, and Death: Intradisciplinary Perspectives on Mortuary Rituals. Meredith Chesson, ed. Pp. 114–131. Archeological Papers of the American Anthropological Association, 10.
2002 The Power to Name and the Claim to Dominion of a Malagasy Sovereign. *In* The Dynamics of Power. M. O'Donovan, ed. Pp. 362–383. Center for Archaeological Investigations Occasional Paper, 30. Carbondale: Southern Illinois University.

Lock, Margaret, and Nancy Scheper-Hughes
1987 The Mindful Body: A Prolegomenon to Future Work in Medical Anthropology. Medical Anthropology Quarterly 1(l):6–41.

Michel-Andrianarahinjaka, Lucien X.
1987 Le système littéraire betsileo. Fianarantsoa, Madagascar: Ambozontany.

Molet, Louis
1979 La conception malgache du monde, du surnaturel et de l'homme en Imerina. Vol. 1. Paris: Editions l'Harmattan.

Ong, Walter
1991 The Shifting Sensorium. *In* The Varieties of Sensory Experience: A Sourcebook in the Anthropology of the Senses, David Howe, ed. Pp. 25–30. Toronto: University of Toronto.

Raison-Jourde, Françoise
1991 Bible et pouvoir à Madagascar au XIXe siècle: Invention d'une identité chrétienne et construction de l'Etat. Paris: Karthala.

Rabearivelo, Jean-Joseph
1960 Poèmes. Antananarivo: Imprimerie Officielle.

Rabemananjara, Jacques
1964 Les Dieux Malgaches. Paris: Henri Maillet.

Rahajarizafy, Antoine
1961 Ny Ombalahibemaso V. Antananarivo, Madagascar: Imprimerie Catholique.

Raombana
1980 Histoires. Fianarantsoa, Madagascar: Ambozontany.

Stein, Gertrude
1935 Lectures in America. New York: Random House.

Stoller, Paul
1997 Sensuous Scholarship. Philadelphia: University of Pennsylvania Press.

Strathern, Andrew
1996 Body Thoughts. Ann Arbor: University of Michigan Press.

Vig, Lars
1977 Croyances et moeurs de malgaches. Vol. 2. Antananarivo: Trano Printy Fiangonana Loterana Malagasy

INDEX

Note: Italicized page numbers refer to figures.

ABOUT THE CONTRIBUTORS

John Baines is professor of Egyptology at the University of Oxford. His research interests include ancient Egyptian art, religion, literature, and biographies; modeling ancient Egyptian society; and comparative approaches to ancient civilizations. His publications include *Cultural Atlas of Ancient Egypt* (with Jaromir Malek; revised edition, 2000) and *Fecundity Figures* (reprinted 2001). He has contributed chapters to numerous interdisciplinary volumes in archaeology and anthropology (www.orinst.ox.ac.uk/staff/bainespb.shtml).

Lawrence S. Coben is the director of Proyecto Inkallakta (Incallajta), a multidisciplinary project centered at the monumental Inka site of that name in central Bolivia. His theoretical interests include the examination of the theatrical characteristics of ritual and public spaces, the relationship between the nature of such spaces and the communicative and emotional import of the performances within them, and the role of such performances in the exercise of power. He is presently completing his doctorate in anthropology at the University of Pennsylvania.

Ian Hodder obtained his Ph.D. from Cambridge University in 1975. After teaching at Leeds University, he returned to Cambridge and taught there until 1999. While at Cambridge he became professor of archaeology and a fellow of the British Academy. Since 1999 he has been at Stanford, where he is Dunlevie Family Professor. His main excavations have been in eastern England and at Çatalhöyük in Turkey. His main books include *Symbols in Action* (1982), *Reading the Past* (1986), *The Domestication of Europe* (1990),

Theory and Practice in Archaeology (1992), and *The Archaeological Process* (1999).

Stephen Houston is professor of anthropology at Brown University and was previously the Jesse Knight University Professor at Brigham Young University. His interests range from Mayan glyphs to the comparative study of writing, along with the nature of divine kingship and courtly systems.

Takeshi Inomata is associate professor at the University of Arizona. After earning an M.A. from the University of Tokyo, he obtained his Ph.D. from Vanderbilt University and taught at Yale University. His current research at the Classic Maya center of Aguateca, Guatemala, examines domestic organization, ancient politics, warfare, and political ecology. He was also director of the Proyecto de Restauración Aguateca, which aims at sustainable development though archaeological conservation and community development.

Susan Kus obtained her Ph.D. from the University of Michigan. She is associate professor at Rhodes College. Working in Madagascar, she has continuous occasion to cross the subdisciplinary boundaries of archeology, ethnohistory, and ethnography. Her current ethnographic work with ritual specialists in central Madagascar is embedded in a larger interest in the force of local knowledge in the face of attempts by early states to coopt local symbols and knowledge for ideological purposes of legitimating state authority.

Jerry D. Moore is professor of anthropology at California State University–Dominguez Hills. He is an archaeologist with ongoing research in Peru and Baja California, projects that focus on the archaeology of place. His books include *Architecture and Power in the Ancient Andes: The Archaeology of Public Buildings*, *Visions of Culture: An Introduction to Anthropological Theories and Theorists*, and *Cultural Landscapes in the Prehispanic Andes: Archaeologies of Place*. He wrote the chapter in this volume during a 2001–2002 fellowship at the Getty Research Institute, Los Angeles.

Victor Raharijaona received his doctorate from INALCO (Institut National de Langues et Civilisations Orientales), Paris, France. He was formerly the assistant director of the Musée d'Antananarivo, Madagascar. He is currently doing independent research on indigenous concepts of sovereignty and the state in the early Merina kingdom of the central highlands of Madagascar. He is also working on the role of orality, gesture, and metaphor in the practice of ritual specialists among the Betsileo in the central highlands of Madagascar.

Adam Smith is assistant professor at the University of Chicago. He is the author of *The Political Landscape* (2003) and coeditor of *Archaeology in the Borderlands: Investigations in Caucasia and Beyond* (2003).

Daniela Triadan is assistant professor of anthropology of the University of Arizona, and a research associate with the Department of Anthropology of the National Museum of Natural History of the Smithsonian Institution. Her research interests are both in the American Southwest and the Maya areas, and she is currently investigating polychrome ceramic production and distribution in Chihuahua, Mexico, and classic Mayan household organization at Aguateca, Guatemala.